Changing Rural Social Systems Adaptation and Survival

FLORIDA STATE
UNIVERSITY LIBRARIES

JUN 19 1997

TALLAHASSEE, FLORIDA

Joseph Allan Beegle

CHANGING RURAL SOCIAL SYSTEMS ADAPTATION AND SURVIVAL

Edited by
Nan E. Johnson and Ching-li Wang

Michigan State University
East Lansing

Copyright © 1997 by Nan E. Johnson and Ching-li Wang

All Michigan State University Press Books are produced on paper which meets the requirements of American National Standard of Information Sciences Permanence of paper for printed materials ANSI Z39.48-1984

Michigan State University Press
East Lansing, Michigan 48823-5202

HT
421
C36
1997

04 03 02 01 00 99 98 97   1 2 3 4 5 6 7 8 9

Library of Congress Cataloging-in-Publication Data

Changing rural social systems : adaptation and survival / edited by Nan E. Johnson and Ching-li Wang.
      p. cm.
Includes bibliographical references (p.).
ISBN (invalid) 0-87013-470-1 (alk. paper)
  1. Sociology, Rural. 2. Sociology, Rural—Research. 3. Rural population—Cross-cultural studies. 4. Rural population—United States. 5. Rural development—Sociological aspects—Cross-cultural studies. I. Johnson, Nan E. II. Wang, Ching-li, 1943-
HT421.C36 1997
307.72—DC21   96-39877
                                                                           CIP

Cover photo: Gateway to the Davis Plantation, Houston County, Georgia. The architect of the greathouse was Pete Davis, who was granted his freedom after supervising its construction. The mansion features three stories, unusual for rural homes in the nineteenth century. (Photo by Nan E. Johnson)

This book is dedicated to our colleague, Joseph Allan Beegle, who was mentor to many and friend to all during his distinguished forty-two years as a faculty member in the Department of Sociology, Michigan State University.

ACKNOWLEDGMENTS

We thank the following sources of financial support for this publication:

Provost Louanna Kimsey Simon, Michigan State University

College of Agriculture (Michigan State University):
    Agricultural Experiment Station Project No. 3350:
    Nan E. Johnson, Principal Investigator
    Ian Gray, Director of the Agricultural Experiment Station
    Donald Isleib, Director of the International Institute of Agriculture

College of Social Science (Michigan State University):
    Dean Kenneth Corey
    Tom W. Carroll, Director of the Center for the Advanced Study of International Development, who made funds available to us through a Title VI grant (acct. # 61-1640) from the U.S. Department of Education
    Jack H. Knott, Director of the International Institute for Public Policy and Social Research
    Christopher K. Vanderpool, Chair of the Sociology Department

Cornelia Butler Flora, Director of the North Central Regional Center for Rural Development

Also, we thank our families, especially Catherine Johnson, Van Johnson, and Ko-Chu Wang for moral support during the conduct of this work.

CONTRIBUTORS

Marilyn Aronoff is Associate Professor of Sociology, Michigan State University.

Daniel C. Clay is Professor at the International Institute of Agriculture, Michigan State University.

George A. Daoutopoulos is Professor of Agricultural Economics, Aristotle University of Thessaloniki, Greece.

Joanne Bubolz Eicher is Regents' Professor of Design, Housing, and Apparel, College of Human Ecology, University of Minnesota.

Rita S. Gallin is Professor of Sociology and Director of the Office of Women in International Development, Michigan State University.

Damian F. Hannan is a researcher at the Economic and Social Research Institute, Dublin, Ireland.

Nan E. Johnson is Professor of Sociology, Michigan State University and Research Affiliate, Population Studies Center of the University of Michigan.

Theobald Kampayana is Analyst, Division des Enquetes et des Statistiques, Ministere de l'Agriculture, de l'Elevage, et des Forets, Kigali, Rwanda.

Jean Kayitsinga is a Ph.D. candidate, Department of Sociology, Michigan State University.

Gaston J. Labadie is Dean of the School of Management and International Affairs, University of the Republic, Montevideo, Uruguay.

William P. O'Hare is Senior Associate, The Annie E. Casey Foundation, Baltimore, Maryland.

Richard W. Rathge is Professor of Sociology, North Dakota State University.

Jon H. Rieger is Professor of Sociology, University of Louisville, Kentucky.

Ching-li Wang is State Demographer, Department of Management and Budget, State of Michigan.

CONTENTS

Part 1. Prologue

1. Introduction   1
   Nan E. Johnson

Part 2. Changing Rural Social Systems: Focus on Familial and Occupational Systems

2. The Poor in Nonmetropolitan America   33
   William P. O'Hare

3. Mechanization in the Western Upper Peninsula
   Pulp-Logging Industry   47
   Jon H. Rieger

4. Development, Women's Work, and Economic Inequality
   in Rural Taiwan   71
   Rita S. Gallin

5. Inequality and the Emergence of Nonfarm Employment
   in Rwanda   93
   Daniel C. Clay, Theobald Kampayana, and
   Jean Kayitsinga

6. Social and Economic Transformation in a Greek
   Farming Village   111
      George A. Daoutopoulos

Part 3. Demographic Adaptation

7. Recent Population Change in Michigan's Metropolitan
   and Nonmetropolitan Areas   137
      Ching-li Wang

8. The Transmission of Information Regarding Population
   Change in a Rural County   155
      Richard W. Rathge

9. Fatal Farm Accidents in Michigan: Implications for
   Research and Policy   173
      Nan E. Johnson

10. Irish Rural-Urban Migration: Post-1960 Changes   189
      Damian F. Hannan

Part 4. Ways to Survive and Thrive

11. Changing Rural Communities: Reconstructing the
    Local Economy of a Nonmetropolitan Community   203
      Marilyn W. Aronoff

12. Social Change and Dress among the Kalabari of Nigeria   223
      Joanne Bubolz Eicher

13. The Call of the Sugar Cane: Agricultural Change,
    Cooperative-Capitalism, and Migrants in
    Northwestern Uruguay   245
      Gaston J. Labadie

Part 1

Prologue

1

INTRODUCTION

Nan E. Johnson

Introduction

The first Department of Sociology in the United States was founded at the University of Chicago by Albion W. Small in 1892. However, it was not until World War II that sociologists achieved a prominent position in science by advising the federal government on effective modes of organizing combat forces. The focus of their early scientific efforts was to explain and solve social problems arising from industrialization, urbanization, and militarization. A common approach was to contrast urbanism with rurality.

Throughout the 1940s and the 1950s, Structural–Functionalism was the dominant paradigm organizing and interpreting this contrast. It viewed social order as possible because norms defined not only common goals, but also appropriate means for reaching them. The ultimate goals (functions) of all social action were said to be the maintenance and survival of the social system.

Toennies (1957), a forefather of Structural–Functionalism, wrote that different types of social systems arise from different kinds of will. He held that Gemeinschaft–like systems are rooted in "natural will" and are governed by sentiment. Within such structures, communication is typically face–to–face, and all communicants give and receive information. Social action linking two communicants takes into account the plurality of roles both play. As such, their interaction often seems to be an end in itself, rather than a means of serving diverse goals that altogether should perpetuate their Gemeinschaft–like social group.

On the other hand, Gesellschaft–like structures are based on "rational will," described by Timasheff (1967, 100) as "the deliberative, purposive form of volition which determines human activity with regard to the future." Within Gesellschaft–like social structures, communication linking two actors serves a few specific (rather than many diffuse) goals, connects fewer roles that the actors share, and thus promotes an experience of impersonality. Access to more resource bases within Gesellschaft–like social structures is supposedly attained through meritorious accomplishments rather than through ascriptive characteristics (e.g., age, sex, or race). In the post–World War II literature, Loomis and Beegle (1950, 1957, 1975) popularized the Gemeinschaft/Gesellschaft contrast as a way of distinguishing rural from urban social systems, but they saw these ideal types of social system as the two poles of a continuum on which all social systems fall. In their view, the farm family and the village are closer to the Gemeinschaft end, while the military unit and the metropolis are nearer the Gesellschaft extreme.

Structural–Functionalism treated the family as the prime example of a social system seeking its own survival and maintenance (and thus preserving the society to which it belonged) by the production and socialization of children (Kingsbury and Scanzoni 1993). The diversity of familial functions geared to these ends was thought to require a specialization of activities into *instrumental* roles, designed to provide the family with outside material resources and to protect it from disequilibrium, and *expressive* roles, meant to nurture and integrate the spiritual and emotional lives of the family. Parsons and colleagues (1955) argued that biological contingencies required men to take on the instrumental jobs, leaving women to perform the expressive roles. In describing the responsibilities of a mother toward her child as "blanket," Loomis and Beegle (1950, 23) implied that the expressive roles were the more functionally diffuse.

Following Merton (1957), Loomis and Beegle argued that threats to the equilibrium of a social system could arise internally, as when generational or gender roles in a family remain vacant or are vacated. Examples of such deviant structures would be found in childless or single–parent families, homosexual unions, and families in which the wife is the primary breadwinner. However, they held that importing more complex agricultural technologies from external, urban sources would inevitably press for change in all rural social systems, Western and non–Western alike. As members of a faculty appointed to a land–grant university that was founded to impart material and nonmaterial science to the agricultural people of Michigan, Loomis and Beegle sought ways to plan rural social change from within the dictates of Structural–Functionalist theory (Loomis and Beegle 1957, 1975). Their mission was courageous, since critics have faulted Structural–Functionalism for emphasizing the systemic "need" for social equilibrium (homeostasis) at the expense of asking how social systems change.

Loomis and Beegle theorized that change occurs in an *enduring* rural social system when a dynamic equilibrium shifts it toward the Gesellschaft pole. Yet the Gemeinschaft–like properties of the rural social system could never entirely disappear, given that all social systems are a complex mixture of both ideal types. They concluded that the best their students, the future change agents, could do would be to plan and implement the dynamic equilibria.

To such ends, Loomis and Beegle used Structural–Functionalism to pose several hypotheses, three of which will be examined here. They reasoned that the social rank of an individual in the occupational system must be congruent with his or her social rank within the family, lest the above–defined benchmark two–parent–family–with–biological–children–of–both–sexes might dissolve from the internal friction produced by the status inconsistencies. For instance, women might challenge patriarchal authority at the farm–home if they outrank their husbands by earning more money from a nonfamilially controlled occupation than men can make from ownership-operation of farms (Hypothesis 1). Also, they argued that the innovations that maximize social integration and cooperation and that minimize the socioeconomic costs of change will be more easily introduced (Hypothesis 2). Similarly, lower–status individuals in any social system should follow the example of higher–status members in adopting new technologies; thus, the change agent should first approach the more highly ranked (who ought then to be the same person in both familial and occupational systems) (Hypothesis 3). The purpose of this chapter is to test these three hypotheses by answering three derivative questions: How have two rural social systems (the familial and the occupational systems) changed? What have been the demographic responses? How does theory help us to understand these dual transitions? The answers will point out ways to revise Structural–Functionalism to bring theory into line with current empirical change. The chapter concludes by examining successfully planned social changes in rural social systems.

Familial and Occupational Systems in Rural Society

From the Structural–Functionalist viewpoint, the type of family system most likely either to disintegrate or to change in a dynamic equilibrium is one that is self–employed. In no other kind of family do the contradictions between a Gemeinschaft–like system's allocation of rank based on ascriptive criteria (especially sex and generation) clash more overtly with the Gesellschaft–like system's rule of awarding status based on achievement. Structural–Functionalism holds that achievement within occupational systems is the attainment of instrumental, not expressive, goals.

The "blanket" responsibility of mothers to their children may be why farm women have not limited themselves to the expressive roles within the family, but have also seized a greater diversity of economic roles on the farm than their husbands. This seizure has been made possible by a tight interweaving of women's farm and home production (Vanek 1980). Farm women not only work in crops, but also tend gardens, raise small animals, process foods, and make clothes or crafts for their families' own consumption; their surplus can be sold for cash to buy other goods that women cannot produce on the farm–home. As far back as 1915, 80 percent of the expenses to provision a farm–home in Michigan were covered by the cash earned by the farm wife (Bailey and Snyder 1921). Farm women have tended to define "leisure" as economically useful activities that could be scheduled at their convenience (e.g., scrubbing dyes off feedsacks before making family clothes from these fabrics). Thus, leisure has been less distinguishable from work in the daily routines of farm wives than farm husbands.

According to Loomis and Beegle, the reservation of a higher occupational rank for the farm husband (generally determined by the level of his earnings) should keep farm wives from commuting to work or having a long–term, salaried job off the farm. Yet Bokemeier and Tickamyer's (1985) study of nonmetropolitan (hereafter *nonmetro*) women in Kentucky found not only that one–third were employed full–time in nonfarm occupations, but also that marital status and farm residence *increased* tenure in their current nonfarm jobs. The reason may be that most farms have become part–time in states like Kentucky, where labor–intensive (rather than capital–intensive) crops such as tobacco predominate (Lobao 1990, 48). Farm householders planting labor–intensive crops and also working in off–farm jobs may exploit themselves, but the female members are rendered more exploitable by their definition as the family's reserve labor force.

Women's labor market experiences are shaped not only by their productive capacities (as reflected in such personal attributes as age, work experience, and education), but also by the demands for their labor from a dual industrial economy. According to Economic Segmentation Theory, two privatized sectors of the capitalist economy emerged at the beginning of the twentieth century. The monopolistic sector became comprised of "core" industries having high capital–to–labor investments, vertical integration, diversified product lines, national markets, wide profit margins, and numerous employees. Examples of core industries are durable manufacturing, wholesale trade, public administration, legal and financial services, and real estate trade. Unionization of employees has become more embedded in core industries, because the large profits and limited competition for market shares make these industries less vulnerable to the demands of organized labor (Lobao 1990, 24). As a result, jobs within core industries tend to offer higher wages, steadier work, paid vacations and other fringe benefits, plus opportunities for working beyond the standard 40 hours per week.

The "peripheral" industries were relegated to the other part of the privatized sector. The many firms within a single peripheral industry compete with each other in supplying the same services or goods and have low capital–to–labor investments, narrow profit margins, a smaller labor force, and a greater vulnerability to market swings (Bokemeier and Tickamyer 1985, 55; Tigges and Tootle 1990, 334). Examples are agriculture, nondurable manufacturing, retail trade, consumer and health services, and education. Peripheral firms (e.g., food franchises) that must purchase inputs from only a few suppliers can become monopolized by core firms (Lobao 1990). As a result, jobs within peripheral firms tend to be lower paid, more seasonal, and more often part–time.

Because female employees are more likely than males to congregate in peripheral industries, Tickamyer and Bokemeier (1988) analyzed sex–specific differences in earnings as reported in the public–use microdata sample (PUMS–D) of the 1980 U.S. Census. An innovation was that political units (e.g., counties) were not used as proxies for Labor Market Areas (LMAs). Rather, LMAs were defined as clusters of counties joined by patterns of commuting to work (which could cut across state lines). In this study, spatial location was treated as a structural factor because core industries have historically avoided more sparsely populated areas or lesser developed regions, where they cannot profit from local economies–of–scale. Therefore, LMAs were characterized as rural if they lacked a city of 50,000 or more inhabitants; and rural LMAs were typified by high employment in either mining (a core industry) or agriculture (a peripheral industry). When Tickamyer and Bokemeier focused only on the 17 LMAs centered in Kentucky, they found different rewards to women and men workers within rural LMAs. Full–time labor force participation rates for women were lower in mining LMAs than in agricultural LMAs, and women received lower earnings than men from employment in core industries in either type of rural LMA. Consequently, women appeared to be more systematically and structurally disadvantaged than men in the rural labor markets of Kentucky. This may have revealed just the tip of the iceberg of gender discrimination in a rural economy, since the data were restricted to those lucky enough to be employed full–time.

The rates of, and earnings from, full–time labor force participation underestimate economic hardship. For example, these rates ignore subemployed people, who have no paying jobs but do not seek work due to their belief that none exists. They are excluded from calculations of unemployment rates because the Bureau of Labor Statistics (BLS) does not define them as members of the labor force. In addition, labor force participation rates hide the underemployment of those working part–time because they cannot find full–time jobs. Poverty (defined by the Department of Agriculture as a household income so low that one–third of its value cannot purchase sufficient food for its members) is certainly a measure of economic stress; however, household income may exceed the poverty line but not by enough to save the household from a fall into poverty, especially if wages are unsteady or if the dollar becomes devalued through inflation. For these reasons, more sensitive indices of economic hardship would be rates of: subemployment, unemployment, low–hours employment (defined by the BLS as less than 35 hours of weekly work by people wanting more hours), and close–to–poverty wages (defined by the Social Security Administration as wages in the past year—adjusted for weeks worked—less than 1.25 times the income–poverty line).

Tigges and Tootle (1990) computed the last three measures for white males in all 382 LMAs (152 were designated as rural) in the 1980 PUMS–D. Concentration of the white male labor force in the core–transformative industries (manufacturing and construction) was negatively related with low–wage and low–hours employment, but positively correlated with higher rates of unemployment, and these relationships were stronger in rural than in urban LMAs. These results showed that even within the same employment sector, white male employees were relatively more disadvantaged if they worked in a rural labor market.

It is striking that greater rates of employment in industries that were highly penetrated by foreign imports were associated with larger unemployment rates for white males (again, this outcome was stronger in the rural LMAs [Tigges and Tootle 1990]). Yet making such industries more competitive in the global economy will not reduce rural unemployment rates to urban levels. U.S. industries seek competitive edges by redefining full–time jobs as part–time jobs through a process of deskilling and relocating the jobs to domestic rural labor markets or to foreign labor markets, whichever are cheaper (Summers 1991).

One example of how this worked for a durable–goods, core–industrial manufacturer (the General Motors Corporation) in the late 1980s came from Gringeri's (1993, 1994) study of Prairie Hills, Iowa, and Riverton, Wisconsin. GMC reduced its labor costs of making automotive vehicles by fragmenting the assembly of small components into a set of simpler tasks, some of which were exportable from Detroit to these two economically depressed communities in the Midwest. The process of deskilling meant that a whole set of steps in the production of an automotive vehicle that was formerly performed by one male union member earning full–time wages and insurance and retirement benefits in Detroit was broken down into subsets performed by several females who were defined as part–time earners of "supplemental" incomes and thus denied the fringe benefits of full–time employment. By narrowly defining "economic development" as the numerical growth of any kind of jobs (regardless of quality), rural community leaders in Prairie Hills and Riverton colluded with GMC in planning a local economic transformation that maximized external corporate profits from the vulnerability of local lower–class women in the labor force.[1] This outcome is predictable from the greater efficiency of changes in rural social systems that minimize the costs (Loomis and Beegle 1957, 16). Indeed, the entry of rural women into part–time employment in these new, urban–governed jobs taxed the rural occupational system minimally, since their low occupational rank was congruent with their subordinate economic power within the rural family system (Loomis and Beegle 1957, 5).

The analyses by Bokemeier, Tigges, and colleagues used data gathered in 1980 and 1981 and focused on whites. More recent inquiry affirms that white males' disadvantages in rural work environments continued during the 1980s. O'Hare (see chapter 2 of this work) shows that the nonmetro/metro gap in the percentages of young adults (aged 18–44) in poverty widened both absolutely and relatively during 1979–86. The expansion of the poverty gap did not signify a deterioration in the quality of the labor force, since there was no decline in the educational attainment or in the proportion of young adults working or looking for jobs. In fact, the poverty rate of these young adults increased between 1979 and 1986, even when they were working full–time. As such, O'Hare rejects the notion that nonmetro young adults became more enmeshed in a culture of poverty. Demonstrating that the industrial and occupational composition of the nonmetro labor force was largely unchanged over the period, he concludes that the expansion of poverty was due to a crumbling structure of rewards to labor.

O'Hare's exclusive focus on the nonmetro population cannot compare the structural sources of poverty between nonmetro and metro residents. McLaughlin and Perman (1991) found that two–thirds of the gap in earnings by white males in nonmetro and metro counties in 1987 came from inferior returns in nonmetro counties to their human–capital "endowments" (education and years of experience in the labor force). The other one–third was largely due to poorer returns to nonmetro white males endowed with better job characteristics (e.g., as tapped by occupational prestige, time commitment required by the job in terms of hours worked per week, and weeks of employment in the past year). Importantly, this study updated Tigges and Tootle's (1990) analysis of 1980 Census data by reaffirming the employment disadvantages of white males in nonmetro environments, and extended earlier analyses by showing that most (but not all) of the disadvantages came from locational inequality in the returns to human capital. Yet the exclusive focus on whites limited the generalizability of this study.

Until recently, Rural Sociology has largely ignored populations of color. The African–American family system in the rural South was perceived as matriarchal and thus as unstable (Loomis and Beegle 1950, 61). Also, since African Americans were ranked lower in rural occupational systems than whites, the latter were thought to be the more plausible audience for change agents (see Hypothesis 3 above). Surely these priorities should have lost force in the 1970s and 1980s, when the patriarchal male–breadwinner–and–female–homemaker form of the conjugal family declined sharply among white Americans (Ahlburg and DeVita 1992) and when the nonmetro blacks and whites of the South became more alike in overall economic hardship (Lichter 1989). The latter racial convergence happened because *employed* blacks became more like whites in the nonmetro South in getting jobs with enough hours to escape unsought part–time employment and enough pay to avoid a plunge into poverty, but blacks there simultaneously became more disadvantaged than whites in escaping joblessness (subemployment or unemployment). In other words, the system of economic stratification in the nonmetro South polarized blacks into "haves" and "have nots" according to how they fared in relation to whites, and the "haves" got an edge. This finding cannot refute an implication of Hypothesis 3: lower–status African Americans follow the leadership of white exemplars. Also, it is consistent with the notion that bringing in more complex technologies of production extends the social stratification ladder in areas heavily dependent on agriculture (Loomis and Beegle 1957), but shows that the extension can mean new rungs added to both ends of the ladder, especially for the one climbed by blacks.

A question raised by Lichter's research was whether the racial convergence in economic hardship also occurred in metro areas. In attempting an answer, Jensen and Tienda (1989) measured absolute rates of poverty as the percentage of all families from a certain racial/ethnic group living below the federal income–poverty line. Relative rates were measured as the percentage of families with annual incomes below one–half or one–fourth the national median for whites. Absolute rates of poverty fell for African–American, Mexican–American, American Indian, and white families in the 1960s and 1970s within nonmetro and metro U.S. counties. However, with the sole exception of American Indians, the relative rates for these minorities improved in nonmetro areas (as Lichter had claimed for Southern blacks) but deteriorated in metro areas. Apparently, the black–white polarization in economic hardship in the metro economy was based on a racially unequal distribution in income rather than on joblessness. This study demonstrated the important duality of metro versus nonmetro occupational systems and the dissimilar outcomes it yielded for upwardly/downwardly mobile persons of different races.

Self–sufficiency, Impoverishment, and Globalization of Rural Economies

The differences in the prevalence of economic hardship by nonmetro and regional locations show that it has spatial fault lines that interact with, but are separate from, the composition of the labor force by age, sex, and race. Therefore, the origins of geographically uneven development must be traced through the spatial organization of the economy.

Lobao (1990) identified three origins. One major root has been the segmentation not only of the nonfarm economy into core and peripheral sectors (defined above), but also of the farm economy into input, production, and postproduction sectors. The agricultural input sector supplies the farmer with fertilizers, pesticides, farm machines, and petroleum while the postproduction sector provides the transportation, processing, and marketing of food and fiber. Agribusinesses in both input and postproduction sectors have formed monopolies, enabling them to control prices paid by and to farmers. To raise profits, farmers have countered by increasingly substituting capital inputs for labor inputs in farming (most of the labor having come from unpaid family workers). The competition that owner–operators of small and medium–sized farm enterprises have faced against large, expanding farms has led to part–time employment by their family members in the nonfarm sector. Obviously, these trends have weakened the economic self–sufficiency of the majority of farm households and led to their tighter integration into, and greater dependence on, the nonfarm zone of the U.S. economy.

The second origin has come from the increasing power of capital over labor from within the nonfarm economy. The Arab Oil Embargo of 1973 raised the price of petroleum so suddenly as to boost monetary inflation within the U.S. economy. In order to reduce overhead, managers within core industries of the nonfarm sector cut the number of full–time domestic jobs, deskilled other full–time jobs into part–time jobs or cottage industries (Gringeri 1993, 1994), and demanded concessions and rollbacks of previous gains from labor unions. Accordingly, membership in nonfarm labor unions plummeted (Lobao 1990, 43).

The success of these managers released nonfarm capital for reinvestment elsewhere. Much of it relocated to nonmetro/rural sites, where workers are less likely to be unionized or unionizable and thus are more exploitable by nonfarm industrial capital. Hence, the third root of unequal economic development in metro/urban/nonfarm versus non-metro/rural/farm economies is the greater mobility of capital created at the former source (Lobao 1990, 47). The opportunities for nonmetro or rural sites to attract external capital depend heavily on having a cheap supply of labor. Yet such new jobs often do not generate capital for subsequent investment in local community infrastructure, since profits are extracted for corporate usage elsewhere and since local plants can be later closed and then reopened in poorer countries where the labor supply is even cheaper.

External corporate developers have been especially attracted by labor pools in remote locations with a history of colonialism or slavery. For example, Saenz and Ballejos (1993) used the concept of "internal colonialism" to define uneven development in the Lower Rio Grande Valley of Texas, where the indigenous Latino population faced colonization by the United States after 1848, when the area was ceded by Mexico's surrender in the Mexican-American War. The structure of agriculture then shifted from small–scale ranching, wherein Latinos owned most of the land, to large–scale cropping, wherein Anglo immigrants seized land ownership through legal and extralegal means and then sealed the poverty of Latinos by hiring and exploiting them as wage laborers. Much more recently, the Border Industrialization Program established by the U.S. government encouraged U.S. firms to set up factory assembly lines on the Mexican side of the border, the prosperity from which would theoretically form a wall retaining would–be emigrants to the United States. Also, wages from these U.S. firms were argued to aid workers living in Mexico but to trickle over the U.S. border when Mexicans came to shop. But the low–skill, low–wage jobs created by U.S. factories on the south side of the border lack stability and fringe benefits; and in search of these resources, Mexicans are now moving northward into the Lower Rio Grande Valley of Texas. The new arrivals contribute to the growth of shantytowns in the Valley, which Saenz and Ballejos (1993) call "colonies within the colony." Likewise, it is telling that the largest share of Hispanics moving out of the Valley between 1975 and 1980 for residences in other U.S. counties were the best educated, whose siphoning into other domestic labor forces creamed off the Valley's most talented potential workers, who otherwise could have founded and funded economic development in this "pocket of poverty."

Another pocket of poverty lies in the remote forests of Ontonagon County in the western Upper Peninsula (UP) of Michigan (see chapter 3 of this work). As is true for extractive industries in many other remote rural areas, the scale of economic organization and the level of decisionmaking have risen up and out from this pulp–logging county. For a large part of its early period, the paper mill in Ontonagon County was fundamentally a local business with local investors or was controlled by a middle-sized concern in nearby Wisconsin. Local farm families could supplement their household incomes by selling specially selected trees off their lands, which they felled and drug themselves to the roadside. Increasingly, the paper mill came under the control of larger and remoter entities and is now owned by the Stone Container Corporation, an international company. As the locus of decisionmaking moved up and progressively away from Ontonagon County, it constrained the options seen by local residents to shape their own destinies. The expensive new technologies developed to fell, de–limb, and haul the trees are now unaffordable by local farmers, who can no longer rely on casual logging to supplement and stabilize the variability in their family incomes from farming. As a result, Ontonagon County is now being impoverished not only demographically by a net outmigration of her youth, but also ecologically by a massive deforestation that thwarts the reappearance of aspen trees, which signal a renewal of the forests in the Upper Peninsula.

These examples from Lower Rio Grande Valley, Texas, and Ontonagon County, Michigan, show that the impoverization of nonmetro or rural U.S. peoples follows their incorporation into a global marketplace, which prevents most families from retaining profits locally. To elaborate this picture, this volume offers three case studies from such diverse places as an Asian village, an African country, and a Greek farming village. These studies show that rural development in nations peripheral to the global economy impoverishes farm households too underendowed with labor, land, or education to technologize the farm or to avail of nonfarm employment.

For example, Gallin (chap. 4) explores the sustenance activities of married women in a Taiwanese village undergoing rural industrialization. Independently of their residence in a conjugal or an extended family, the most often reported and subjectively significant sustenance activity for married women was housekeeping. This activity was less frequently acknowledged by wives in extended families than by those in conjugal (nuclear) families (33 percent vs. 48 percent of the wives) and served different economic ends in each family type. The housekeeper wives in extended families typically lived with married sons and daughters–in–law; their housekeeping and childcare services freed the daughters–in–law to farm or to work for wages in the off–farm labor force. And there was an effective demand for such young female laborers, who would work cheaply in the seven small satellite factories in the village. For housekeepers in conjugal families, home maintenance may have been the "master role," but these women typically performed a diverse set of jobs, such as piece working, tending a small family store, or farming (if their family was even lucky enough to own land). Therefore, the economic status of grandmothers was becoming bifurcated into those who were poorer because they lived in conjugal units versus those who were richer because they benefited from the pooled off-farm earnings of coresident male kin and their wives. Since extended familism allows complex divisions of labor between married women of different generations, its prevalence in the village is increasing.

Clay et al. (chap. 5) examine the impacts of government policies to stimulate rural development in Rwanda, where (as in Taiwan) land fragmentation and scarcity have forced many families to try to supplement their farm incomes with wages from the nonfarm sector. But growth in nonfarm employment opportunities has interacted with control over adequate farmland to polarize rural households into two classes. Farm households endowed with larger landholdings (more than two hectares) and more male members have been able to implement a household economy of scale. Namely, some males can be spared from farmwork to obtain schooling sufficient to qualify them for wages as artisans, merchants, or functionaries; and these monies can then be remitted to the farm household to buy or rent more farmland and to hire farmworkers. As in Taiwan, Rwandan farm families who are underendowed with farmland must sell their only other asset (labor), usually to do the manually intensive fieldwork for the richer farm families. Consequently, the policies to foster a growth of jobs in the rural nonfarm labor force have resulted in uneven economic prosperity in Rwanda.

Daoutopoulos (chap. 6) describes how land scarcity aggravated uneven agricultural development in a Greek farming village. After the visit of several tobacco exporting companies in 1966, six or seven farmers in the village of Aghios Loukas (St. Luke) decided to plant burley tobacco. Adoption required the farmer to make heavy initial investments in a tractor, herbicides, mist irrigation machinery, sprayers, and a curing barn. To seek a profit, the farmer then spread these start-up costs over as many hectares as possible; and the returns per unit of cultivated land proved unusually high. Another reason why burley tobacco is land-intensive is that it can be planted in the same field only in alternating years. Since, for historical reasons, most farms in the village are rather small, the adopters of burley tobacco had to increase their operational holdings by renting other fields.

The labor-intensive nature of growing tobacco (despite the costly, labor-saving technology) required tobacco growers to hire seasonal farmworkers from outside the household. Farm owners of very small plots could not follow suit because they could not secure loans sufficient to mechanize their operations, nor could they obtain machinery on contract from large–scale farmers, who were disinterested in the small profits available in this way. In addition, the small farmers found it increasingly difficult to obtain temporary seasonal labor through the traditional systems of labor exchange, since it became more profitable to sell one's labor to the large–scale farmers than to reciprocate it for work in one's own field (especially if that field were rented out). In sum, the technological, economic, and social demands foisted by burley tobacco upon its cultivators bifurcated village farmers into two agricultural classes. The antagonisms emerging along these class lines defeated efforts to organize local farm cooperatives (such as the one described by Labadie in chap. 13 of this volume) that might have spread the new wealth more evenly. Apparently, the scarcity of farmland in these diverse farming areas of Taiwan, Rwanda, and Greece disproportionately benefits the cultivators who can control larger plots of arable land.

Demographic and Social Responses

The sections above have described shifts within the rural American household away from a family–owned economy to a dependency on work controlled by others who often live outside the local community and fail to invest in its human capital or infrastructure. At the community level, the rural occupational system has witnessed a decline in agricultural employment and a rise in nonfarm jobs in the peripheral sector of the economy. In this section, we explore how these changes have affected mortality, migration, and fertility in rural America and ultimately the composition of the rural American population by sex and age.

Crime

Poverty is a major axis of social cleavage that segregates families and individuals from the community–at–large. The social isolation of the poor is more profound in rural communities of the United States, where stronger traditional values dignifying hard work and self–reliance stigmatize the impoverished as "moral failures." To hide their poverty, rural residents are less likely to rely on welfare (Jensen and Tienda 1989); but when they do, they exit these programs more swiftly than urbanites (Rank and Hirschl 1988). Yet the stress of poverty, combined with the stress from social isolation, results eventually in social disruption. Wilkinson (1984a, 1984b) argued that since forms of nonlethal violence (e.g., aggravated assault, robbery) are more common between persons related to each other in weak social ties and since urbanites have a higher proportion of weak ties than rural people do, the crime rate for nonlethal violence should be higher in urban areas. On the other hand, since homicides, suicides, and divorces typically reflect conflict between persons with strong social ties and since strong ties represent a higher proportion of one's interpersonal networks in rural areas, we would expect higher rates of homicide, suicide, and divorce in rural America. Wilkinson's data, gathered in the mid–1970s for a large number of counties in the northeastern United States, were consistent with these hypotheses.

An analysis of data from the National Crime Victimization Survey (NCVS, which obtains information not necessarily reported to the police) suggested that some of these relationships are not peculiar to the northeast. Consistently with Wilkinson's theory, the national rate of victimization for nonlethal violence (broadly defined as rape, robbery, aggravated assault, or simple assault) was highest for residents of central cities and lowest for residents of nonmetro areas in the 1980s (Bachman 1992).

The findings for *lethal* violence are less compatible with Wilkinson's research. On the one hand, Schroeder and Beegle (1953) described the rural suicide rate as almost twice the urban rate for Michigan males in the late 1940s, and Dennis (1967) reported that the rural suicide rate for white men remained above the urban level during 1955–65. On the other hand, about one–third of the rural white men committing suicide in Michigan in the late 1940s were farmers, while two–thirds were rural men engaged in urban–oriented jobs. Houser and Beegle (1951) speculated that rural men in urban jobs are especially prone to confusion and disorientation brought on by the clash between traditional and modern values in the workplace.

The clash may also be heard in other developed nations: Kurosu (1991) reported higher suicide rates existed in less urbanized areas of Japan at the beginning of the 1960s and strengthened for the next 20 years. Rapid economic development in Japan during these decades favored urban places, fostered rural–to–urban migration of young adults, and left many elderly Japanese farm residents with no one to carry on their farm, to manage their financial affairs, or to provide them with companionship.

As will be analyzed in more detail below, nonmetro U.S. residents do tend to be older than their metro counterparts; thus, we must age–standardize nonmetro and metro rates of lethal violence before comparing them. Accordingly, Potter and Galle (1990) held the effects of age, race, and sex constant, but then saw almost identical proportions of metro and nonmetro residents committing suicide in the southern United States. A second contradiction of Wilkinson's theory is that U.S. counties with *higher* percentages of the population in rural–farm or rural–nonfarm locations yielded *lower* rates of homicide in 1979-81 (Kowalski and Duffield

1990). Two ways to reconcile these discrepancies between a theory of violence and its test are first to see suicide and homicide as different sides of the same coin for physical violence (internal versus external aggression); and second, to recognize the differences in lethality of the chosen weapon. A firearm, the most efficient weapon of death, is more widely available in rural than in urban locations (Wilkinson 1984a), if now only to facilitate game hunts. But the wider current access to, and knowledge of how to use, firearms in the South may stem also from the Civil War (1861-65), which was primarily waged in southern territory and which perhaps required even civilians (women and children) to learn how to shoot, if only in self-defense. If this skill was truly broadened by the Civil War and then taught by one generation to the next, we might reasonably expect suicide to be as common in contemporary urban areas as in rural parts of the South (Potter and Galle 1990) and homicide rates in that region to exceed those in other regions (Jacobson 1975; MacKellar and Yanagishita 1995).

School Dropouts and the Inheritance of Poverty

The poverty rate of U.S. children was higher in nonmetro than in metro areas in 1990 (respectively, 21.1 percent and 18.2 percent of children under age 18 and living with at least one parent; see Lichter and Eggebeen 1992); and both rates were higher in 1990 than in 1980, mainly due to a rise in the number of female–headed families. Family income from all sources for female–headed families with poor children was almost identical in nonmetro and metro areas in 1979 (as measured in constant 1989 dollars), and fell in both areas over the decade, but dropped more sharply in nonmetro areas (Jensen and Eggebeen 1994). Yet regardless of family–headship status, the percentage of children lifted above the income-poverty line by public assistance (including food stamps) was lower in nonmetro than in metro areas throughout the 1960–90 period because nonmetro poverty was so much deeper (Jensen and Eggebeen 1994). Indeed, longitudinal studies (e.g., Garrett, Ng'andu, and Ferron 1994) have found that rural children born into poverty are more likely than similar urban children to remain in poverty. Youths experiencing chronic poverty may come to question the value of a high school diploma as a way to climb up. Discouragement over unalleviated poverty may be why impoverished youths are much more likely to drop out before finishing their high school diploma if they live in rural areas (Lichter, Cornwell, and Eggebeen 1993). Unfortunately, this result means that poverty is more likely to become transgenerational if it is rural.

Changing Rural Social Systems

Figure 1. This stone schoolhouse was built in the nineteenth century in a rural area just outside Ann Arbor, Michigan. Surrounded by a suburb, the school is now a nursery school. (Photograph by Nan E. Johnson.)

Rural–Urban and Urban–Rural Migration

People living in areas lacking economic opportunities can move to more favorable locations. But does rural–to–urban migration really help young people climb out of poverty or unemployed youths to find jobs? One analysis of these two questions tracked rural adults aged 18-23 with longitudinal data covering 1980-88 (Wenk and Hardesty 1993). A proportional hazards model of those with at least one poverty spell controlled the respondent's marital status, educational attainment, and number of children in the household at the beginning of the first spell, any change in status on these three variables during the first spell, any first–time migration to an urban county and its date of occurrence, and the number of years the first poverty spell lasted. The importance of using statistical models allowing a change in a predictor variable was underscored by the fact that rural white men and women stayed in poverty longer if the number of children in their household changed during the poverty spell. Moving to an urban area shortened the poverty spell for white and black rural women and the duration of unemployment for rural men of either race. This longitudinal study confirmed that rural–to–urban migration did alleviate economic hardship for rural youths in the 1980s. However, this migration selected the better educated youths (Lee 1970) and thereby perpetuated the spatial inequality of human capital.

Given that the nonmetro poverty rate has been persistently higher than the metro rate (Task Force on Persistent Rural Poverty 1994), the net inmigration to nonmetro counties that emerged during the 1970s (to the surprise of most Rural Sociologists) and then reappeared in the 1990s (Johnson and Beale 1994, 1995) seems economically irrational until we realize that it was caused by the territorial mobility of middle–aged and elderly adults. Young adults aged 20–29 have manifested net outmigration from nonmetro to metro counties unfailingly since the 1940s (Johnson 1993). In other words, job opportunities for young adults trying to establish themselves in the labor force have been better all along, and have been perceived as such, in metro counties. And because economic opportunities have been much scarcer for women than men in nonmetro America, young women have been more likely than young men to forsake their nonmetropolitan origins (Fuguitt, Brown, and Beale 1989).

Figure 2. Beginning in the nineteenth century, trains transported not only agricultural products but also rural labor to urban marketplaces. For every pioneer moving westward, twenty farm people moved to town. (Photograph by Nan E. Johnson)

The majority of nonmetro counties in the United States reverted to population losses in the 1980s, but Michigan was one of the few states where the percentage of population change in nonmetro counties remained positive and greater than that in metro counties. Wang's analysis of Michigan's "deviancy" (chap. 7) distinguishes nonmetro counties according to whether they are located in the Southern Lower Peninsula (SLP), the Northern Lower Peninsula (NLP), or the Upper Peninsula (UP). Since all of the metro counties are located in the SLP, these three intrastate regions represent a scale of decreasing proximity to metro areas. He finds that the only type of nonmetro county with net inmigration during the 1980s was in the NLP, and this gain occurred mainly because these counties attracted retirees and residents seeking resort communities. Also, he finds that the core metropolitan counties (containing the central city of the Metropolitan Statistical Area) faced population loss associated with a steep decline in jobs in manufacturing in the 1980s. Wang concludes that the expatriation of jobs in the global automotive industry headquartered in Michigan caused net outmigration not only from the metro and their adjacent nonmetro counties in the SLP, but also from the nonadjacent nonmetro counties in the UP. As such, Wang's work shows that nonmetropolitan population gains from inmigration reflect only a new mode of regionalization controlled by decisionmakers in the metropolitan centers.

A companion chapter by Rathge (chap. 8) analyzes the content and the placement of articles published in a weekly newspaper during the 1970s that interpret the social impacts of rapid population growth in a nonmetro county in Michigan's NLP. He reports that many articles discussed how the exploding number of retirement and recreation homes inflated property values and property taxes beyond the level that many indigenous people could afford in "Pine Tree County." This trend may have increased homelessness or forced the sale of homes. Certainly, the number of county recipients of public assistance increased 155 percent between 1972 and 1980, a rate exceeding that for all other nonmetro counties in the state. The modal category of articles and the majority of those appearing on the front page claimed that population influx burdened the local government's efforts to prevent and solve crimes and to offer other public services. Inmigration was blamed for boosting the number of seasonally occupied homes, which facilitated vandalism, and for raising the number of school–aged youths, who were most likely to become the vandals. Consequently, chapter 8 reinforces Lichter's (1993) claim that a net inflow of people to a nonmetro county does not lift the economic well–being of all. Rather, it suggests that a net inflow of people creates more distance between the rich and the poor, by importing more of the former, who then create more disadvantages for the latter.

The substitution of machines for hands in doing farmwork coexisted with the net influx of people to nonmetro counties in Michigan in the 1970s and 1980s because the inmigrants were not going into farming. Rather, the mechanization of farming has been simultaneously a cause of, and a response to, the loss of farm workers (whether or not they stayed in nonmetro places) and a root of the de–familialization of the farm labor force. Since heavy machines can kill and since concerns for safety vary with who faces risk, farming has become more perilous in the current agricultural economy of the United States. At the same time, farms have emerged as recreational sites where hunters, fishermen, or spectators confront potential mishaps. Johnson's analysis (chap. 9) of death certificate data for Michigan shows that most people dying from accidents on farms in 1989–91 were not farming at the moment of the mishap, and most of those killed in the line of farm duty were farming only part–time. The annualized rate of accidental deaths per farm was somewhat higher in metro than nonmetro counties in Michigan, and this appeared partly due to variations in the social structure of agriculture between the two types of county. Farm laborers, who had the highest rate of on–the–job accidents, outnumbered farm operators and managers only in metro counties.

The net inflow of migrants to rural locations in the 1970s was not peculiar to the United States, for it also occurred in a number of countries in northwestern Europe (Vining 1982). In chapter 10, Hannan attributes rural Irish population growth in the 1970s (which was more rapid in the open countryside than in urban centers) to state policies that promoted tuition–free secondary schooling, raised agricultural prices through membership in the European Economic Community, and promoted the spread of industrial jobs in the rural nonfarm sector. Ironically, he finds the propensity for outmigration, which had been lowest in the hinterlands in the 1960s, had become highest there in the mid–1980s because the severe decline in farm–sector employment had not been sufficiently matched by a rise in nonfarm–sector jobs. He decides that the relationship between locality and inequality remains strong in the Republic of Ireland, even after 20 years of national policies aimed at the opposite effect.

Nuptiality and Fertility

Several important demographic and socioeconomic consequences have followed from the pattern of greater net outmigration of young women than young men from rural to urban places in the United States. In 1990, the sex ratio (the number of males per 100 females) was highly feminized (i.e., much below 100) in urban places within either metro or nonmetro counties. The sex ratio was lowest (89.3 males per 100 females) in small cities of 2,500-9,999 inhabitants in nonmetro counties partly because

Table 1.
Demographic Characteristics of the 1990 U.S. Population by Type of Place of Residence.

Place of Residence	No. of Residents	Median Age	%<18 Years	%>64 Years	DR	% Now Married of Females 15-24	CWR
United States	248,709,873	32.9	25.6	12.6	61.7	17.9	367.6
Metro:	192,725,741	32.6	25.3	11.9	59.2	16.7	360.8
Central city (CC)	77,843,533	31.6	24.7	12.4	59.0	15.6	358.7
Not in CC:	114,882,208	33.3	25.7	11.6	59.5	17.6	362.3
Inside urbanized area (UA)	79,755,134	33.3	25.0	11.8	58.2	16.5	353.7
Outside UA	8,684,794	32.1	27.1	13.5	68.4	21.0	405.9
Rural	26,442,280	33.8	27.3	10.5	60.8	19.8	375.8
Nonmetro:	55,984,132	33.8	26.6	14.7	70.5	22.1	394.7
Inside UA	1,520,259	31.8	24.0	14.2	61.8	17.1	355.6
Place of 10,000+ outside UA	9,873,345	31.7	25.1	14.9	66.7	17.6	374.0
Place of 2,500–9,999 outside UA	9,458,347	34.2	26.1	17.6	77.6	21.6	409.1
Rural	35,132,181	34.4	27.4	13.9	70.4	24.3	399.0

Source: Data are from tables 15 and 38 in: U.S. Bureau of the Census. 1990 *Census of Population, General Population Characteristics, United States*. Washington, DC: U.S. Government Printing Office, 1992.
Note: DR = Dependency Ratio, the number of persons aged less than 18 or over 64 years as a percentage of those aged 18–64. CWR = the Child–Woman Ratio, the number of children under age 5 per 1,000 women aged 20–44

elderly farm widows are more likely than elderly farm widowers to move to town (Fuguitt, Brown, and Beale 1989, 123). On the other hand, the sex ratio was nearly balanced (almost 100) in rural areas of metro and nonmetro U.S. counties (101.5 and 99.2, respectively). One reason is that persons who move out of rural areas are more likely to be single than either those they leave behind or those who move into rural areas.

This difference in the sex ratios has structured different marriage markets for young women in nonmetro and metro locales. McLaughlin, Lichter, and Johnston (1993) used the 1979–86 National Longitudinal Survey of Youth (NLSY) to track the age at which young (18–28 years old) females married for the first time. Geocodes from the NLSY were used to link a residence to demographic data on that place as collected by the 1980 Census. In this way, the authors calculated the ratio of the number of unmarried, noninstitutionalized males aged $x–2$ to $x+9$ per 100 unmarried, noninstitutionalized females in the same age range and associated it with a respondent aged x living in that area. This placed a respondent in a 12–year age group of potential husbands and rivals in that marriage market. If the respondent moved, the sex–ratio was updated to reflect the new marriage market. Not only was the mean marriage–market sex ratio for these never–married women much higher in nonmetro than metro areas (119 vs. 106), but also the much greater availability of men relative to women in the nonmetro locales was a major factor in the earlier age at nonmetro females' first marriage. That the higher sex ratio still facilitated earlier female marriage in nonmetro areas at the end of the 1980s is indirectly shown by the higher percentage of nonmetro than metro females aged 15–24 who were currently married at the time of the 1990 Census (22.1 vs. 16.7 percent, table 1). Note that the largest fraction of females aged 15–24 who were currently married in 1990 (nearly one in four) were those living in rural sections of nonmetro counties.

An earlier age at a woman's first marriage generally means that her births will be spaced more closely and that she will have a larger total number of births in her lifetime (Pratt et al. 1984; Fuguitt, Brown, and Beale 1989). Indeed, the earlier first marriages of nonmetro women have preserved a higher Total Fertility Rate[2] in nonmetro than in metro counties, despite falls in both TFRs below the replacement level (Fuguitt, Beale, and Reibel 1991). By 1986, a nonmetro woman could expect an average of 1.92 births in her lifetime, while a metro woman could expect 1.81 (Fuguitt, Beale, and Riebel 1991).[3] While there is not much difference left in these fertility rates between nonmetro and metro women, Fuguitt and colleagues (1991) reported that a large difference remains in how these births are timed. To wit, the age–specific rates of bearing first or second children are much higher for nonmetro women before age 25, but much higher for metro women aged 25 or older. Fuguitt, Beale, and Reibel (1991) speculated that the earlier average age at motherhood in nonmetro America reveals nonmetro women's aversion to abortion.

Population Aging

The decline of the birth rate in both nonmetro and metro areas is the main reason why the U.S. population–at–large is aging; but this process is being hastened in nonmetro areas by the persistent exodus of young adults, particularly women in the prime childbearing ages of 20–29. (These outmigrants contribute births to metro instead of nonmetro areas and thus help to keep metro populations "young.") Also, net inmigration to nonmetro counties has favored the elderly since the 1960s (Johnson 1993). Motivations of these elderly inmigrants are a search for the scenic beauty or the recreational sports at isolated mountains and lakes and a wish to return to the rural residence of one's childhood. As a result, not only was the percentage of children under age 18 higher in nonmetro/rural than in metro/urban places, but the percentage of persons aged 65 or older was also, according to the 1990 U.S. Census (table 1).

While the 1993 poverty rate of 12 percent for elderly persons (aged 65+ years) equals that for working–age adults (18–64 years), elderly adults in poverty are less likely to climb out (Treas 1995). Hence, the greater proportion of the nonmetro population that is elderly and the higher poverty rate of the nonmetro than the metro elderly (16.1 percent vs. 10.8 percent in 1990; see Glasgow et al. 1993) are two factors sustaining the greater material disadvantage of *all* nonmetro peoples. In fact, seniors' poverty places strong economic cross pressures on nonmetro adults of labor-force age, who try to offer material support to their elderly parents while at the same time caring for their children.

One way of meeting multigenerational needs is to pool resources through coresidence. Indeed the majority of the elderly respondents to a survey in rural North Carolina felt their children should give them shelter if need be (Powers and Kivett 1992). Yet elderly respondents to the 1982 National Long–Term Care Survey (NLTCS) were more likely to live with their children if they were in cities of 50,000 or more inhabitants (Lee, Dwyer, and Coward 1990). This unexpected finding may have resulted from a failure to control either the race of these respondents (blacks are more likely than whites to live in three–generation households in metropolitan areas) or the sex of the child they expected to provide the coresidence (traditional sex roles designate *daughters* as principal caregivers) or from the restriction of the 1982 NLTCS to elders with at least one chronic physical disability (obviously, chronic physical disability requires more complex help than economic disability alone). On the other hand, since more rural than urban adults of labor–force age head nuclear families who are sheltered, yet teetering on the edge of homelessness, the former may be more hesitant to invite parents or grandparents to live under such a precarious roof (Fitchen 1992).

Implications for Theory and Public Policy

The praxis of American Rural Sociologists is to conduct research with immediate applications promoting the human welfare. From the 1970s to the 1990s, their efforts were challenged by uneven social and economic development, which widened inequalities between the rural and urban family based on the sex and race of its headship and the ages of its members and by the globalization of the rural occupational system, which expropriated decisionmaking and profits from local control. Can Structural–Functionalism be revised to account for adverse changes in these rural social systems? Can theoretical revisions then guide new forms of rural development in which communities rebuild familial and occupational systems so that social inequalities converge?

The answer to both questions invites new propositions on how rural social systems (familial and occupational) are organized. In their extreme forms, rural social systems embody Gemeinschaft–like principles, which organize social relationships to promote not only the narrow economic aims, but also the broader goals of social solidarity and religious sacredness and, in the process, create "communities of common fate" (Loomis and Beegle 1975). Yet social change need not inevitably shift rural social systems toward the urban pole on the continuum, having antonymous (Gesellschaft–like) rules of organization. Rather, changes in rural social systems have historically fluctuated back and forth on the continuum and will likely remain in a state of flux between its two poles (Wilkinson 1991). Acknowledging this likelihood frees us to consider many more options for empowering rural social change in familial and occupational systems.

Rural capital must be created if rural laborers and their families are to be empowered. Also, the integration of American rural and urban occupational systems into the global marketplace means that rural U.S. communities must recognize and accept their ties to these larger geo–social spheres. For such reasons, Wilkinson (1991, 86) called for the planning of a futuristic "rural–urban community," uniting the most empowering features of social organization found at both rural–Gemeinschaft and urban–Gesellschaft extrema. In service to this goal, we hold that new theoretical guidelines are offered by Neo–Functionalism and World Systems Theory.

Classic dialectical theory, as given by Karl Marx, addresses the struggle of individuals against such stressors as poverty, which ought to impinge differently on each one according to sex, race, and age. But Neo–Functionalism goes on to ask how an individual's selfish interests or burdens, as structured by sex, race, and age, can be negotiated within one's family without leading to estrangement. As such, Neo–Functionalism pushes contemporary sociological theory to see stress as a collective (familial), not just an individualistic, phenomenon (Kingsbury and Scanzoni 1993) and seeks answers to the first question above through viewing intrafamilial compromise as the synthesis of a dialectical contradiction. According to Pauline Boss's (1987) approach to Neo–Functionalism, which we follow, an important question becomes: how can rural families maintain a higher level of stability than urban families, despite a higher level of economic stress? This a question worthy of further research.

World Systems Theory is likely to offer new insights into how rural occupational systems can be reorganized in ways that do not inevitably lead to the exploitation of rural workers. World Systems Theory acknowledges that capital will seek to maximize profit anywhere, even in rural areas (Falk and Lyson 1993). Therefore, the challenge to rural economic planners is to attract capitalistic investment that builds on and reinforces the social and economic strengths of the rural population.

An example of how that can work is given in chapter 11. Here, Marilyn Aronoff assumes that communities can continue to exist and have separate identities even when they become interdependent with external social systems. Communities can self–direct development by creating or recreating unique, positive local identities that enable them to attract external resources to benefit their residents. Aronoff analyzes this process for Gratiot County, Michigan, a nonmetro county that faced industrial collapse after several mobile home manufacturing plants were closed in 1973–74. Then, in 1976, the county's largest employer, a chemical manufacturing plant, was closed when it was discovered to be the source of polybrominated biphenyl (PBB), a toxic substance that was accidentally added to commercially produced cattlefeed and led to mass extinction of herds in the state. Collapse of the agricultural sector of the county's economy continued with a downturn in the world demand for U.S. farm products in the early 1980s and was exacerbated by a major flood in 1986. With initial funding from the State of Michigan, the Greater Gratiot Community Development, Inc. (GGDI) was formed in 1978 to facilitate and coordinate economic recovery.

To these ends, its leaders have cultivated ties with the local college (a "piece of the outside world" inside the county) and with state legislators. To and through these links to external resources, GGDI has distributed brochures portraying the county as offering the advantages of proximity to metropolitan institutions (medical facilities, universities, cultural centers) without the penalties of urban life. The assets offered by its rural labor force to external investors are depicted as industriousness, efficiency, and warmth. Having had one of the highest rates of unemployment in the state in the 1970s, Gratiot County is now the only county of fewer than 140,000 inhabitants to have three industrial parks. In addition, GGDI has secured state and local monies to fund a "business incubator" to nurse fledgling entrepreneurial activities. As such, external resources are being used not only to boost the local stock of jobs, but to stimulate internal commerce further.

Similarly, a non–Western rural society can use its linkages into the global economy, not to obliterate, but to sponsor local identity and commercial vitality. In chapter 12, Joanne Bubolz Eicher describes how this process has been engaged by the Kalabaris, a riverine people of Western Nigeria, who entered the global economy in the fifteenth century through trading contacts with the Portuguese. The Kalabari people have obtained textiles and items of clothing by barter with Europeans, South Indians, and other Western Nigerians and then have exercised "cultural authentication" to make these imports into material symbols of local identities. A path to cultural authentication has been to combine European accessories (e.g., Bowler hats, scarves, and canes) with West African main dresses in ways to create a distinctive Kalabari ensemble.

Finally, in chapter 13, Gaston J. Labadie studies the hinterlands of Bella Union, Uruguay, in the Department of Artigas, the only department showing rural population growth in the 1985 census. The stimulus to this net inmigration was economic development based on sugar cane production and refinement. With initial funding from Spain, local producers organized the refinery as a cooperative in the mid–1960s to process sugar for the national market. A profit of 20 percent over production costs is guaranteed to the sugar cane growers by national law, and half of this is paid as dues by the producer–member to the cooperative. The forward vertical integration of the production with the processing of sugar cane has allowed profits to be retained locally for investments in other infrastructures.

Two examples derive from technological investments that have diversified farming, boosted agricultural productivity, and increased the demand for farm labor in the rural hinterlands of Bella Union. These include a rural electrification program, which has led to the irrigation not only of sugar cane fields, but also of citrus groves and grape vineyards; and a sponsorship of agricultural research to increase yields and growing seasons. Thus, Bella Union is a model of relatively even agricultural development from which all social classes have benefited.

More importantly, the story of Bella Union is a tale of how spatial location can augment the profits of capital investors. Its close proximity to the borders of Argentina and Brazil forms a double black marketplace, where the value of the Uruguayan peso can be stretched. As such, future theoretical and applied work on changing rural social systems and their demographic sequelae must treat physical/social geography as a significant factor attracting or repelling venture capital, shaping the occupational systems of its interiors, and determining the fates of families who must sell their skills within labor markets constrained by space.

Notes

1. Since Prairie Hills and Riverton are representative of other rural communities experiencing externally controlled rural "development," we are not surprised that core industries headquartered in metropolitan areas have devised profit–saving strategies damaging to union employment. The percentage of the labor force belonging to unions fell from around 30 in the early 1970s to under 20 in the mid–1980s (Lobao 1990, 43).
2. To obtain the Total Fertility Rate (TFR), all the age–specific fertility rates (ASFRs) per woman for a particular calendar year in a population must be summed; the sum is then multiplied by the number of years in the age intervals used to calculate the ASFRs. This product (the TFR) represents how many children a woman would bear in her lifetime if she bore children on this schedule throughout her fecund lifespan.
3. To replace a population exactly, given the current mortality conditions in the United States, a woman must bear an average of 2.1 children in her lifetime. A TFR of 2.1 is necessary to assure the replacement of the woman and her partner and to allow for the fact that some women will never marry and some live births will not survive to reach childbearing age.

References

Ahlburg, Dennis A., and Carol J. DeVita. 1992. New realities of the American family. *Population Bulletin* 47(2): 1–44.

Bailey, Ilena, and Melissa Snyder. 1921. A survey of farm homes. *The Journal of Home Economics* 13: 346–56.

Bachman, Ronet. 1992. Crime in nonmetropolitan America: A national accounting of trends, incidence rates, and idiosyncratic vulnerabilities. *Rural Sociology* 57(4): 546–60.

Bokemeier, Janet L., and Ann R. Tickamyer. 1985. Labor force experiences of nonmetropolitan women. *Rural Sociology* 50(1): 51–73.

Boss, Pauline. 1987. Family stress. In *Handbook of marriage and the family*, ed. M. B. Sussman and S. K. Steinmetz, 695–724. New York: Plenum Press.

Dennis, Ruth E. 1967. Suicide differentials in Michigan: A replication. Master's thesis, Department of Sociology, Michigan State University, East Lansing.

Falk, William W., and Thomas A. Lyson. 1993. Forgotten places redux. In *Forgotten places: Uneven development in rural America*, ed. T. A. Lyson and W. W. Falk, 257–69. Lawrence: University Press of Kansas.

Fitchen, Janet M. 1992. On the edge of homelessness: Rural poverty and housing insecurity. *Rural Sociology* 57(2): 173–93.

Fuguitt, Glenn V., Calvin L. Beale, and Michael Reibel. 1991. Recent trends in metropolitan–nonmetropolitan fertility. *Rural Sociology* 56(3): 475–86.

Fuguitt, Glenn V., David L. Brown, and Calvin L. Beale. 1989. *Rural and small town America*. New York: Russell Sage Foundation.

Garrett, Patricia, Nicholas Ng'andu, and John Ferron. 1994. Is rural residency a risk factor for childhood poverty? *Rural Sociology* 59(1): 66–83.

Glasgow, Nina, Karen Holden, Diane McLaughlin, and Graham Rowles. 1993. The rural elderly and poverty. In *Persistent Poverty in Rural America*, ed. Task Force on Persistent Rural Poverty, 259–91. Boulder, Colo.: Westview Press.

Gringeri, Christina E. 1993. Inscribing gender in rural development: Industrial homework in two Midwestern communities. *Rural Sociology* 58(1): 30–52.

_____. 1994. *Getting by: Women homeworkers and rural economic development*. Lawrence: University Press of Kansas.

Houser, Paul M., and J. Allan Beegle. 1951. Mortality differentials in Michigan. East Lansing: Michigan Agricultural Experiment Station Bulletin No. 367.

Jacobson, Alvin L. 1975. Crime trends in Southern and non–Southern cities: A twenty–year perspective. *Social Forces* 54(1): 226–42.

Jensen, Leif, and David J. Eggebeen. 1994. Nonmetropolitan poor children and reliance on public assistance. *Rural Sociology* 59(1): 45–65.

Jensen, Leif, and Marta Tienda. 1989. Nonmetropolitan minority families in the United States: Trends in racial and ethnic economic stratification, 1959–1986. *Rural Sociology* 54(4): 509–32.

Johnson, Kenneth M. 1993. Demographic change in nonmetropolitan America, 1980 to 1990. *Rural Sociology* 58(3): 347–65.

Johnson, Kenneth M., and Calvin L. Beale. 1994. The recent revival of widespread population growth in nonmetropolitan areas of the United States. *Rural Sociology* 59(4): 655–67.

_____. 1995. The rural rebound revisited. *American Demographics* 17(July): 46–54.

Kingsbury, Nancy, and John Scanzoni. 1993. Structural–functionalism. In *Sourcebook of family theories and methods: A contextual approach*, ed. Pauline G. Boss, William J. Doherty, Ralph LaRossa, Walter R. Schumm, and Suzanne K. Steinmetz, 195–217. New York: Plenum Press.

Kowalski, Gregory S., and Don Duffield. 1990. The impact of the rural population component on homicide rates in the United States: A county-level analysis. *Rural Sociology* 55(1): 76-90.

Kurosu, Satomi. 1991. Suicide in rural areas: The case of Japan 1960–1980. *Rural Sociology* 56(4): 603–18.
Lee, Everett S. 1970. Migration in relation to education, intellect, and social structure. *Population Index* 36(4): 437–44.
Lee, Gary R., Jeffrey W. Dwyer, and Raymond T. Coward. 1990. Residential location and proximity to children among impaired elderly parents. *Rural Sociology* 55(4): 579–89.
Lichter, Daniel T. 1989. Race, employment hardship, and inequality in the American nonmetropolitan South. *American Sociological Review* 54(3): 436–46.
_____. 1993. Migration, population redistribution, and the new spatial inequality. In *The demography of rural life*, ed. David L. Brown, Donald R. Field, and James J. Zuiches, 19-46. University Park, Penn.: Northeast Regional Center for Rural Development.
Lichter, Daniel T., Gretchen T. Cornwell, and David J. Eggebeen. 1993. Harvesting human capital: Family structure and education among rural youth. *Rural Sociology* 58(1): 53–75.
Lichter, Daniel T., and David J. Eggebeen. 1992. Child poverty and the changing rural family. *Rural Sociology* 57(2): 151–72.
Lobao, Linda M. 1990. *Locality and inequality: Farm and industry structure and socioeconomic conditions.* Albany, N.Y.: SUNY Press.
Loomis, Charles P., and J. Allan Beegle. 1950. *Rural social systems.* New York: Prentice–Hall, Inc.
_____. 1957. *Rural Sociology: The strategy of change.* Englewood Cliffs, N.J.: Prentice–Hall, Inc.
_____. 1975. *A strategy for rural change.* New York: John Wiley & Sons.
MacKellar, F. Landis, and Machiko Yanagishita. 1995. Homicide in the United States: Who's at risk? *Population Trends and Public Policy* 21: 1–20.
McLaughlin, Diane K., Daniel T. Lichter, and Gail M. Johnston. 1993. Some women marry young: Transitions to first marriage in metropolitan and nonmetropolitan areas. *Journal of Marriage and the Family* 55 (November): 827–38.
McLaughlin, Diane K., and Lauri Perman. 1991. Returns vs. endowments in the earnings attainment process for metropolitan and nonmetropolitan men and women. *Rural Sociology* 56(3): 339–65.
Merton, Robert K. 1957. *Social theory and social structure.* Glenco, Ill.: Free Press.
Parsons, Talcott, and Robert Bales (with James Olds, Morris Zelditch, Jr., and Phillip Slater). 1955. *Family socialization and interaction process.* New York: Free Press.
Potter, Lloyd B., and Omer R. Galle. 1990. Residential and racial mortality differentials in the South by cause of death. *Rural Sociology* 55(2): 233–44.
Powers, Edward A., and Vira R. Kivett. 1992. Kin expectations and kin support among rural older adults. *Rural Sociology* 57(2): 194–215.

Pratt, William F., William D. Mosher, Christine A. Bachrach, and Marjorie C. Horn. 1984. Understanding U.S. fertility: Findings from the National Survey of Family Growth, Cycle III. *Population Bulletin* 39(5): 1–42.

Rank, Mark R., and Thomas A. Hirschl. 1988. A rural–urban comparison of welfare exits: The importance of population density. *Rural Sociology* 55(2): 190–206.

Saenz, Rogelio, and Marie Ballejos. 1993. Industrial development and persistent poverty in the Lower Rio Grande Valley. In *Forgotten Places: Uneven development in rural America*, ed., T.A. Lyson and W.W. Falk, 102-24. Lawrence: University of Kansas Press.

Saenz, Rogelio, and John K. Thomas. 1991. Minority poverty in nonmetropolitan Texas. *Rural Sociology* 56(2): 204–23.

Schroeder, W. Widick, and J. Allan Beegle. 1953. Suicide: An instance of high rural rates. *Rural Sociology* 18 (March): 45–52.

Summers, Gene F. 1991. Minorities in rural society. *Rural Sociology* 56(2): 177–88.

Task Force on Persistent Rural Poverty. 1994. Poverty in rural America: Trends and demographic characteristics. In *Persistent Poverty in Rural America*, 20–38. Boulder, Colo: Westview Press.

Tickamyer, Ann, and Janet Bokemeier. 1988. Sex differences in labor market experiences. *Rural Sociology* 53(2): 166–89.

Tigges, Leann M., and Deborah M. Tootle. 1990. Labor supply, labor demand, and men's underemployment in rural and urban labor markets. *Rural Sociology* 35(3): 328–56.

Timasheff, Nicholas S. 1967. *Sociological theory: Its nature and growth*. New York: Random House.

Toennies, Ferdinand. 1957. *Community and society—Gemeinschaft and Gesellschaft*. Translated by Charles P. Loomis. New York: Harper and Row.

Treas, Judith. 1995. Older Americans in the 1990s and beyond. *Population Bulletin* 50(2): 1–45.

Vanek, Joann. 1980. Work, leisure, and family roles: Farm households in the United States, 1920–55. *Journal of Family History* 5(4): 422–31.

Vining, Daniel R., Jr. 1982. Migration between the core and the periphery. *Scientific American* 247(6): 44–53.

Wenk, DeeAnn, and Constance Hardesty. 1993. The effects of rural–to–urban migration on poverty status of youth in the 1980s. *Rural Sociology* 58(1): 76–92.

Wilkinson, Kenneth P. 1984a. A research note on homicide and rurality. *Social Forces* 63(2): 445–52.

_____. 1984b. Rurality and patterns of social disruption. *Rural Sociology* 49(1): 23–36.

_____. 1991. The future of the rural community in rural areas. In *The future of rural America*, ed. Kenneth Pigg, 73–89. Boulder, Colo.: Westview Press.

Part 2

Changing Rural Social Systems: Focus on Familial and Occupational Systems

2

THE POOR IN NONMETROPOLITAN AMERICA[1]

William P. O'Hare

Introduction

Higher poverty rates in nonmetropolitan (nonmetro) areas are certainly not new. The 1940 Census showed that the proportion of nonmetro people in poverty[2] was over 150 percent that of metropolitan (metro) people (83.4 percent and 54.7 percent, respectively; Ross, Danziger, and Smolensky 1985). To some extent these rates represented the disproportionate impact of the Great Depression of the 1930s on nonmetro people.

Economic recovery from the Great Depression began with, and continued after, World War II, but metro Americans benefited much more. The decline in the poverty rate in metro America (to 15 percent by 1959) was so much faster than that in nonmetro America (to 33 percent by 1959), that the poverty gap widened to a factor of 220 percent ([33/15] x 100) in favor of metro Americans. However, the nonmetro poverty rate fell more rapidly than the metro rate in absolute and relative terms during 1960-79, so that by the end of the 1970s, the nonmetro rate was only 127 percent of that in the metro population (13.8 percent and 10.7 percent, respectively).

From this absolute and relative convergence, many experts predicted a virtual disappearance by the 1980s of the poverty gap separating metro and nonmetro America. For example, Hawley and Mazie (1981, 20) concluded: " . . . events in industrial movements, local government changes, the shifting status pattern, and the growing inclusiveness of the organizational structure of the nation point toward a convergence of nonmetro and metro sectors." Johnson (1985, 159) argued: "There is little chance that demographic trends will revert to the pre–1970 pattern because the economic and industrial structure of contemporary nonmetropolitan counties is quite different from that of earlier times."

Despite these predictions, many trends in the metro and nonmetro populations are no longer converging: indeed, the gap between metro and nonmetro poverty rates widened again during the 1980s. In 1986, the poverty rate in the nonmetro population was 147 percent that of the metro population (18.1 percent and 12.3 percent, respectively).

The shift from converging rates of poverty in metro and nonmetro areas during the 1960s and 1970s to diverging rates during the 1980s poses many interesting questions regarding the underlying causes of the recent increase in nonmetro poverty. In the following analysis, I address these questions from two conflicting theoretical perspectives.

The first perspective, known as the Culture of Poverty Theory, argues that adults are poor because they lack certain personal characteristics or values; such as, job skills, proper motivation, or good work habits. In other words, people are poor not because they cannot find work, but rather because they do not have the right training or motivation. The origins of this perspective are found in: Lewis 1966a and 1966b; Banfield 1968; and Auletta 1982. Similarly, Murray (1984) invoked this perspective in suggesting that the cause of American poverty is a dependence on welfare since the liberal reforms of the 1960s.

The second perspective, known as the Structural Poverty Theory, holds that poverty is rooted in a social structure that does not yield enough jobs, hours, or wages to provide people with adequate sustenance. This view suggests that individuals are typically poor not because they are intrinsically different from the rest, but because the social structure has failed to generate appropriate job opportunities. Proponents of this latter interpretation are: Harrington (1984); Kasarda (1985); and Wilson (1987).

These opposing theoretical views of poverty have different policy–related implications. Public policy prescriptions for reducing poverty would focus on changing the skills, values, and habits of individuals under the Culture of Poverty Theory, but would concentrate on modifying major social institutions and opportunity structures under the Structural Poverty Theory. Also, most recent work has concentrated on the metropolitan poor (Mead 1986; Murray 1984; and Wilson 1987). In the present study, I examine roots of nonmetropolitan poverty in the 1979–86 period from the two theoretical perspectives

Data Sources and Definitions

Most of the data are from the Demographic Supplement to the 1980 and 1987 March Current Population Survey (CPS) conducted by the U.S. Bureau of the Census. The CPS is a nationwide household survey that collects demographic and socioeconomic information from approximately 60,000 households each month. The CPS obtains the numbers and ages of people in the participating household and the total household income from all sources in the preceding year. Therefore, these two surveys can be used to determine whether a responding household was in poverty in the preceding year, 1979 or 1986. The federal income poverty index, constructed by the Social Security Administration, gauges the adequacy only of money income (e.g., it excludes the value of Food Stamps) in light of the household's size and composition. The poverty threshold is recalculated each year to take into account changes in the Consumer Price Index or inflation. In 1986, the poverty threshold was $11,203 for an average family of four people.

Metropolitan Statistical Areas (MSAs), formerly called Standard Metropolitan Statistical Areas (SMSAs), are determined by the U.S. Office of Management and Budget (OMB) in consultation with the Bureau of the Census. MSAs are comprised of counties that surround large cities (typically a city of 50,000 or more) including outlying counties that are socially and economically tied to the core county. The nonmetropolitan counties are all those that are not part of a Metropolitan Statistical Area.

Interpretation of the changes in the nonmetropolitan population in the 1980s is confounded somewhat by a changing definition of what constitutes a metropolitan area, a reclassification of metro areas based on data from the 1980 Census, and most importantly, a change in the CPS sampling frame. In 1984, the CPS sampling frame was redesigned to account for changes in metro areas since 1972. This abruptly altered the residential location status of about 20 million Americans from nonmetro to metro. Consequently, analysis of changes between 1979 and 1986 must be based on changing proportions or rates, rather than on raw numbers.

There is some contention that the redefinition of metropolitan areas in 1983 by the OMB and the redesign of the CPS sampling frame biased the rate of nonmetro poverty upwardly by reclassifying many of the most prosperous nonmetro counties as metropolitan. However, the nonmetro poverty rate was 18.3 percent both in 1983 and in 1985.[3] This stability suggests that the redesign of the CPS sampling frame in 1984 did not increase the observed rate of rural poverty.

The March 1980 CPS contained records for 19,816 nonmetro respondents aged 18 to 44 who represented 24.2 million persons. The March 1987 CPS sample contained records for 15,166 persons between the ages of 18 and 44 who resided in nonmetro areas and who represented 20.5 million persons. The sample cases were weighted to provide estimates that are consistent with several important characteristics of the national population. The samples were drawn to be representative of all states and therefore of the regions and census divisions containing them.

Analysis

The Culture of Poverty Theory and the Structural Poverty Theory both seek to explain poverty occurring among able–bodied people of working age. Consequently, this analysis will focus on the changes in poverty between 1979 and 1986 among nonmetro persons aged 18 to 44 (hereafter called "young adults"). Young adults were more vulnerable than older adults of working age (45 to 64 years) to employment–related economic hardships during the recession of the early 1980s (see O'Hare 1988). Reasons include the relative lack of time in developing the seniority and job–related employment experiences that would protect workers from layoffs or job terminations. Also, the economic hardships confronted by young adults were more likely to affect other family members; such as children under age 18.

Young adults comprised 34 percent of the poor in nonmetro areas in 1986.[4] The poverty rate for this group increased from 10.2 percent in 1979 to 15.8 percent in 1986; for workers in this group, the poverty rate went from 7.6 percent in 1979 to 12.7 percent in 1986. From the Culture of Poverty Theory, the rise in the poverty rate of young nonmetro adults (including the "working poor") would imply a reduction in rates of labor force participation, a decline in educational attainment and work effort, increased reliance on government assistance, and a shift in the reasons why poor young adults were not working. These implications can be examined with data from the CPS.

Labor Force Participation

The Culture of Poverty Theory would lead one to expect a decrease in labor force participation among young adults in nonmetro areas between 1979 and 1986. However, the share of young adults in nonmetro areas that worked or looked for work actually increased from 83.5 percent in 1979 to 85.7 percent in 1986 ($p < 0.10$). In 1979, those who worked or looked for work made up about two–thirds of the young poor in nonmetro areas, but by 1986 they comprised 70.1 percent. In other words, despite the increase in the nonmetro poverty rate over this seven–year period, there was no decline in the willingness to work. In fact, the poverty rate rose both for part–time and for full–time workers (table 1).

Educational Attainment

If the Culture of Poverty Theory is correct, we would expect a general decrease in the educational attainment of young adults in nonmetro areas during the years of the study, but this expectation is generally inconsistent with the data in table 2. The share of young nonmetro adults that had not

Table 1.
DISTRIBUTION OF YOUNG NONMETRO ADULTS BY NUMBER OF WEEKS WORKED DURING THE YEAR AND NUMBER OF HOURS WORKED PER WEEK: 1979 AND 1986.

	1979		1986	
	Percent in Category	*Poverty Rate in Category*	*Percent in Category*	*Poverty Rate in Category*
1–20 weeks worked in the previous year:				
1–34 hours/week	5.6%	15.9%	6.5%	26.8%
35+ hours/week	8.2%	19.4%	7.2%	31.3%
21 or more weeks worked in the previous year:				
1–34 hours/week	11.6%	9.8%	15.0%	15.2%
35+ hours/week	74.6%	5.1%	71.3%	7.6%

Source: Population Reference Bureau Analysis of Census Bureau Public Use Files from the March 1980 and March 1987 U.S. Current Population Survey
Note: In 1979, the number of poor people was 1,478,000 and total N was 19,990,000. In 1986, the number of poor was 2,007,000 and the total N was 17,128,000.

finished high school went from 24 percent in 1979 to 20 percent in 1986, and this drop was statistically significant at $p < 0.05$. There were small upward shifts in the share of young nonmetro adults who had completed 12 years of education as well as in those with 13 to 15 years of education, and a small decline in the share of young nonmetro adults who had completed 16 years of education, but these shifts are not statistically significant at the 0.10 level.

If the education-specific rates of poverty that were observed in young nonmetro adults in 1979 had remained constant until 1986, the poverty rate for young nonmetro adult workers would have been 9.6 percent, instead of the observed rate of 15.8 percent.

Welfare Reliance

One major element in the Culture of Poverty Theory is the reliance of the poor on public welfare assistance, often resulting in intergenerational

Table 2.
Years of Education Completed by Adults Ages 18 to 44 in Nonmetro Areas and Poverty Rates by Year of Education Completed: 1979 and 1986

	1979		1986	
	Percent in Category	*Poverty Rate in Category*	*Percent in Category*	*Poverty Rate in Category*
Years of Education Completed				
Fewer than 12 (Fewer than High School)	24.0	22.5	20.0	32.8
12 (High School Grad.)	40.5	7.6	43.7	14.3
13 to 15 (Some College)	21.8	5.6	23.3	10.1
16 or more (College Grad.)	13.7	3.4	13.0	4.8

Source: Population Reference Bureau Analysis of Census Bureau Public Use Files from the March 1980 and March 1987 U.S. Current Population Survey

transference of welfare dependence. This theory would argue that the increase in the poverty rate of young adults in nonmetro counties between 1979 and 1986 would be accompanied by increased reliance on welfare by this population.

This issue is more difficult to address, because one would expect the share of the whole population receiving welfare to increase because the number of poor increased, making more of them eligible for welfare assistance. Thus, I have elected to examine changes in the share of the poor that receive welfare benefits (table 3). It is evident that there were no major shifts in the extent to which poor young adults in nonmetro areas relied on public assistance. Two of the programs (Cash Public Assistance and Food Stamps) showed slight decreases in the percentage of the poor being served, and three of the programs (Medicaid, Public Housing, and

Table 3.
PARTICIPATION IN PUBLIC WELFARE PROGRAMS BY POOR YOUNG ADULTS IN NONMETRO AREAS: 1979 AND 1986

	Percentage of Poor Receiving Benefits from Program	
	1979	1986
Cash Public Assistance	21	18
Food Stamps	48	47
Medicaid	29	33
Public Housing[a]	12	13
Free School Lunch[b]	79	80

Source: Population Reference Bureau Analysis of Census Bureau Public Use Files from the March 1980 and March 1987 U.S. Current Population Survey
Note: This table includes all respondents, regardless of their work status. N was 2,459,000 in 1979 and 3,248,000 in 1986.
[a]Homeowners are not included in calculating this percentage.
[b]Only households with members ages 5 to 17 are included in this calculation.

Free School Lunch) showed slight increases. But none of these changes was statistically significant at the 0.10 level.

Reasons for Not Working

People without a job were asked to give the major reason why they were not working (table 4). The share of nonworking young adults in nonmetro areas that said they did not work because of home or family responsibilities declined from 65.3 percent in 1979 to 51.6 percent in 1986 ($p < 0.001$). At the same time, the category with the largest increase was those who claimed they looked but could not find a job (from 5.6 percent in 1979 to 13.5 percent in 1986; $p < 0.001$). This result is consistent with the rise in the unemployment rates seen in nonmetro areas during this time period. The only other category that increased noticeably during the period was those who did not work because they were ill or disabled (from 10.5 percent in 1979 to 14.6 percent in 1986; $p < 0.10$). These findings contradict the Culture of Poverty Theory.

The Structural Poverty Theory would not predict a change in the work–related characteristics of young nonmetro adults, but would predict that the recent rise in poverty among young adults in nonmetro counties

Table 4.
DISTRIBUTION OF YOUNG NONMETRO ADULT RESPONDENTS' REASONS FOR NOT WORKING: 1979 AND 1986.

	1979	1986
Ill or Disabled	10.5	14.6
Home or Family Responsibilities	65.3	51.6
Going to School	15.1	16.5
Can't Find a Job	5.6	13.5
Other	3.5	3.7
N	4,206,000	3,381,000

Source: Population Reference Bureau Analysis of Census Bureau Public Use Files from the March 1980 and March 1987 Current Population Survey

has been accompanied by changes in major social institutions, such as rural economies. Changes in several dimensions of the rural economic structure can be examined using the CPS files.

There are two possible interpretations of the Structural Poverty Theory that would lead to different expectations about changes between 1979 and 1986. One interpretation would predict that there was a shift in occupations and industries that resulted in a workforce more concentrated in the jobs with high poverty rates. The second interpretation would imply that in light of shifting national and international economic patterns, a general restructuring of rural economies raised the poverty rates for most rural workers, regardless of occupation or industry of employment. But none of the changes in the distribution of young nonmetro workers by industry (table 5) or occupation (table 6) between 1979 and 1986 was statistically significant ($p > 0.10$). It can be calculated from table 5 that if the industrial mix present in 1979 had experienced the industry–specific poverty rates of 1986, the overall poverty rate for young nonmetro workers would have been 12.5 percent, not much lower than the 12.7 percent actually observed in 1986. Hence, the rise in the poverty rate for young nonmetro members of the labor force was driven by a pervasive intraindustry and intraoccupation rise, not by a change in the division of labor within the rural economy.

Table 5.
DISTRIBUTION OF YOUNG NONMETRO ADULTS BY INDUSTRY OF EMPLOYMENT: 1979 AND 1986

	1979		1986	
	Percent in Industry	Poverty Rate in Industry	Percent in Industry	Poverty Rate in Industry
Agriculture and Mining	7.5	14.9	7.5	24.1
Construction	7.8	8.6	7.2	15.3
Manufacturing	25.7	6.7	23.1	9.9
Transportation/ Communications	4.3	6.4	4.2	6.5
Trade	19.1	8.7	21.6	14.4
Finance/Insurance/ Real Estate	3.9	3.5	3.4	5.4
Services	25.8	6.7	28.0	12.8
Government/ Public Utilities	5.8	4.1	5.0	7.0
N	19,302		16,622	

Source: Population Reference Bureau Analysis of Census Bureau Public Use Files from the March 1980 and March 1987 Current Population Survey.

Discussion

The rise in poverty among young adults in nonmetro counties from 1979 to 1986 did not result from a decay in their social capital, as would be indicated by a decline in the willingness to work, a withdrawal from the labor force, a rise in laziness (operationalized by an increase in dependence on welfare), or a drop in educational attainment. Rather, it appeared to respond to changes in the structure of the rural economy.

Resource–based industries have historically been the economic foundations of rural areas. A major structural transformation in the rural economy has been the decline in employment by such industries, although agriculture, forestry, fisheries, and mining continue to employ a disproportionate share of rural workers. Unfortunately, jobs in resource–based industries are expected to fall by 6.4 percent between the mid–1980s and

Table 6.
DISTRIBUTION OF YOUNG NONMETRO ADULTS BY OCCUPATION: 1979 TO 1986

	1979		1986	
	Percent in Occ.	*Poverty Rate in Occ.*	*Percent in Occ.*	*Poverty Rate in Occ.*
White—Collar[a]	42.9	4.0	42.6	6.9
Blue—Collar[b]	39.0	8.0	37.3	12.6
Service	12.6	12.7	14.2	23.2
Farming/Fishing	5.5	21.0	5.8	30.0

Source: Population Reference Bureau Analysis of Census Bureau Public Use Files from the March 1980 and March 1987 U.S. Current Population Survey.

Note: For 1979 the total number of workers examined was 19,332 and the total number in poverty was 1,466. For 1986, the total number of workers examined was 16,620 and the total number in poverty was 2,110.

[a] White-collar occupations include executives, managers, professional specialties, technical and related support, sales, administrative support, and clerical.

[b] Blue-collar occupations include precision production workers, craftsmen, machine operators, assemblers, transportation workers, materials movers, handlers, and laborers.

---

the mid–1990s; this drop will probably create a disproportionate economic hardship on the labor force in rural areas.

Resource–based industries are increasingly dependent on international relationships that are controlled by the federal government. For example, the health of the agriculture, mining, and timber industries relies heavily on trade agreements, tariffs, and foreign exchange rates. Decisions regarding these issues are made in Washington, D.C. and overseas capitals, not in nonmetro counties. Furthermore, with the growth of national and multinational corporations, more and more of the resources in nonmetro areas are controlled by peoples and organizations located in metro areas.

The dominance of one industry within many nonmetro counties, coupled with the geographic isolation of many of these counties, creates a single–industry dependency that makes rural areas more vulnerable to swings in the economy. Most nonmetro areas lack the industrial and occupational diversity to buffer economic shocks from near or far. Consequently, the recession of the early 1980s had a more adverse impact on nonmetro areas than on metro areas.

Many of the nonmetro counties with growing populations in the 1980s depended on tourist dollars or retirement incomes, much of which came from Washington. But urban–generated acid rain, industrial pollution, and toxic wastes may destroy the forests and pollute the lakes and soils that endow these nonmetro counties with natural amenities attracting outsiders to visit or settle. Therefore, the long–run economic vitality of such nonmetro counties is uncertain, given that the sources of revenues and of environmental hazards are mainly extralocal.

Another important structural change was the attraction of new manufacturing industries to nonmetro counties during the 1960s and 1970s. More nonmetro workers are now employed in manufacturing than in farming. But the expansion of the manufacturing sector of the labor force living in nonmetro counties occurred mainly for nondurable goods (e.g., foods, textiles, apparel, or furniture). Nondurable manufacturing industries require less skilled labor for tasks such as garment inspection, repetitive assembly work, or simple machine operation (McGranahan, 1987) and the nonmetro labor force will work for lower wages.

On the other hand, factories using high technology to produce more complex products (e.g., chemical or electrical goods) remained physically centered in urban areas, where the resident labor force is more educated. Consequently, while the percentages of metro and nonmetro residents in the labor force and in manufacturing were nearly identical by the mid–1980s (16.5 percent and 17.6 percent, respectively), their distributions according to the complexity of the work tools became more polarized. About half of the metro residents working in the manufacturing sector were involved in the complex manufactures, where the number of jobs is expected to rise by 17.8 percent between 1984 and 1995.[5] Over half of the nonmetro residents working in the manufacturing sector were using the work tools of simple technology, where the jobs are expected to decline by 3 percent by 1995. Even within the same industry, workers in metro areas were more likely than their nonmetro counterparts to be employed in high–paying white-collar or administrative occupations, because industry headquarters are typically located in major cities, even when production facilities are based in rural areas. Industry leaders are thus able to remove profits from the nonmetro points of creation, and nonmetro laborers are relatively powerless to bargain for its retention and investment locally.

During the first half of the 1980s, the exportation of U.S. jobs within the nondurable manufacturing industries was chiefly from nonmetro U.S. counties to Third World countries, particularly to Mexico, Taiwan, Korea, and the Philippines, where the wage–price of labor is only a fraction of that in the United States. However, even in manufacturing jobs remaining in the United States, low–skilled workers were and are more likely than the highly skilled to be replaced by machines. All these structural transformations have maintained and may sustain the relative economic disadvantage of the nonmetro or rural labor force.

Notes

1. An earlier version of this chapter was presented at the annual meeting of the Rural Sociological Society, Athens, Georgia, August 1988.
2. The 1940 Census collected data only on income earned from employment, so those who might have been lifted out of poverty by income from other sources, such as government assistance or investments, are erroneously classified as poor in this analysis.
3. Between 1983 and 1985, metro poverty rates went from 13.8 percent to 12.7 percent.
4. Children under 18 and elderly persons (aged 65 or older) made up 51 percent of the nonmetro poor in 1986, and adults of mature labor–force ages (45 to 64 years) comprised 15 percent.
5. Less than one–third of nonmetro residents working in factories are employed in plants using the tools of high technology.

References

Auletta, Kenneth. 1982. *The underclass*. New York: Random House.
Banfield, Edward C. 1968. *The unheavenly city*. Boston: Little, Brown and Co.
Harrington, Michael. 1962. *The other America*. New York: Macmillan.
──────. 1984. *The new American poverty*. New York: Holt, Rinehart, and Winston.
Hawley, Amos, and Sara Mills Mazie. 1981. *Nonmetropolitan America in transition*. Chapel Hill, N.C.: University of North Carolina Press.
Johnson, Kenneth M. 1985. *The impact of population change on business activity in rural America*. Boulder, Colo.: Westview Press.
Kasarda, John. 1985. Urban change and minority opportunities. In *The new urban reality*, ed. P. E. Peterson, 33–67. Washington, D.C.: Brookings Institution.
Lewis, Oscar. 1966a. The culture of poverty. *Scientific American* 215(41): 19–25.
──────. 1966b. *La vita*. New York: Random House.
McGranahan, David A. 1987. The role of rural workers in the national economy. In *Rural economic development in the 1980s: Preparing for the future*, ed., David Brown and Kenneth Deavers, pp. 2–1 through 2–23. Washington D.C.: U.S. Department of Agriculture: Economic Research Service.
Mead, Lawrence. 1986. *Beyond entitlement*. New York: Free Press.

Murray, Charles. 1984. *Losing ground*. New York: Basic Books.
O'Hare, William P. 1988. *The rise of poverty in rural America. Population trends and public policy* No. 15. Washington, D.C.: Population Reference Bureau.
Ross, Christine, Sheldon Danziger, and Eugene Smolensky. 1985. The level and trend of poverty, 1939 to 1979. University of Wisconsin: Institute for Research on Poverty.
U.S. Bureau of the Census. 1987. *Current population reports*. Series P–60, No. 157.
Wilson, William Julius. 1987. Chicago: University of Chicago Press.

3

MECHANIZATION IN THE WESTERN UPPER PENINSULA PULP-LOGGING INDUSTRY

Jon H. Rieger

Introduction

An accepted truism in modern society is that technology has been the key to economic expansion, improvement in the quality of life, and the maximization of prosperity. As that technology has expressed itself in the economy of rural America, it has meant the introduction of machinery and equipment on an ever-increasing scale, and a progressive reduction in the amount of labor required in agriculture, mining, forestry, and other rural industries. This chapter reports on a case study of the impact of technological developments in the pulp-logging industry in a local community in Michigan's Upper Peninsula. In reviewing the growth of technology in the logging industry in this community, account will be taken of the "appropriate technology" critique inspired by E. F. Schumacher's work of the early 1970s (Schumacher 1973).

Modern Technology and Appropriate Technology

The development of improved technology in the extractive industries (agriculture, forestry, mining, fishing) is recognized as the essential element that made possible the expansion of other industries and the growth of cities. Technology has come to be thought of popularly as a largely unmitigated good, fostering the development of a better life for all whose lives it touches. The implementation of modern technological development has followed a characteristic path—that of increasing scale, complexity, and energy intensiveness. Increasing scale and complexity refer to both the equipment and the social organization that accompanies it. This can be easily seen in the case of agriculture, an industry that has been characterized by continual expansion in the size and sophistication of the equipment used and in the growth, and increasing dominance of, progressively larger operating units, including corporate farms.

Modern technology adopted by agriculture and forestry has been capital- and energy-intensive. Machinery and petroleum have replaced muscle and sweat, with a consequent rise in output per man–hour of labor. The increased productivity has led to liberally stocked markets and relatively cheap prices for many commodities.

The assumption of a perpetual, upward spiral in the relationship between technological growth and economic growth and well–being was sharply challenged by Schumacher (1973). He contended that many human costs were ignored in evaluating the benefits of technological growth, particularly among local indigenous populations. Other critics (Lovins 1976, 1977; Lovins and Nash 1979) cited environmental damage and the accelerated exhaustion of nonrenewable energy resources as additional consequences of unmitigated and thoughtless introduction of technological innovation. The notion of an unending cycle of technology and development was criticized as ultimately self–defeating, in that it both undermined the economic viability of local populations and degraded the environment. On either account, the *modern technology* growth strategy was judged as not "sustainable" over the long run.

The critics argue that things do not have to proceed this way since there is an alternative—that is, the implementation of, or reversion to, *appropriate technology:*

> Systems that are small–scale, decentralized, resource conserving, and that use local and renewable resources are considered appropriate because of desirable social impacts. These technologies create meaningful work (particularly for less skilled workers), supply basic needs, allow self–sufficiency, and create an ecologically sustainable and higher quality of life. (Lodwick and Morrison 1982, 46)

In this chapter, I describe the technological changes in the pulp-logging industry in the western region of Michigan's Upper Peninsula and discuss how these bear on the modern technology–appropriate technology debate.

The Western Upper Peninsula Pulp–Logging Industry

The pulp industry has been an important element in the economy of the western Upper Peninsula of Michigan since early in the century. The development and transformation of this industry is one of the most significant events in the recent social history of this region. It is an area whose population has long struggled with economic uncertainty—with periodic expansion and contraction of local industry—and the changing dynamics of the local pulp industry have epitomized the challenges and perils of rural industrialization (see also Bald 1961, Jamison 1965, and Johanson 1985).

The site of this study, Ontonagon County, Michigan, is on the southern shore of Lake Superior. Because it is geographically the third-largest county in the state, its sparse population yields a density of only about seven people per square mile. The Porcupine Mountains comprise much of its western border, while the Keweenaw Peninsula is located to the northeast. The largely forested areas of Gogebic County form the southern and western borders, and Houghton and Iron Counties lie to the east and southeast, respectively.

In 1923, a small paper mill built near Ontonagon Village (the county seat) made the cutting of pulpwood for the manufacture of paperboard a significant economic activity in the area. The mill operated on and off under a succession of owners until 1953, when it abruptly closed (Johanson 1985). Reopened in 1956 under new ownership, it has grown fairly steadily under various owners.

The present review of developments in the pulp-logging industry is based on my knowledge derived from years of fieldwork in this area, augmented by my interviews with key local informants. I chose the interviewees for their direct knowledge and familiarity with the woods industry. They include, among others, the paper mill manager, executives of the largest pulpwood suppliers in the area, three loggers, and the present and former cooperative extension agents for the county.

Early Structure and Practice in the Pulp-Logging Industry (1923-45)

The years from the opening of the mill in 1923 to the end of World War II constitute the "early days" of the pulp industry in this region. The paper mill was, by all accounts, a modest operation during the early period. After several false starts it was acquired by Marathon Paper Mills of Wausau, Wisconsin, and, by 1925, was producing paperboard steadily. As the Depression came, the continuation of papermaking fell back largely on the efforts of local people as the mill was reorganized to become the Ontonagon Fiber Corporation. The company barely hung on through the 1930s, but substantially improved its position during World War II (Johanson 1985).

The period through 1945 was essentially a premodern era of logging in the North Woods. It was not utterly devoid of mechanization, since farm tractors were used by some operators to drag or "skid" the logs out of the forest, and trucks or the railroads were used for hauling, but it was a period in which a great deal of the work was done by hand and with the aid of draft animals. Trees were harvested to fill various needs: some were used for fuel; but most were used for lumber or pulp. Wood that was sent to nearby sawmills or to the paper mill was usually trucked, and some material was bought by brokers and transported out of the area by rail. By more recent standards, production levels were low.

The pulp mill purchased its raw material from local loggers, farmers, and other nearby landowners. The quantity of pulpwood bought by the mill was not large, and the geographic radius of its suppliers was relatively short. Much of the cutting of pulpwood was done in the spring of the year, when the bark could be easily stripped off. Pulp–cutting operations tended to be very small, a typical crew consisting of two or three persons—often a farmer and his wife and, perhaps, one of their teenage children. The trees to be cut, rarely more than two feet in diameter, were felled with the two-man crosscut saw, in such a manner that the fall would position the tree for the subsequent operations. Delimbing was done with an axe, and the bark was peeled off with a specially made hand tool that somewhat resembled a pick, consisting typically of a sharpened segment of automobile leaf-spring onto which a handle had been welded. The log was struck with the sharpened end of the tool so as to split the bark, and the blade was slid around inside, gradually separating the bark from the log until it popped off like a stiff wrapper. The logs were subsequently secured at one end with a cable noose or *choker*, and dragged by a horse or horse team to the loading point, usually the edge of the road. There they were cut to length (typically about eight feet) by hand and stacked for transport to the mill.

Farmers who owned tractors generally used them to skid the logs, but tractors were not always an advantage over horses. Horses were more desirable in places where the terrain was too steep or rough for a tractor, or where the objective was to be selective of certain trees while leaving others. Many woods operations made use of horses into the 1950s. Hauling from the roadside was done by truck. Loggers generally owned their own or made a contract with a trucker. Farmers sometimes hauled their own pulpwood if they owned a truck, but often they contracted a trucker with larger equipment to transport the pulp to the mill (Toivonen 1986).

The loading of the pulpwood onto a truck was another labor–intensive step. In the early days the wood was loaded by hand. Some operators built crude loading ramps, but the shifting location of the woods operation often left such structures too far away. Eventually the loading process was made somewhat easier with homemade *jammers*, primitive power–cable devices fabricated from an old car axle/differential assembly, and connected to the power take–off on a tractor or the truck itself. Similarly powered *boom–loaders* were also used, in which the cable came down over the back of the truck from the end of a boom and could be used to pull the logs up skids to the truck bed (Brusso 1986).

The production rate that could be achieved by a two–person crew in the woods with a crosscut saw and a tractor or team of horses was nearly five cords per day (a cord weighs about 5,000 pounds), delivered to roadside. In the typical stand of timber in the Ontonagon County area, that means a harvest of about one–half acre. The early period of the industry was the era of the small independent logger or farmer–logger. Most woods operations were small, usually one or two crews, and the principal form of differentiation, to the extent that it existed, was the split between those who worked in the woods and those who hauled the material to the mill. Farmers who cut pulp were more likely to make use of contract haulers than were the loggers, who often owned their own equipment. The loggers operated by buying *stumpage* (standing timber) from land owners. Not all of the timber taken off the land was pulpwood, of course. Some species, such as yellow birch, were considerably more valuable as *sawlogs*, that is, logs that could be used for lumber or made into veneer; those logs were channeled to the saw mills rather than to the pulp mill in Ontonagon. (The wood used for pulp during this period was softwood, particularly balsam, hemlock, and fir, and some hardwoods, such as aspen.)

The Transitional Period (1946–72)

The transitional period is characterized by gradual mechanization. The first really significant change occurred in the 1940s with the arrival of the power saw.[1] With this new tool, a single sawyer could now do the work of a two–person team, and could do it much faster. A sawyer could actually cut the wood down faster than it could be delimbed and skidded out, especially if it had to be peeled (debarked). Thus the size of the operation tended to get bigger—crews of five or more were not uncommon—and the work roles became more specialized (Toivonen 1986).

A second important technological innovation took place in the loading of material for transport to the mill. Pickup trucks had long since given way to larger flatbed trucks, and by about 1959 the *knuckle boom* loader appeared in the western Upper Peninsula. This was a truck–mounted, hydraulically powered, articulated device with caliper–like jaws on the end

Changing Rural Social Systems

Figure 1. An early example of the power saw in use (ca. 1950). The saw was big, bulky, and dangerous. Note that the operator is not using protective eyewear or a safety helmet. (State Archives of Michigan.)

that could be maneuvered to load the sticks of pulpwood from the roadside stack to the truck bed. This equipment made it possible for the truck operator to load material without assistance and made the process much faster. A little later the trucks were equipped with outriggers to stabilize them during the loading process. The effect of the loader on the woods operation was immediate: the hydraulic loader not only increased the production by simplifying the loading process, but it fostered differentiation (Brusso 1986). The equipment was expensive enough that most farmers and other landowners, as well as many loggers, found it more sensible to hire a trucker to transport their pulpwood than to buy a truck with a loader and haul it themselves (Toivonen 1986).

A third development was an improvement in the tractor used to move the material out of the woods: around 1965, a more specialized tractor, called a *skidder*, began to make its appearance in the area. This tractor was articulated in the middle and had a power winch with a cable, and was

Figure 2. William Weisinger and his truck equipped with hydraulic knuckle boom loader (ca. 1965). Courtesy of Mrs. William Weisinger.

better adapted to the specific needs of woods work. The skidders were two or three times as expensive as farm tractors, or the small crawlers some operators used, and so tended to be bought mainly by full–time loggers. They were more powerful than an ordinary tractor, however, and, with three or four chokers, could drag a considerable load out of the forest.

During the transitional period the pulp mill changed hands several times. It was acquired in 1945 by the National Container Corporation and manufactured kraft liner board product until 1953, when the company stopped all production activity at the plant. The facility was idle until 1956, when it was purchased by new investors led by a Chicago entrepreneur, Alvin Huss, and reopened as the Huss Ontonagon Pulp and Paper Company. New equipment was installed and the operation shifted to a hardwood pulp paper process (Johanson 1985, 153).

The mill contracted loggers to harvest the hardwoods on its land and bought wood from practically anyone who drove a truckful onto the company's scale at the mill. It maintained a huge inventory of pulp logs stacked in a large yard beside the plant. The company operated a chipper, a large piece of machinery, to grind "round wood" into small chips for the papermaking process.

In 1962 the mill was bought by the Hoerner Box Co. of Keokuk, Iowa, and in 1967 Hoerner merged with Waldorf Paper Products of St. Paul, Minnesota. The company operated as the Hoerner–Waldorf Paper Company until 1976.

Figure 3. A feller–buncher in Ontonagon County, Michigan (winter 1985–86). Moving on a crawler base and operated by a single worker, this equipment harvests trees literally by the bunch. Powered by hydraulics, the articulated arm grips a tree at its base and snips it off with shears in about eight seconds. The tree is held fast in the fixture as the operator moves to the next tree. The fixture can hold up to six trees. The bunch is deposited in a pile by slewing the hydraulic arm to a cleared area beside the machine and angling the fixture horizontally before opening its jaws. (Courtesy of J.H. Rieger.)

The Modern Period (1973 to the Present)

The area's pulp–logging industry was consolidated in the modern period. Through the early 1970s, the mill continued to buy pulp logs from many small local suppliers. This practice was sometimes problematic, from the mill operator's standpoint: The reliability of the supply was sometimes in doubt, depending on the season and economic conditions. The suppliers typically brought in too little material during the winter and too much during the summer. If the price was not high enough, they might not bring in any at all (Howard 1985; Toivonen 1986).

In a fateful move for the industry in this area, the mill management decided in the early 1970s to export the chipping component of its operation. The company's own equipment had never been very reliable or efficient, and it seemed that the business could be made more profitable by buying the raw material in chip form. Because a chipper cost well over $200,000, this policy innovation greatly favored the largest suppliers of pulpwood, since only they were likely to have the capital or credit essential to obtain such equipment. The mill implemented its decision, reportedly by financing, in part, the purchase of chippers by several local operators. The most prominent of those, and the most successful, is Turpeinen Brothers, Inc., of Alston, Michigan.

The premise of a successful chipper operation is high–volume business, and the acquisition of such equipment by Turpeinen Brothers, Inc., went hand in hand with a contract with the mill to become its major Ontonagon–area supplier (Turpeinen 1986). The mill contracted two additional, but smaller, sources of chips, the Pestka Company, in Ontonagon, and Eli Miljevich, in Wakefield, near the Wisconsin border. These three operations now supply virtually all of the raw material, other than saw mill scrap, used by the mill.

A description of the Turpeinen operation will illustrate the contemporary technology of pulp logging in the North Woods. The mobile chipper that the Turpeinens acquired could be taken to the site of the woods operation. The chipping of the pulpwood in the woods with this equipment produced several other changes. First, it meant that the logging truck with its expensive paraphernalia (hydraulic loader, outriggers, etc.), was no longer needed—the chips could be hauled by conventional semitrailer trucks with no special equipment. Second, it impelled a significant expansion of investment in other equipment, since one chipper could devour the output of several skidders and cutting operations.

In the years since the Turpeinens started, they have greatly enlarged their operation and have continually acquired the latest innovations in equipment. At the leading end of their woods operation the trees are cut

Figure 4. A modern grapple skidder pulling a load of logs out of the forest south of Military Hill in Ontonagon County, Michigan (winter 1985–86). The pulp logs are secured in the hydraulically operated grapple jaws on the rear of the fourteen-ton skidder. Belching a puff of diesel exhaust, the skidder pauses on its trip to the chipper in order to get the trees delimbed. In this operation, a flail approaches from the rear and rides briefly up on the heads of the trees, knocking off the small branches and some of the bark with its rapidly rotating chains. (Courtesy of J.H. Rieger.)

and stacked in a single operation utilizing a very heavy, powerful, and sophisticated piece of equipment called a *feller–buncher*. This is a large caterpillar–style tractor with a heavy–duty hydraulic knuckle boom that can reach to a distance of almost 30 feet. On the end of the boom are mounted hydraulically operated shears, and jaws that can hold up to six trees at once. The feller–buncher can cut trees up to a foot–and–a–half in diameter in a few seconds. When the jaws are filled to capacity, the tractor is swiveled on its chassis and the boom manipulated to stack the load in a *bunch* where it can be conveniently picked up by a skidder. This equipment, operated by a single worker, can cut and stack trees fast enough to

Figure 5. A mobile chipper in Ontonagon County, Michigan (winter 1985–86). With the aid of a hydraulically operated grappler arm, the chipper digests whole trees in less than a minute, spewing the chips into the waiting semi–trailer truck for transport to the mill. Another truck is always kept standing by in order to minimize the interruption of operations. (Courtesy of J.H. Rieger.)

keep several skidders busy. The large skidders currently used by Turpeinen, Inc., are known as *grapple skidders*: the driver can simply back up to the cut ends of a stack of up to fifteen trees and grasp the bunch with huge, hydraulically powered caliper–shaped jaws suspended from the rear of the skidder, instead of having to secure a choker by hand to each tree. (Skidders such as these, powerful enough to drag a dozen or more whole trees at once over rough terrain as much as a half mile to the chipper, weigh upward of ten tons and cost approximately $150,000.)

The trees are skidded to the chipper and, en route, are attacked by a *flail*, a large prime–mover tractor equipped with a front–mounted delimbing unit. The delimber consists of a rapidly revolving transverse axle to which lengths of heavy chain are attached. The chains are swung against the tree tops, knocking off most of the smaller branches, along with much of the foliage. The trees are then fed into the chipper with the aid of a large hydraulically operated boom attached to the chipper itself. The chips fly from a chute at the other end of the chipper into waiting semitrailer trucks, which have a capacity of about thirty tons. Enough trucks are used that the operation is nearly continuous.

This drama of cutting, pulling, and chipping is augmented by considerable other activity. Roads must be built into the forest to sustain these operations; and for this purpose the Turpeinens own and operate bulldozers, fifty-ton lowboys, motor graders, and dump trucks. The equipment must be serviced and refueled, for which the company maintains a forty-foot shop van and a number of smaller service, lubrication, and fuel trucks. All of the equipment is radio controlled. The company owns twelve semitrailer trucks with which to haul chips. It operates repair shops in Alston to handle major repairs and overhaul of equipment (Knight 1985).

Moving and operating such a mass of large equipment has meant that the parcels of forest that can be profitably cleared have had to be larger than in former times, using older methods. The Turpeinens bid on stands no smaller than about ten acres—about a day's work at the present scale of their highly mechanized operation. Such a production rate is unprecedented in this area of the western Upper Peninsula: in 1986 the company was delivering to the mill, in chip form, between 4,500 and 5,500 cords per month (from between 280 and 340 acres of stumpage, clear-cut), and claimed it could actually harvest up to 400 cords per day, if necessary (Turpeinen 1986).

The rise in output reflects, and is directly tied to, the increasing production at the paper mill over the recent decade. In 1976 the mill was bought by the Champion International Corporation and, under this new ownership, its output continued upward. The mill facility itself was enlarged several times. By the mid-1980s it averaged approximately 640 tons of paper product per day, an enormous increase over the 50 tons-per-day rate of the early years (Johanson 1985, 154). In 1986 the mill was sold to the Stone Container Corporation, based in Chicago. Since the new company has not yet acquired substantial forest acreage in the area, the mill has relaxed, at least for the time being, its resistance to the purchase of some round wood from independent suppliers. These purchases account for only a small fraction of its total raw material consumption, however, and it is unclear how long this practice will continue.

The Ramifications of Mechanization

Changes in the Nature of "Woods Work"

Most obviously, the mechanization of the pulp–logging industry in the western Upper Peninsula has changed the nature of "woods work." In the early period, woods work required great physical struggle. Human and animal muscle were needed literally to wrestle the material out of the forest. All of the work was manual: each tree was felled and delimbed. Then the lengths were marked off, and the trunk was debarked. It was dragged to the loading point, cut to length, and stacked. Later it was hand–loaded for transport to the mill. Such work was physically exhausting and dangerous. Continually exposed to the elements, the woods workers labored under conditions of extreme isolation, far from help in the event of an accident or other emergency.

Steel and petroleum have now been substituted for muscle and sweat. The workers now concentrate on controlling the equipment that handles the logs, rather than grappling with them directly.

Changes in Employment and Opportunity

Mechanization has brought a dramatic change also to the woods employment picture in Ontonagon County. At the same time that it was greatly adding to the volume of supply of pulpwood to the mill, mechanization was steadily reducing the number of workers needed to produce it. Thus, as the amount of acreage being harvested rose, employment opportunities in the woods were actually decreasing. Particularly hard pressed were the small independent operators, and the farmers and other landowners who pulped mostly on a part–time basis. Most of them were simply driven out of the business (Brusso 1986; Toivonen 1986).

With the shift of the mill's policy from buying on an open market to buying on contract, the opportunities left to small operators became fleeting: to stay in business, the independent logger had to find a market outside the area and a way of keeping the transportation costs low enough to make it pay (Brusso 1986). Not only the loss of the local market but also the rise in production costs have made the small operation uneconomic (Turpeinen 1986).

Mechanization has reduced the number employed in woods work in the Ontonagon County area to under 100, according to the estimates of those directly involved.[2] What has happened to the people who formerly worked in this industry? Some have gone to work at the paper mill. The mill workforce increased very slowly until the beginning of the modern period, but grew rapidly thereafter. In the decade following the purchase of the mill by Champion International in 1976, its employment rose by almost 75 percent—from 174 to 303. There were definite attractions for woods workers in employment at the mill: the hours are regular and pay rates steady, employees have fringe benefits and a retirement program, and working conditions are far better than they were in the woods. A few workers gained employment with one or another of the contract suppliers of the mill. The remaining workers either drifted into other pursuits or left the area (Brusso 1986).

Increases in the Scale of Organization and Market Control

As is the case with other industries in many other rural areas, the scale of economic organization and the level of decisionmaking have obviously risen in the pulp–logging industry in the western Upper Peninsula. For a large part of the early period the mill was fundamentally a local business with local investors or under the control of a middle–sized concern in nearby Wisconsin. During the transitional period the mill fell into the hands of larger and remoter entities and, of course, is presently owned by the Stone Container Corporation, which, like Champion, is a company doing business on an international scale. As the locus of decisionmaking moved up and progressively away from Ontonagon County, it increased the alienation of local residents:

> Exploitation has always been the economic pattern for the Ontonagon Country with the outside world taking what the area has to offer and giving in return employment and sustenance to the people living here, but only so long as the profits remain high enough to justify the expense! (Johanson 1985, 151)

A similar pattern of upward and outward movement might be said to have occurred in the supply end of the industry, that is, in the woods. The situation has changed from one in which the raw material was supplied by many small local entrepreneurs to one in which woods work is dominated by a multimillion-dollar corporation with a contract. Turpeinen Brothers, Inc., is not based in Ontonagon County, but to the east, at Alston, in Houghton County. (The second-biggest supplier, Miljevich, is headquartered to the west, in Gogebic County.) While most of the Turpeinens' pulp chips still come from Ontonagon County, the company gets material from as far away as the Marquette area, especially during the spring "break–up," and it acknowledged that its workforce is distributed as widely as its sources of pulp (Turpeinen 1986). The consequence of this is that employment income from woods work that was once concentrated in the area immediately surrounding the mill is now diffused over a far larger region. The small number still employed in the woods industry may have steadier work and higher incomes, but they are spread over a much wider territory.

With unemployment remaining at high levels in the Upper Peninsula generally, and particularly in the sparsely populated area of Ontonagon, Houghton, and Baraga Counties in the west, companies such as Turpeinen Brothers, Inc., are placed in a highly advantageous position. They are relatively free to set wage levels so as to insure profitability and are, at the same time, relatively less vulnerable to local political and economic considerations.

The combination of advanced mechanization and the economy of scale, exercised over a broad region of the western Upper Peninsula, has given Turpeinen Brothers, Inc., substantial control of the pulp business in this area. Such control is not absolute and total, however, since the mill also buys from Miljevich in Wakefield, and a smaller additional volume from Pestka in Ontonagon (Pestka 1989). Still, the company acknowledges that it has no real competition in the area at present (Turpeinen 1986). Furthermore, the same techniques used to achieve such control can be utilized to maintain it: by mechanizing so heavily, Turpeinen Brothers has minimized the unit–cost of chips effectively to keep anyone from starting up a competing operation (Brusso 1986).

Under the present circumstances, there are few bidders on stumpage other than Turpeinen Brothers, since, except for an occasional sawlog, it is so difficult to find a market for it. Has that market power been used to depress the price paid for stumpage? Not according to the company: by clear–cutting and harvesting the whole tree, and by converting it to chips onsite, the yield is increased to almost double that attained by earlier methods. The recovery is so complete that it brings the seller's price up to about $5.00 per cord, so that, even though the price per ton has not changed much over the years, the income per acre of stumpage is greater because of the new technology (Turpeinen 1986).

Increasing Reliance on Federal Timber Resources

The U.S. Forestry Service from time to time auctions off blocks of timber in the Ottawa National Forest, which blankets much of the territory in the western Upper Peninsula, including Ontonagon County. Some in the area feel that this practice keeps the price of pulpwood low and at public expense.[3] The loggers have, through the purchase of rights to harvest federal timber, a relatively cheap alternative to buying stumpage from private landowners. Many small operators feel that the Forest Service is too cozy with the big companies who bid for such timber or who are major users of it as raw material. It is pointed out, for example, that decisions about opening tracts for harvest in the Ottawa Forest are made in the USDA regional office in Milwaukee, Wisconsin. But those decisions issue from recommendations submitted by a Forestry Advisory Committee in the local area, key members of which are the owners of the sawmills and Board members of the paper mill.

Small operators complain that the Forestry Service seems to open more land to harvest any time the level of demand threatens to raise the market price, and that the way it administers the process favors large logging companies. Since federal land is a major source of pulpwood in the area, the Forest Service's practices can indeed have a significant impact on the structure of the pulp industry. The blocks of forest land opened up for logging have gotten progressively larger in size in recent years. Small operators cannot afford to bid on such large contracts and, in any event, the blocks are too big for them to clear, even within the three-year limit normally established (Toivonen 1986). As it happens, the largest single percentage of the Turpeinen Brothers' business comes from cutting on Forestry land and the company acknowledged that it would have a struggle surviving without such access (Turpeinen 1986).

Negative Impacts on Local Farmers

The structural changes and mechanization in the industry that have led to a near monopoly by a few corporations have certainly been the main drama unfolding during recent decades. But the shift of the paper mill from open purchase of pulpwood to near–exclusive contracting may have had another, and somewhat subtler, impact in addition to the devastation of many small independent logging operations. The business was largely shut off, not only to the independent loggers and truckers, but to the many farmer–loggers who did such work on a part–time basis. While it cannot be proved, some of our informants believe that this hastened the demise of agriculture in the area (Brusso 1986; Slye 1986). Agricultural employment in the north country has been marginal in recent decades, but the local farm economy is likely to have been further undermined by the loss of the pulp market (Domitrovich 1986).

The use of pulping as a fallback source of income had been a tradition in the county for generations. Woods work has been frequently mentioned as a source of income during layoffs in other industries or other periods of unemployment among the residents surveyed through the years of our research in this area. For many of these individuals and their families, pulping served as an alternative to subsidization at public expense during periods of under– or unemployment, or simply as a means of income augmentation (Brusso 1986).

As mechanization and the contract system overtook the industry, such part–time players were put out of the game. Nonetheless, a few have managed to continue earning a side income from woods work as a result of a fortuitous development: the dramatic increases in the cost of petroleum that began in the early 1970s. Wood has come to be widely used in the area as a substitute for other fuels, mainly for home heating. Thus some entrepreneurs support themselves in part by the cutting and selling of firewood. Apart from the fact that this activity essentially brings no new money into the local economy, it seems to offer a very limited opportunity even to those who pursue it. The production of firewood is labor intensive: only certain types of wood are desirable as firewood and, once found, it must be cut into short lengths and split, and then dried. Sales are generally in very small lots, often less than a cord, and the product must be delivered to the customer's door. As a former logger said, selling firewood might carry a person for awhile, if the equipment needed were already on hand, but it would not yield enough income at current prices to make it very profitable or to cover the cost of any new equipment (Domitrovich 1986).

Ecological Consequences

Beyond the consequences of the changes in the nature of the pulp industry for the political economy of woods work, are the ecological implications of those changes. There is no question but that the overall environmental impact of the operations in the North Woods has risen—one need only consider the enormous increase in the sheer *amount* of wood being cut to recognize that. Moreover, in the early period, when much of the material taken was by owners off their own lands and by other small operators, harvesting could be selective. Private landowners' motives were to preserve the productivity of their land, so it made sense to pull only the mature trees and to leave the others. Thus, under ideal conditions, the forest could be made to be more or less continuously productive while, at least superficially, appearing little changed.

The switch in the mode of woods work from a system of many small operators whose total production was relatively modest to domination by a handful of large, highly mechanized operations has made the environmental impact of the industry far more obvious and, perhaps, more problematic. The current, mechanized approach to woods work makes the selective cutting that was common in the days of crosscut saws and horse teams less physically and economically feasible. Substantial roads must be cut into the forest to support the heavy equipment used to do the work and the trucks needed to haul away the material, once it is harvested. The procedure universally preferred by such companies is *clear–cutting*. Basically, this means that everything within the designated tract is cut, and nothing remains standing. Clear–cutting has been a controversial procedure and while efforts have been made to soften its apparent impact upon the forest environment, it remains a fairly drastic process. In the North Woods the clear–cutting operations of the Turpeinen Brothers, Inc., create, initially, scenes of considerable devastation.

Critics of clear–cutting also argue that it is wasteful of precious resources. The belief that clear–cutters unselectively chip everything in their path, including valuable sawlogs, is fairly widespread among the more traditional loggers (Domitrovich 1986; Brusso 1986), and it may be that some are guilty of the practice. The Turpeinens insist that they save the sawlogs, despite the inconvenience; it would make little sense for them to take wood that can bring $100–200 per thousand board feet and run it through the chipper for one–fourth of that return (Turpeinen 1986).

The dominance of aspen in many of the second-growth stands in the North Woods is itself a basis for some of the criticism of the practice of clear–cutting. Aspen is the characteristic "first generation" regrowth forest in such places. When the original, varied–species forest is clear–cut, it is the aspens that come back first, in great abundance. "They'll come up so fast and so thick that it's like a hairbrush—you can barely walk in it" (Moilanen 1986). Critics complain that the varied forest thus becomes replaced with a "monoculture," an ecologically less–sound and resilient forest than the one it replaced.

The Loss of Tradition

The recent evolution of the pulp–logging industry in the North Woods has wrought changes in other aspects of the culture of the region, besides those in the industry itself. Woods work has been very much a part of the traditional culture of the area and was part of the cultural heritage of the Finns who populate much of the region. The forests were abundant and pervasive, and many people participated in one degree or another in the woods economy. Even those who did not directly participate were generally familiar with the industry, since practically everybody had relatives or acquaintances who were involved. The woods industry has been an important economic enterprise across this sparsely settled region. For a goodly number of people it was a primary source of income. It is not romanticizing to say that people who grew up in this area loved the North Woods—as a place to live and as a source of sustenance. The forest has been integrally a part of the formative experience of many local citizens.

As the industry has become concentrated in the hands of a few large operators, the economic and emotional anchorage in the woods is being eroded for many who formerly worked there. There is a distinct "aging–out" process that is taking place among the great cadre of local people who used to work in the woods, and the skills that went with that work are disappearing (Brusso 1986).

Changes in Income Distribution

With concentration in the woods business has come, inevitably, a concentration in fewer hands of the wealth from woods work. Some local citizens see this development as adversely affecting the welfare of a broad segment of the population, even though the incomes of those employed in the new industry have gone up. Poverty is pervasive in the western Upper Peninsula, and the loss of woods work by many has aggravated the level of rural under– and unemployment, with a negative effect on the rest of the economy.

Some of those who are working in the industry in its new incarnation are counting on a "trickle–down" effect for the local economy (Howard 1985), but that is not a hope that is universally shared among local residents. Except for the wages of those directly involved, they see little coming back directly to the community from the woods. A sharp distinction is thus made between the paper mill itself and the woods operations of outfits such as Turpeinen Brothers: the mill is very much integrated into the Ontonagon economy and pays local taxes, while those paid by Turpeinen Brothers, Inc., go to another jurisdiction. This expression of local chauvinism can be dismissed without obscuring the point that as the benefit base of the industry can become less concentrated in any one area.

Changes in Corporate–Community Relations

While much of the local sensitivity about the change in the structure of the pulp industry centers around the rise of the Turpeinen Brothers, with their big contract, it is easy to lose sight of the fact that it was the mill's decision to export the chipping process that ushered that change in. Interestingly, a very significant modification in the mill management's attitude and policy toward the community roughly parallels, in time, its shift of buying practice for raw material. As the mill was progressively shutting out independent sources of supply of pulpwood, it embarked on a campaign of building community goodwill and encouraging employee participation in community affairs and organizations. Any insinuation of a direct connection between these events is subject to challenge, however, since the community relations program came with the buyout of the mill by Champion International, while the shift to the purchase of chips had already begun under the previous ownership. An emphasis on good community relations was claimed to be a standing company policy and the mill manager proudly reported that a quarter of his employees were actively involved in a community organization (Howard 1985). In addition, the company maintains a special fund to support worthy community projects. This change of orientation of the mill operators toward the community is a self–conscious program of image management and is an acknowledged reversal of the previous posture of aloofness and isolation.

Vertical Integration

The success of the mill in its community relations campaign does not obviate the reality that it is the most powerful player in the area's woods economy. While Turpeinen Brothers, Inc., may seem like an octopus to the few other woods operations still attempting to hang on in the business, it is nonetheless largely a captive supplier of the mill, and its production rises and falls on the basis of the needs of the mill. This vulnerability is well understood by the Turpeinens and seems to be accepted with realism and humility (Turpeinen 1986).

By its arrangement with the Turpeinens, Miljevich, and Pestka, the mill has come close to achieving total vertical integration of the industry in the area, and the likelihood of its return to a substantially more open, and therefore inevitably more uncertain, supply system similar to that of the previous era would seem quite unlikely.

Traditionally, woods work was a craft that required considerable and varied skills. Yet, while it had many of the characteristics of a craft, it was organized since the early days along entrepreneurial lines. The many small operators who pursued woods work in this region were never effectively organized to protect their interests as a group. When change came, they reacted to it individually. Most of those who still work in the North Woods have now been transformed from entrepreneurs into employees. The sophistication and mystery of the woods craft is disappearing rapidly, and the woodsmen are being replaced by a platoon of machine operators, and the assault on the forest goes on year–round. As one retired former woodsman observed, "It's almost never quiet out there anymore."

Technology and North Woods Pulp Logging

The recent transformation of the pulp–logging industry in the North Woods would seem to exemplify economic development through the adoption of "modern technology." The earlier system was certainly closer to what the critics in the technology debate would consider an "appropriate technology." It was small–scale, relatively decentralized structurally, depended on mostly local resources, and relied heavily upon renewable energy sources. It might be said to have had "desirable social impacts" on the local population by providing "meaningful work, supply[ing] basic needs, allow[ing] self–sufficency," (Lodwick and Morrison 1982, 46) and preserving valued traditions and skills.

Changes in the industry followed the characteristic path to higher capitalization: greatly increased scale, complexity, and centralization. Mechanization displaced many local workers from their jobs and produced a certain amount of alienation. As the scale of operations rose, the industry became more resource–intensive and resource–depleting. The present style and intensity of the woods operations are certainly more environmentally destructive than formerly and may at some point—if not already—exceed the recovery capacity of the local timberlands. The drive to modern technology has certainly dominated the process of change in the North Woods.

The extraordinary transformation in the industry took place one step at a time, and over a period of several decades. It resulted from the incremental effects of the diffusion of new technology into the local area, and the adaptation to such change on the part of the many players in the drama. Those players, as exemplified by our study informants, were driven not by greed or malice, but by the imperatives of competition in a changing marketplace. While they disagree on important issues, there is an awareness among them that the forces that produced change in their industry went well beyond the North Woods. As far as the technology debate is concerned, the question that arises is whether the path of development that has occurred was the only alternative, or whether other strategies might have been possible, or might yet be options for the future. The *appropriate technology* critique, as it applies to the circumstances described in this case study, would focus mainly on the heavy reliance on nonrenewable energy inputs, such as fossil fuel, the potential environmental consequences of the emerging system of harvesting raw material, and the scale of organization, especially in the degree to which control of the industry moved out of the hands of local participants.

How could fossil-fuel costs of woods work be minimized except by reversion to the use of crosscut saws and horses? (It is doubtful that mere reversion to chainsaws and pickup trucks would be any more energy–efficient, or even as efficient, as the present system. In terms of the amount of fuel consumed per ton of chips, it is highly questionable that any saving would be achieved by returning to that technology.) The other kinds of energy sources sometimes suggested by appropriate technologists, solar and wind power, would seem to have scant possibility of implementation in this type of work.

A switch back to draft animals and hand labor, accompanied by other appropriate changes, might make it possible once again to harvest the forest selectively, so as to avoid the huge cataracts that are the outcome of the present procedures. A change of this type would drastically increase the labor–intensiveness of woods work, however, and would necessitate the recruitment and training of a large cadre of workers. It would also almost certainly mean the revival of agriculture in the area to supply the feed necessary for the many animals that would be required.

Because the wood must be reduced to chips if it is to be made into paper, a chipping operation must be sustained, and since part of the appropriate technology doctrine is the maintenance of local autonomy and control, it is easy to imagine that the chipping operation might be cooperatively owned by the local woods operators. It may be possible that even a chipping operation could be made to operate on some alternative source of energy, that is, something other than petroleum.

Could the industry, at this stage of its history, revert in the direction of reduced capital-intensity, scale, complexity, and centralization, perhaps along the lines described above? Would it really be feasible to revive the presumably more environmentally benign harvesting strategies and practices that apparently characterized the earlier era in the woods? Could such drastic changes be inaugurated without reducing present production levels? Are such scenarios any more than idealistic fantasies?

The appropriate technology critics argue that our present level of consumption of commodities such as pulp paper is excessive, wasteful, and environmentally unsustainable. The reduction of production, as well as the adoption of alternative systems of production, may ultimately be mandatory. From an appropriate technology standpoint, the issue is not one that can be addressed only, or even primarily, at the local level: It is an issue that transcends local conditions, and requires adjustments at a broader, societal level.

A reduction in production not compensated for by other employment opportunities might be rather devastating in its effects on the people of this region and on the local economy. From the standpoint of local people, a reversion to the earlier technology would clearly make woods work a more strenuous and dangerous occupation once again, a daunting prospect. A system that theorists might advocate as energy–conserving and environmentally "responsible" is quite another thing to the people who would once again have to venture into the woods with saws and axes.

Such a solution is likely to be implemented in the North Woods only when there is no fuel left at all or where there is absolutely no other alternative.

The conditions that would have to exist for appropriate technology to be considered potentially viable would include: (1) that it were somehow cheaper and therefore competitive with the existing technology, or (2) that it were implemented as part of a wider set of changes taking place in the society at large. There is simply no way that the local population could survive if the changes that were made resulted in the uncompetitive pricing of the materials and products that are the basis of their livelihood. Hence, the adoption of new appropriate technologies for forestry must be consistent with the broader changes in the larger economy. The question of how to adopt new and appropriate technologies is inevitably one that must be answered at the macrolevel, which stretches beyond the North Woods.

Notes

1. Johanson (1989) claims that the power saw first made its appearance in the county in 1937. Nonetheless, it was apparently the mid–forties before power saws were widely used in the area.
2. These estimates may well be fairly accurate: the 1980 Census counted only 56 persons over age 16 in the county employed in "forestry and fisheries." Since commercial fishing is an all–but–nonexistent industry in this locality, we may assume that most of those listed were working in the woods.
3. This is a view shared by other critics of the industry. Michael Kellett, Michigan representative of the Wilderness Society, was quoted as follows: "What the public doesn't realize is that the (national and state forest) timber programs lose money. It costs more money to manage the timber programs than the programs bring in, so the taxpayer is subsidizing these programs. . . . Lots of cheap, subsidized timber does not promote community stability. There is no shortage of trees in Michigan. There is a vast amount of timber owned by private interests. But it is more trouble to go to private owners so the forest service is hit for more timber" (Hoover 1986, 5B, 8B).

References

Bald, F. Cleaver. 1961. *Michigan in four centuries, revised and enlarged edition*. New York: Harper & Brothers.

Brusso, Dallas. 1986. Personal interview. (Farmer, independent logger, Ontonagon County, Mich.).

———. 1989. Personal interview.

Domitrovich, Carl. 1986. Personal interview. (Logger, sawyer, Ontonagon County, Mich.).

———. 1989. Personal interview.
Hoover, Barbara. 1986. A light through the forest: timber offers a fiber of hope for U. P. *Detroit News*, 16 November, B1, B5, B8.
Howard, Ron. 1985. Personal interview. (Manager, paper mill, Ontonagon County, Mich.).
Jamison, James K. 1965. *This Ontonagon country: The story of an American frontier*. Calumet, Mich.: Roy W. Drier.
Johanson, Bruce H. 1985. *This land, the Ontonagon*, 2d ed. Ontonagon, Mich.: Ontonagon Herald Co.
———. 1989 Personal interview. (Local historian, Ontonagon County, Mich.).
Knight, D. K. 1985. Turpeinen brothers: A very thorough story. *Timber Harvesting* 33 (February): 18–20.
Lodwick, Dora G., and Denton E. Morrison. 1982. Appropriate technology. In *Rural society in the U.S.: Issues for the 1980s*, ed. Don A. Dillman and Daryl J. Hobbs, 44–53. Boulder, Colo.: Westview Press.
Lovins, Amory B. 1976. Energy strategy: the road not taken? *Foreign Affairs* 55(1): 65–96.
———. 1977. *Soft energy paths: Toward a durable peace*. Cambridge, Mass.: Ballinger Publishing Co.
Lovins, Amory B., and Hugh Nash. 1979. *The energy controversy: Soft path questions & answers*. San Francisco, Calif.: Friends of the Earth, Inc.
Miljevich, Eli. 1989. Personal interview. (Forest material jobber, Gogebic County, Mich.).
Moilanen, K. J. 1986. Personal interview. (Retired County Agricultural Extension Agent, Ontonagon County, Mich.).
Pestka, Norman. 1989. Personal interview. (Forest materials jobber, Ontonagon County, Mich.).
Schumacher, E. F. 1973. *Small is beautiful: Economics as if people mattered*. New York: Harper & Row.
Slye, Allan. 1986. Personal interview. (County Natural Resources Agent, Ontonagon County, Mich.).
———. 1989. Personal interview.
Toivonen, Ernest. 1986. Personal interview. (Independent logger, Ontonagon County, Mich.).
———. 1989 Personal interview.
Turpeinen, Robert. 1986. Personal interview. (Manager, Turpeinen Brothers, Inc., Alston, Mich.).
———. 1989. Personal interview.

4

DEVELOPMENT, WOMEN'S WORK, AND ECONOMIC INEQUALITY IN RURAL TAIWAN

Rita S. Gallin

The Taiwan model of development is assumed to produce an equitable distribution of wealth. Emerging evidence, however, suggests otherwise. Officials in Taipei have announced that the rich are getting richer in the Republic of China (ROC) and that the gap between the rich and poor is widening (*Free China Journal* 1988, 3). Further, Hsiao's 1987 study of income inequality in Taiwan between 1953 and 1983 found that while the proportion of capitalist owners has remained constant, the share of family–owned businesses has declined and the percentage of workers has increased—a trend suggesting class polarization.

Perhaps because the questioning of conventional wisdom is so new a phenomenon, little research has been conducted to analyze the substance and meaning of economic inequality in Taiwan. (For an exception, see Schak 1988.) The purpose of this chapter is to *explore* this issue in Hsin Hsing, a village that has changed over the past 30 years from an economic system primarily based on agriculture to one predominantly dependent on off–farm employment.[1]

I emphasize the word *explore* because the chapter does not include a standard measure of income or class. Rather, it uses the occupations of married women as marks of village families' positions in the economic hierarchy. This usage is based on the premise that, in rural Taiwan, a woman's work reflects a family's strategy to secure its subsistence or to pursue its mobility; her work, therefore, indicates her family's niche in the class structure. I argue that development in Taiwan has created a set of new social categories, including an underclass of poor in which the elderly are disproportionately represented (see also *Free China Journal* 1990, 3; Gates 1979).

I begin the chapter by describing development in Taiwan and in Hsin Hsing village to show how the transformation of the island's economy was accompanied by changes in the community. Then, I examine how demographic and economic changes in Hsin Hsing were related to married women's work. In the final section, I discuss the results of my analysis and consider what the impoverization of the elderly in Hsin Hsing suggests about the futures of today's young families in Taiwan.

Development in Taiwan

When the nationalist government retreated to Taiwan in 1949, it found the island to be mainly agricultural, with conditions not consistently favorable to development. The strategies it adopted to foster economic growth have been documented in detail elsewhere (Ho 1978; Lin 1973; Pang 1987). Here, I need only say that the government first strengthened agriculture to provide a base for industrialization, pursued a strategy of import substitution for a brief period during the 1950s, and then in the 1960s adopted a policy of industrialization through export.

The latter policy produced dramatic changes in Taiwan's economic structure. The contribution of agriculture to the net domestic product declined from 36 percent in 1952 to only 7 percent in 1986, while that of industry rose from 18 to 47 percent over the same period. Trade expanded greatly, increasing in value from US$303 million in 1952 to US$64 billion in 1986. The contribution of exports to the volume of trade also rose dramatically, from US$116 million (38 percent) in 1952 to US$40 billion (63 percent) in 1986 (Lu 1987, 2).

To achieve this transformation, Taiwan's planners did not depend primarily on direct foreign investment. Rather, they relied on capital mobilization within the domestic private sector and an elaborate system of subcontracting to spearhead the growth of manufactured exports. As a result, Taiwan's industrial development is based on and sustained by vertically integrated and geographically dispersed small–scale businesses.

As early as 1971, for example, 50 percent of the industrial and commercial establishments and 55 percent of the manufacturing firms in Taiwan were located in rural areas (Ho 1976).[2] Most such businesses are small–scale operations that produce for domestic and international markets; more than 90 percent of the island's enterprises employ fewer than 30 workers each (Bello and Rosenfeld 1990, 219) and, in 1987, these small businesses employed almost three–quarters (74.2 percent) of Taiwan's labor force (DGBAS 1988, 116–17).

The predominant form these small enterprises take is the family firm. It is estimated that 97 percent of all businesses owned by Taiwanese are family organized (Greenhalgh 1980, 13). These firms were founded with capital drawn almost exclusively from the informal money market of domestic savings and personal loans. They are fueled by the unpaid labor of family and the underpaid labor of hired workers. Taiwan's economy, in sum, is sustained by a multitude of small firms that traverse the island and provide income for the majority of the population—a population that, in terms of wealth, is becoming increasingly unequal.

Development in Hsin Hsing

Hsin Hsing is a nucleated village approximately 125 miles southwest of Taiwan's capital city, Taipei, and located beside a road that runs between two market towns, Lukang and Ch'i-hu. Its people are Hokkien (Minnan) speakers, as are most in the area; their ancestors emigrated from Fukien, China, several hundred years ago. Within the village, the basic socioeconomic unit is the family, the *chia*. Such a family takes one of three forms: conjugal, stem, or joint. The conjugal family consists of a husband, wife, and their unmarried children; the joint family adds two or more married sons and their wives and children to this core group. The stem family—a form that lies somewhere between the conjugal and joint family types—includes parents, their unmarried offspring, and one married son with his wife and children.

The registered 1958 population of the village was 609 people in 99 households or economic families (*chia*). Approximately four-fifths of the population was between the ages of one and 44 years, and slightly less than half was male (see table 1). Conjugal families predominated, accounting for 66 percent of village families (56 percent of the population). In contrast, only 5 percent of village families (10 percent of the population) was of the joint type, while the remaining 29 percent of families (35 percent of the population) lived in stem units.

During the 1950s, when no significant industries or job opportunities existed locally, land was the primary means of production. Almost all families were agriculturalists, deriving most of their livelihood from two crops of rice, marketable vegetables grown in the third crop, and, in some cases, wages from farm labor.[3] Men worked in the fields, taking care of tasks such as plowing, harrowing, transplanting, irrigating, and harvesting, and assumed responsibility for the care of oxen, which provided the major draft power in plowing and hauling, as well as "backyard fertilizer," to meet agricultural demands. Women managed the house and children, weeded fields and dried rice, preserved crops, raised poultry, and, in their "spare time," wove fiber hats at home to supplement the family income.

The situation in the village began to change in the mid-1950s and early 1960s as the growing population pressure on the land created problems of underemployment and farms too small to support family members. Increasing numbers of men began to migrate to the larger cities of the province to seek jobs and supplemental income (Gallin and Gallin 1974). The stream of migrants continued throughout the 1960s and labor shortages became acute, farm profits decreased, and agricultural production declined. (In Taiwan as a whole, production leveled off and varied by only a small amount from year to year in the late 1960s [see CEPD 1979, 59].) The stream of migration and decline in production might well have continued in Hsin Hsing, but for certain national and international developments in the 1970s.

The government's policy of export–oriented industrialization had brought about rapid urbanization and migration from rural areas to cities during the 1960s. Large segments of the rural population had been absorbed by urban industry, and the value of a farmer's production in 1972 was only one–fifth that of an off–farm worker's production (Huang 1981, 3). To stem the stagnation of agriculture, in 1972 the government abolished the rice–fertilizer barter system;[4] in 1973 it instituted a guaranteed rice price and enacted the Accelerated Rural Development Program (Yu 1977). The implementation of these policies created a climate in which farmers believed they could derive profits from the cultivation of their land, and it accelerated the move of industry—which had begun in the 1960s—to the countryside.

These attempts to invigorate agriculture were followed by the oil crisis of 1974 and the world recession and inflation of 1974–75. The pace of industrialization in Taiwan's cities slowed (CEPD 1979, 78), and more than 200,000 urban workers lost their jobs (Huang 1981, 163) when some factories shut down and others cut back production. The city began to lose the aura of opportunity as the countryside began to acquire one of promise.

A comparison of the structure of the village population in 1979 with the population in 1958 suggests one of the outcomes of these developments. By 1979 only 382 people lived in Hsin Hsing, but the sex ratio had increased to 113 percent (see table 1). In part, this increase reflected a decline in male emigration and a rise in the migration of unmarried women to urban areas.[5]

Although the sources of data contained in the table differ, correlations with other statistical materials confirmed the accuracy and comparability of the two data sets. These materials included enumerations based on our own surveys and interviews with individual village families cultivating land, maintaining livestock, and owning farm implements.

Further examination of the data suggests another way in which the villagers responded to national and international developments. By 1979,

Table 1
POPULATION OF HSIN HSING BY PERIOD AND AGE, 1958-1979.

Age	1958 N	1958 %	1979 N	1979 %
1–15	269	44.2	151	39.5
16–44	235	38.6	129	33.8
45–64	90	14.8	78	20.4
65 and older	15	2.5	24	6.3
TOTAL	609	100.0	382	100.0
Sex ratio (m/100f)		95		113

Sources: 1958, Household Record Book, Puyen Township Public Office; 1979, Field Interviews

Note: The figures for 1958 are for all people registered as members of Hsin Hsing households, regardless of whether they were resident or only registered there. An estimated 509 people actually lived in Hsin Hsing in 1958. The figures for 1979 record only people resident in the village; 606 people living in 170 households, however, were registered in the records of the township office in 1979.

conjugal family households no longer predominated in Hsin Hsing; only 45 percent of households (30 percent of the population) were of the simple type. Fully 18 percent of family households (34 percent of the population) were of the joint type, while the remaining 37 percent of family households (36 percent of the population) were of the stem form.

The reasons for this increase in complex families have been documented in detail elsewhere (Gallin and Gallin 1982a; Gallin 1984a, 1984b). Suffice it to say that villagers believed that this type of family provided the means for socioeconomic success in a changing world. A family that included many potential wage workers, as well as other members who could manage the household, supervise children, and care for the land, had a better chance of diversifying economically than did a family of small size.

Economic change also accompanied national and international developments. Labor–intensive factories, service shops, retail stores, and construction companies burgeoned in the local area. By 1979, seven small satellite factories, three artisan workshops, and 26 shops and small businesses had been established in the village, and resident families derived 85

Table 2.
AGES OF MARRIED WOMEN IN HSIN HSING BY LIVING ARRANGEMENTS, 1979.

Age	Living Arrangements					
	Conjugal		Extended		Total	
	N	%	N	%	N	%
20–29	4	33.3	8	66.7	12	100.0
30–39	12	48.0	13	52.0	25	100.0
40–49	12	66.7	6	33.3	18	100.0
50–59	8	42.1	11	57.9	19	100.0
60 and over	10	41.7	14	58.3	24	100.0
Total	46	46.9	52	53.1	98	100.0
Mean age	46.6		48.3		47.4	

Source: Field Interviews, 1979

percent of their income from off–farm employment (Gallin and Gallin 1982b). Work in the agricultural sector, however, was not abandoned. Fully 84 percent of village households continued to farm, and households engaged in both farming and off–farm work were by far the most common.

The change in the villagers' mode of employment was not simply a response to rural industrialization. Despite implementation of new policies, agriculture remained an unprofitable venture; on the average, Hsin Hsing farmers realized less than NT$2,000 (US$52.63) from the rice they grew on one *chia* of land in 1979. Nevertheless, they continued to cultivate the land because: (1) it was a source of food (rice); (2) the mechanization and chemicalization of agriculture obviated the need for either a large or a physically strong labor force (see Gallin and Ferguson 1988); and (3) the decreased size of family farms—in 1979 the average land size tilled per farming household was 0.63 *chia*—required less labor. (For Taiwan as a whole, the average tillage was less than 1 hectare [*Free China Journal* 1990, 3.])

Women's Work in Hsin Hsing

1979, 98 married women lived in the village as members of either extended or conjugal households (see table 2).[6] Their mean age was 47.4 years, and approximately half fell below and half above this average. The majority of the women identified their primary activity with nontraditional

Table 3.
PRIMARY ACTIVITY OF MARRIED WOMEN IN HSIN HSING BY LIVING ARRANGEMENTS, 1979.

Primary Activity	Living Arrangements					
	Conjugal		Extended		Total	
	N	%	N	%	N	%
Wage laborer	11	23.9	11	21.1	22	22.4
Entrepreneur	2	4.4	3	5.8	5	5.1
Worker in family business	1	2.2	1	1.9	2	2.0
Farmer	10	21.7	12	23.1	22	22.4
Housekeeper	22	47.8	17	32.7	39	40.0
Retired	—	—	8	15.4	8	8.1
Total	46	100.0	52	100.0	98	100.0

Source: Field Interviews, 1979
Note: To determine women's primary activity, they were asked: What do you do most of the time?

roles: over one–quarter said they were wage laborers and entrepreneurs, and slightly fewer listed themselves as farmers or assistants in family businesses (see table 3).

While it might be argued that farming and helping with a family business fall within the traditional definition of the female role, in the past such activities were considered secondary to Hsin Hsing women's primary responsibility for the household. Despite this changed view of what was appropriate work for women, their labor nevertheless continued to be part of a family strategy to secure its subsistence or to pursue its mobility. Being an off–farm worker, farmer, or housekeeper thus was intimately linked to a household's niche in the economy.

Off–farm Workers

Twenty–nine women said that off–farm work was their primary activity; 15 belonged to extended households and 14 to conjugal units.[7] Those from extended households tended to be younger (see table 4) and to be married to men who were also employed off the farm. Twelve of these 15 working women had been encouraged by their parents to enter the industrial labor force. Realizing that their off–farm employment furthered the

Table 4.
AGES OF MARRIED WOMEN IN HSIN HSING BY LIVING ARRANGEMENTS AND PRIMARY ACTIVITY, 1979.

Primary Activity	Living Arrangements			
	Conjugal		Extended	
	Age Mean	Age Range	Age Mean	Age Range
Wage laborer	47.6	36–66	34.3	21–56
Entrepreneur	43.0	38–48	31.0	26–37
Worker in family business	49	—	24.0	—
Farmer	39.7	31–60	49.2[b]	39–60
Housekeeper	49.2	20–79	47.4[c]	25–70
Retired	—	—	73.8	62–86

Source: Field Interviews, 1979

[a]The 56-year-old woman was a mother–in–law. If she is omitted from the calculation, the mean age of wage laborers in extended households decreases by 2 years to 32.1 years.

[b]Six of the farmers were mothers–in–law; their mean age was 54.0 years, with a range of 48 to 60 years. The mean age of daughters–in–law who farmed was 44.3 years, with a range of 39 to 53 years.

[c]Nine of the housekeepers were mothers–in–law; their mean age was 60.1 years, with a range of 54 to 70 years. The mean age of the eight daughters–in–law who were housekeepers was 33.0 years, with a range of 25 to 51 years.

to enter the industrial labor force. Realizing that their off-farm employment furthered the mobility of the family, their mothers-in-law had assumed some of their role responsibilities during the daytime; such as, supervision of the children and work on the family land.

The demand for inexpensive labor is high in rural areas undergoing industrialization. Women, who are willing to work for less money than men, are often the preferred employees. Empirical support for this scenario comes from the lives of the 14 female off–farm workers who belonged to conjugal households. Contrary to their counterparts in extended families, these wives were middle–aged or older (Table 4) and their husbands were not members of the off–farm labor force.

Two women in their sixties worked for wages while their husbands farmed their small landholdings (mean = 0.25 *chia*), and one woman in her fifties from a landless family labored in a factory to support herself and her unemployed husband. In the case of two women, contributions to the family treasury from their unmarried children did augment their meager earnings. But the cost of this contribution was high. "I have no money to marry off my son," said one woman. "We need his wages to survive." One other woman in her fifties, who also worked in a local factory, was a widow whose two married sons lived and worked in Taipei with their families. Neither sent money to her—"they live in poverty," she reported—and she barely survived at a subsistence level.

Not all women workers in conjugal units, however, lived as precarious an existence as these four older women. Four wage laborers in their forties were married to men who also worked for remuneration, and their unmarried adult children were employed off-farm as well. A fifth woman, a 48-year-old widow, operated one of the three village stores. Her married sons worked and lived in Taipei with their families, but they regularly remitted money home to her, and one had sent his preschool-age daughter to live in the village so that, she said, "I could have company."

The remaining two wage laborers in their forties were both married to farmers who worked the families' small landholdings (mean 0.4 *chia*). Neither of the women had children old enough to enter the off-farm labor force and both considered themselves the mainstay of their families. One, in fact, when asked what her husband did most of the time, replied, "He doesn't do anything." While this was not entirely true, the resources she provided in behalf of the family far outweighed his small contribution.

Only three (out of 16) women in their thirties who lived in conjugal units worked off farm. One woman was a 38-year-old barber who operated a small shop at the front of the village. Two of her unmarried sons worked for wages and she and her husband, a factory worker, tilled the family's 0.77 *chia* of land. The second woman was a 36-year-old factory worker who was married to a mainlander, an army officer stationed in a large city who remitted money to her regularly; she lived in the village with her three school-age children and 69-year-old father, who tilled the family's 0.15 *chia* of land.

The third young woman working off farm was a 38-year-old landless widow whose husband, a policeman, had died in 1973. She had migrated to Taipei to seek employment, leaving behind her eight-year-old son in the village with her brother-in-law and sister-in-law; they charged her for his room and board. She returned to the village in 1976 and, after working in a factory for a short period, she purchased a sewing machine so that she could earn money working at home. In 1979, she and her son subsisted on the NT$1950 (US$51.32) a month she earned and a small government pension. "I have to rely on myself," she said. "I don't want to ask my brother-in-law for help."

To summarize, women worked off farm either to promote their families' futures or to secure their livelihoods. Young women who were members of extended families and middle–aged women living in conjugal units tended to work for remuneration in order to help advance the household's mobility. Older women, in contrast, were likely to seek paid employment to guarantee the family's survival.

Farmers

Twenty–two women identified farming as their primary activity. Twelve lived in extended households, which tilled an average of 0.78 *chia* of land. Ten were members of conjugal units whose families farmed approximately the same amount of land (mean = 0.73 *chia*).

Half of the women farmers in extended households were mothers–in–law and, as might be expected, they were older, on average, than daughters–in–law who farmed (54.0 and 44.3 years, respectively). Five of the six mothers–in–law had daughters–in–law who worked off–farm (see table 5). The sixth was the mother of a 37–year–old woman, said to be slow mentally, whose adopted–in–husband worked in the city and sent remittances to the family in Hsin Hsing.

The village–resident sons of four of the five farmers, like their wives, worked off–farm; one woman's son was in the army. In addition, two of the farmers' husbands worked for wages; the husbands of the other four identified themselves as farmers. What this means is that two–thirds (four out of six) of the mothers–in–law farmed in partnership with their husbands, thereby releasing married children to pursue employment off–farm, and one–third assumed primary responsibility for the farm, while all other adults in the family worked off–farm.

Daughters–in–law who farmed, not surprisingly, had mothers–in–law who identified themselves as either retirees or housekeepers (see table 5); their mothers–in–law were older, on average, than mothers–in–law who farmed (72.5 and 54.0 years, respectively). Three of these farmers were married to men who worked off–farm, while the husbands of the three others identified themselves as farmers who earned wages as farm laborers and also worked at sporadic jobs off–farm.

The families of the three daughters–in–law with farming husbands tilled, on average, more land than those in which the women's husbands worked off–farm (0.86 *chia* and 0.59 *chia*, respectively). Yet these three farming families did not consider their earnings from the land sufficient, since the women's husbands also took occasional agricultural and nonagricultural jobs in order to earn income. The decision to remain a farming family may, in two instances, have reflected the fact (1) that the husbands in these families were only sons whose fathers had "died many years

Table 5.
Primary Activity of Mothers–in–Law (N=24) in Hsin Hsing by Primary Activity of Daughters–in–Law (N=28), 1979.

Daughters–in–Law Primary Activity	Mothers–in–Law Primary Activity				
	Wage Laborer	Farmer	Housekeeper	Retired	Total
Wage laborer	—	4	2	2	8
Entrepreneur	—	—	1	—	1
Worker in family business	—	1	—	—	1
Farmer	—	—	3	3	6
Housekeeper	1	1	3	3	8
Total	1	6	9	8	24

Source: Field Interviews, 1979

ago," and/or (2) that the wives were relatively young women who were unable to pursue paid employment because they had preschool–age children.

The factors that underlay the third family's decision to remain a farm family are unclear; it tilled only about half as much land as the two other farming families (0.6 *chia* in comparison to 1.0 *chia*). Small remittances from the family's two unmarried, migrant sons did little to supplement income from the land, and their married son rarely sent them money. "How can he [the married son] send money home to his parents," his mother asked rhetorically, "when he earns only [NT]$80.00 [US$2.10] a day and must spend much of his earnings to repair his old truck and to pay the doctor's bills for his two children who are frequently sick?" The family had never attempted to rent additional land—as the two others had—to augment its meager landholdings. Perhaps the decision to remain a farm family had been based on the hope that the mother would raise filial sons who would assume responsibility for supporting their parents in old age. The dream, however, had not been realized and the woman faced an old age similar to that of the two older female farmers who lived in conjugal households.

One of these women was 60 years old, married to a farmer, and the mother of two married sons who lived and worked in Taipei. The older couple farmed 0.3 *chia* of land but, reported the woman, "We don't produce enough to sell or eat and we have to depend on my sons to send money home to meet expenses." In the changing world of the 1970s, however, remittances were not always forthcoming and the woman and her husband eked out a precarious living from the land. They were one of 11 families in the village without a refrigerator: "We have nothing to put in," she said.

The second older farmer, 50 years old and also married to a farmer, did not own a refrigerator either.[8] She and her husband tilled 0.4 *chia* of land, did not produce enough rice to sell, and subsisted on income from a variety of sources, as the following quote illustrates:

> Our daily expenses to live come from the sale of vegetables in the third crop. But we make little profit since we must pay trucking and marketing charges. My daughter [16 years old] works in a factory in Lukang and earns [NT]$2,000 a month [US$52.63] . . . and my sons are in the military. One was conscripted but the other enlisted in the Air Force Academy so we get a subsidy of 22 kilograms of rice a month. Soon we'll apply for a 50 percent reduction in our electricity bill which costs about [NT]$135 a month [US$3.55]. We can apply because I've got two sons in the military.

This woman's account provides empirical substance to the villagers' view of farming as an unprofitable venture—and it helps explain the roots of the gender division of labor in the eight other conjugal households in which the women were farmers. These eight women were young (mean age 35.9 years) and tilled an average of 0.83 *chia* of land; six of them were married to men who worked off–farm. The husbands of the two other women farmers identified their primary activity as farming, but both men were diversifying economically in the agricultural sector: one raised over 500 chickens for the wholesale market, and the second used his own power tiller to plow other people's land for wages.

In actuality, then, the families of only two female farmers depended on agriculture for their sustenance. The remaining 20 derived their livelihoods from a combination of sources and, in over half (11 out of 20) of these households, women's assumption of primary responsibility for the farm had enabled other family members to work for wages in the industrial sector. Those farmers who were members of large family units played a crucial role in the construction of a diversified family economy—an economy necessary for success in a transformed rural area. Those young farmers who were members of small family units labored to contribute to their families' livelihood. Furthermore, in order to survive, those farmers who were older tilled the land their children refused to cultivate. The labor of female farmers, in sum, was an important facet of a family's strategy to improve its status or to subsist.

Housekeepers/Retirees

Thirty–nine women identified themselves as housekeepers—17 lived in extended units and 22 in conjugal units—and eight women identified themselves as retirees. As might be expected, retired women were members of extended households and among the oldest women in the village (see table 4). One of the eight women summed up the meaning of retirement when, in response to being asked what she did most of the time, she replied, "Eat and play [with pocket money married children supplied]." These women, because they had married children in the village, enjoyed the prerogatives of old age.

Having married children in the village, however, did not guarantee that an older woman could command the labor of her daughters–in–law to lighten her own workload. Six other women (considered elderly at mean age 65.2 years) also had adult children living in Hsin Hsing. But these women, four of whom lived in extended households, with daughters–in–law who farmed or worked off–farm, and two of whom lived in conjugal units, identified themselves as housekeepers.

The lives of the two women who lived in conjugal units were similar to, but in important ways different from, those of the women who considered themselves retired. Like retirees, these two women neither cooked—since they ate with the families of their daughters–in–law on a rotating basis—nor farmed, and both also received "pocket money" from their sons. In contrast to retirees, however, these two women, by living in conjugal units, were required to maintain the household and to do piecework on a part–time basis to earn the money they needed. (One complained that the NT$900 [US$23.68] she and her husband received monthly "was not enough.")

Five other elderly women (mean age 66.4 years) also identified themselves as housekeepers, but they had no married children in the village. Their lives provided stark evidence that support of parents was not automatic in this changing world. In addition to keeping house and doing piecework, three helped their husbands farm the land (mean 0.76 *chia*) their city–based children refused to till. Two were from landless families: one woman did piecework to supplement sporadic remittances from her sons, which she and her husband depended upon for their sustenance; the second woman helped her husband manage the small grocery store they operated in the village. She openly reported that they had established the business because "we have to depend upon ourselves." Her husband, however, was embarrassed to acknowledge the unfiliality of their children, as the following quote illustrates:

> I was a junk peddler in Taipei for seven years [1967–73] but I returned to the village because I was too old for the work. While I

was away my wife stayed in the village tilling the land, but when she could no longer farm we sold it and she worked for others, weeding and harvesting vegetables. We opened the store because we thought we could help our sons by making our own living—we wouldn't have to eat with them. We don't want to bother them for food and pocket money. We make enough to live on. Our profit is about [NT]$2,000 a month [US$52.63] and sometimes we can make almost [NT] $50.00 [US$1.32] a day cleaning snow peas.

In addition to the 11 housekeepers in their sixties, 11 women in their fifties (mean age 54.7 years) also were housekeepers: six were members of extended households and five lived in conjugal units. Two of the housekeepers living in extended households were mothers–in–law who kept house and cared for their grandchildren while their daughters–in–law worked off-farm. The third was the daughter–in–law of the 86-year-old retiree. Her two sons were students and, in addition to keeping house, she farmed with her husband, who operated a small trucking business.

The remaining three housekeepers living in extended households had daughters–in–law who also identified themselves as housekeepers. In one case, the mother–in–law and daughter–in–law were members of Hsin Hsing's wealthiest family; it operated a large rice mill. In the second, the daughter–in–law and her infant son lived with her mother–in–law, while her husband worked in a nearby city and remitted money home. In the third case, the mother and daughter kept house while the younger woman's adopted–in–husband farmed the family's 1.0 *chia* of land and operated an itinerant vegetable business.

The five housekeepers in their fifties who lived in conjugal units also had married children, but they had no daughters–in–law resident in the village. One woman kept house and cared for her four grandchildren while her widowed son worked for wages. The other four women managed the village house, in addition to helping their husbands with the farm, while their daughters–in–law maintained homes in the city for their own husbands and children. In contrast to housekeepers in their sixties who had no adult children in the village, however, these women's lives were not fraught with uncertainty. Their married sons sent them money on a regular basis. The women were from land–poor families (mean 0.42 *chia*), but they had secured themselves material support by providing capital for the enterprises their sons operated.

Four housekeepers were in their forties (mean age 46.0 years) and, although their lives were different, they shared two characteristics: none had married sons, and all earned income doing piecework in their homes or working at odd jobs on and off the land. Two of these housekeepers were married to men who identified themselves as farmers, and their families were among the most land–poor in the village (tilling 0.2 and 0.3 *chia*, respectively). They subsisted on rice they produced, remittances from unmarried daughters, and money the women and their husbands earned working part–time. The third woman also was from a land–poor family (0.3 *chia*) but her husband, three of her unmarried sons, and a single daughter worked off–farm. The fourth woman, the youngest in the cohort, was married to a farmer who was diversifying economically in the agricultural sector. She worked with him, tilling their 1.4 *chia* of land, and wove straw belts at home on a part–time basis to supplement their income.

Finally, 13 women in their twenties and thirties (mean age = 29.6 years) identified themselves as housekeepers. Seven lived in extended households and six were members of conjugal units. Three housekeepers living in extended households had mothers–in–law who also were housekeepers, while two others had mothers–in–law who either worked off–farm or farmed (see above). The remaining two housekeepers living in extended units were the daughters–in–law of retirees. Both women had preschool–age children and, in addition to keeping house, they farmed the land (mean 0.63 *chia*) with their husbands, who worked full–time for remuneration in the industrial sector.

Five of six young housekeepers living in conjugal households were also the mothers of preschool–age children. The sixth woman was childless, the twenty–year–old wife of an twenty–year–old wage worker; she had married her husband when his brother, to whom she was engaged, was killed in a motorcycle accident. Her family was the second–largest landholder in the village and she worked the unit's 1.7 *chia* with her father–in–law, who identified himself as a farmer.[9]

The families of three other young housekeepers also had land, and the women tilled it with their husbands, who were off–farm workers. In contrast to the families of the six women in their age cohort who identified farming as their primary activity, however, the families of these three women were land–poor. On average, they tilled 0.38 *chia* of land. The fourth and fifth young housekeepers were members of landless families. One was married to an entrepreneur who operated a machine shop in the village—much to the annoyance of neighbors living near the shop—and she worked with him in his business. The other was married to a man who manufactured inexpensive suitcases for sale wholesale.

To summarize, 47 women reported that they occupied roles traditional for women: eight were retirees and 39 were housekeepers. Nevertheless, almost three–fifths (23 out of 39) of the housekeepers also were engaged in production, either as auxiliary workers in the farm labor force or as part–time wage laborers and pieceworkers. What this means is that few families could afford to have women engaged only in reproduction—and such families tended to be extended units and to include off–farm workers, who provided the cash needed to insure the family's security. Housekeepers from simple units, in contrast, either contributed some labor to farm production or earned small amounts of money on a sporadic basis to help secure their families' sustenance. Women's reproductive and productive work, in short, was a critical component in the strategies families devised to support their current subsistence and to construct their hoped–for future prosperity.

Summary and Discussion

The focus of this chapter has been development, women's work, and economic inequality in rural Taiwan. Data collected over a thirty-year period show how the land lost its ability to sustain life, how cash became a necessity for survival, and how village women who primarily had performed domestic roles were transformed into workers in the agricultural and industrial sectors. The data also show that the entry of women into the farm and off-farm labor forces was a response to both changes in the economy and the needs of the family.

The mechanization and chemicalization of agriculture led to a shift from human to fossil energy, thereby obviating the need for either a large or physically strong labor force, and the dispersion and expansion of rural industry created a demand for low-cost labor. Both changes acted as centripetal forces, drawing women into activities formerly dominated by men. Family considerations, in contrast, acted as centrifugal forces that propelled women into agriculture and industry. To secure their subsistence or to advance their fortunes, families pressed women into nontraditional roles.

The assumption of these roles varied across households and cohorts of women. In extended families, young women tended to be off-farm workers, while older and middle-aged women were farmers. In conjugal households, by contrast, young women were likely to farm, while older and middle-aged women worked off farm. These differences were shown to be a reflection of a family economic strategy and related to the unit's niche in the economy.

Extended families were large (with a mean size of 9.5 people), enabling a division of labor in which older women assumed responsibility for the work of others in order to release them for remunerative work off farm.[10] The cash these workers contributed to the family treasury bought their household a relatively comfortable standard of living and built the foundation for their future prosperity. Conjugal units, in contrast, were small (with a mean size of 4.9 people) and unable to develop a division of labor in which responsibilities were delegated between older and younger members of the family. The present and future of these simple units differed, however.

Households with women in their twenties and thirties usually included only one wage earner, the male family head. Because they had preadolescent children, the women of these households engaged in some production, frugally managed the home on a tight budget, and put their hope for their futures in the sons they were raising. The situation of the families with women in their forties tended to be more diverse. Some units included several wage earners who provided a reliable source of cash and the potential for a prosperous future. Others had only one member who was able and willing to sell labor power, and these families struggled to subsist and dreamed of economic solvency. Finally, the households with women in their fifties and sixties, because they tended to include few potential wage laborers, were among the poorest in the village, and the older women and their husbands lived lives fraught with insecurity and devoid of future prospects.

A key issue, then, is whether the families of today's young women will be able to realize the secure futures they hope to build with their hard work and frugality. The Taiwan "miracle" has been constructed by means of export-oriented industrialization—a policy predicated on the "self-exploitation" of the Chinese family (Gates 1979). Land no longer is the primary means of production, and cash is needed for survival as well as to improve a family's economic status. Monthly incomes in Taiwan, however, are low—with little potential for capital accumulation—and few rural families are able to maintain their solvency or to achieve mobility without many family members to earn money.[11]

Yet any number of older women and men in rural Taiwan live in households that lack sufficient labor power to sell (see also Hu 1984, 188). Moreover, because security is derived from income earned in a capitalist economy and not from land controlled by family elders, and because few older people have investment capital available to improve their sons' employment opportunities, the majority lack the resources necessary to pressure adult children to discharge their filial responsibilities. In the absence of a universal state-supported social security system, then, the rural elderly must depend on themselves to survive.

To the extent that Taiwan continues its current policy, economic development may continue to perpetuate the povertization of the old. Appreciation of the Taiwan dollar, competition from developing countries catching up with Taiwan's production level, and increasing disputes between labor and management in the aftermath of political liberalization have unfavorably affected the island's comparative advantage. In combination with international protectionist sentiment, increasing manufacturing costs, and the ROC-U.S. trade deficit, these phenomena all cast a shadow on Taiwan's future economic health. More importantly, they bode ill for the small-scale, labor-intensive industries that are owned by the rural petty bourgeoisie and that employ the rural proletariat and subproletariat of Taiwan. The village families of today's young women, in sum, may find their lives in old age as poor and vulnerable as those of the current elderly of Hsin Hsing.

Notes

1. The research for this paper covers the period from 1957 to 1982. The first field trip in 1957-58 involved a seventeen-month residence in Hsin Hsing. This was followed by two separate studies, in 1965-66 and 1969-70, of out-migrants from the area. The most recent research spanned two months in 1979 and one month in 1982. During these visits, Bernard Gallin and I collected data using both anthropological and sociological techniques, including participant observation, in-depth interviews, surveys, censuses, and collection of official statistics contained in family, land, school, and economic records.
2. The dispersal of industry to the countryside has been explained as a product of industry's desire to be near the sources of low-cost labor and raw materials (Ho 1976). While true, the government encouraged this movement by refraining from protecting agricultural land until the goal of industrialization had been achieved and farm productivity had declined. In November 1975, the government promulgated a law barring the use of certain agricultural lands (i.e., grades 1-24) for purposes other than farming. (Before this law, only land grades 1-12 had been so regulated.)
3. Despite implementation of the Land Reform Program and changes in the tenancy/ownership ratio, most families cultivated small farms: 45 percent of the village families cultivated below 0.5 hectare, and 84 percent cultivated below 1.0 hectare. (Approximately one hectare (0.97) equals 2.4 acres or 1.0 *chia*.) For a detailed discussion of the village in the 1950s, see Gallin 1966.
4. The rice-fertilizer barter system, begun in 1950, was a government program through which farmers received chemical fertilizer on the basis of land cultivated by exchanging fixed amounts of rice through local Farmers' Associations acting as agents for the Provincial Food Bureau. Ho (1978, 181) argues that "the high price of fertilizer was in part a consequence of the government's policy to subsidize industrialization at the expense of agriculture."
5. In 1979, 34 unmarried women 16 years of age and older were considered members of families resident in Hsin Hsing. Half were living and working in cities outside the local area.

6. As will be seen in the following, a woman's occupation was a product of the type of family in which she lived, as well as her age. More specifically, the presence or absence of another woman in the household was implicated in what a woman did.

   For the purpose of the following discussion, therefore, I have merged joint and stem families and use the term extended family or household, defining it as one in which two married women of different generations were in residence. A conjugal unit is thus one in which only one married woman was in residence. Thirteen of the women categorized as living in conjugal units considered themselves to be members of stem or joint families. Nine, however, had no daughters-in-law living in the village, and the mothers-in-law of four women were dead.

   The concepts young, old, and middle-aged also are used in the discussion that follows. Young is defined as 20 to 39 years of age; most married women in the village begin and complete child bearing during these years. Old is defined as 50 years of age and older; villagers consider the marriage of sons and the birth of grandchildren to mark the beginning of old age, and most Hsin Hsing women achieve this status by age 50. Middle-age—the residual category—is defined as 40 to 49 years of age.
7. Almost all women who worked for remuneration were members of families that cultivated land. Fewer extended (one out of 15) than conjugal (3 out of 14) units, however, were landless, and extended households tilled more land on average (0.82 *chia*) than conjugal households (0.3 *chia*).
8. Of the remaining nine families that did not own refrigerators, one was the extended family of the 41-year-old farmer whose husband, an only son, also farmed. Two others were the conjugal families of women who worked off-farm: a 35-year-old deaf mute, married to a farmer 25 years her senior, and a 40-year-old woman whose husband also worked off-farm. The remaining six families were also of the simple type, and the mean age of the women living in these units was 59.8 years: five women were housekeepers in their sixties, while one was the 56-year-old widow who worked off-farm.
9. The largest landholding in the village was 2.3 *chia*. It was operated by the son and daughter-in-law of the 86-year-old retiree.
10. Joint families were larger than stem families, including an average of 14.3 compared to 7.2 people, respectively.
11. In 1988, approximately two wage earners were needed to enable a family to achieve the per capita GNP. According to the Taiwan DGBAS (1989), this figure stood at US$6,053 in 1988, while the minimum wage for that same year was US$280 per month (Cohen 1988, 131). Thus, in 1988, 1.8 people "each" had to earn US$3,360 per annum to realize the island's average family income. It is unlikely that the wages of the working women, or even of most of the working men, in Hsin Hsing have risen to this level since 1979.

References

Bello, Walden, and Stephanie Rosenfeld. 1990. *Dragons in distress: Asia's miracle economies in crisis.* San Francisco: The Institute for Food and Development.

Cohen, Marc J. 1988. *Taiwan at the crossroads.* Washington, D.C.: Asia Resource Center

Council for Economic Planning and Development (CEPD). 1979. *Taiwan statistical data book.* Taipei, Taiwan: Council for Economic Planning and Development, Executive Yuan.

Directorate General of Budget, Accounting and Statistics (DGBAS). 1988. *Yearbook of manpower statistics, Taiwan area, Republic of China.* Taipei, Taiwan: Executive Yuan.

_____. 1989. Statistical data ROC on Taiwan. *Free China Journal,* 17 April:7.

Free China Journal. 1988. Hard to slow a rich man down in the ROC. 11 August, 3.

_____. 1990. As Taiwan modernizes agriculture's face wrinkles. 9 August, 3.

Gallin, Bernard. 1966. *Hsin Hsing, Taiwan: A Chinese village in change.* Berkeley, Calif: University of California Press.

Gallin, Bernard, and Rita S. Gallin.1974. The integration of village migrants in Taipei. In *The Chinese city between two worlds,* ed. Mark Elvin and G. William Skinner, 331-58. Stanford, Calif: Stanford University Press.

_____. 1982a. The Chinese joint family in changing rural Taiwan. In *Social Interaction in Chinese Society,* ed. Richard W. Wilson, Sidney L. Greenblatt, and Amy Wilson, 142-50. New York: Praeger Publishers.

_____. 1982b. Socioeconomic life in rural Taiwan: Twenty years of development and change. *Modern China* 8(2): 205-46.

Gallin, Rita S. 1984a. The entry of Chinese women into the rural labor force: A case study from Taiwan. *Signs* 9(3): 383-98.

_____. 1984b. Women, family and the political economy of Taiwan. *The Journal of Peasant Studies* 12(1): 76-92.

Gallin, Rita S., and Anne Ferguson. 1988. The household enterprise and farming system research: A case study from Taiwan. In *Gender Issues in Farming Systems Research and Extension,* ed. Susan Poats, Marianne Schmink, and Anita Spring, 223-35. Boulder, Colo: Westview Press.

Gates, Hill. 1979. Dependency and the part-time proletariat in Taiwan. *Modern China* 5(3): 381-408.

Greenhalgh, Susan. 1980. Microsocial processes in the distribution of income. Paper presented at the Taiwan Political Economy Workshop, East Asia Institute, Columbia University, New York, N.Y., 18-20 December.

Ho, Samuel P. S. 1976. Decentralized industrialization and rural development: Evidence from Taiwan. *Economic Development and Cultural Change* 28(1): 77-96.

_____. 1978. *Economic development of Taiwan, 1946-1970.* New Haven: Yale University Press.

Hsiao, Wey. 1987. Changes in class structure and rewards distribution in postwar Taiwan. In *Research in social stratification and mobility*, vol. 6, ed. Robert V. Robinson, 257-78. Greenwich, Conn.: JAI Press.

Hu, Tai-li. 1984. *My mother-in-law's village: Rural industrialization and change in Taiwan*. Taipei, Taiwan: Institute of Ethnology, Academia Sinica.

Huang, Shu-min. 1981. *Agricultural degradation: Changing community systems in rural Taiwan*. Washington, D.C.: University Press of America, Inc.

Lin, Ching-yuan. 1973. *Industrialization in Taiwan, 1946-1970*. New York: Praeger Publishers.

Lu, Min-jen. 1987. Promotion of constitutional democracy government's goal. *The Free China Journal* 5 October: 2.

Pang, Chien-kuo. 1987. The state and economic transformation: The Taiwan case. Ph.D. Diss., Department of Sociology, Brown University.

Schak, David. 1988. *A Chinese beggars' den: Poverty and mobility in an underclass community*. Pittsburgh, Penn.: University of Pittsburgh Press.

Yu, Terry Y. H. 1977. The accelerated rural development program in Taiwan. In *Industry of free China*, 2-16. Taipei, Taiwan: Council of Economic Planning and Development, Executive Yuan.

5

INEQUALITY AND THE EMERGENCE OF NONFARM EMPLOYMENT IN RWANDA

Daniel C. Clay, Theobald Kampayana, and Jean Kayitsinga

Introduction

Off–farm employment has long been seen by farm residents as a way to cover income deficits arising from stagnating farm production and growing population pressure. In Rwanda, where population density in certain regions approaches 400 persons per square kilometer, subdivision and further fragmentation of land has led many households to supplement their incomes through employment in the nonfarm sector of the rural economy. Government awareness of the need to stimulate nonfarm employment opportunities for the rural poor has grown recently, as demonstrated by a well–known presidential address on this question (Rwanda 1986a) and by the official declaration of 1988 as the "Year of Raising Farm Incomes." Hope abounded for converting such slogans into reality. Promotion of small enterprises, cooperatives, new sources of credit, and employment training were some alternatives studied (Rwanda 1988a).

Yet beyond its contribution to the overall growth of farm residents' incomes, expansion of jobs in the nonfarm sector can alleviate income inequalities in the agricultural sector that result from an unequal distribution of landholdings. To the extent that poor farm households with little access to land can obtain the training, capital, and credit to facilitate their participation in the nonfarm sector, their relative economic position will likewise be enhanced. Indirectly, households that rely on agricultural wage labor as their main source of income also benefit from an expanding nonfarm sector, since the creation of employment alternatives shrinks the size of the agricultural labor pool and drives up the prevailing agricultural wage rates.

This chapter examines the structure of income inequality among farm households in Rwanda. It asks how inequalities in the distribution of landholdings might bifurcate the rural social classes into households who own relatively large farms and hire agricultural laborers versus the nearly landless householders who must become the hirees. Of particular concern is how emergent nonfarm employment opportunities might implement a more even form of rural development, reducing inequality in the income of rural households. We hypothesize that farm households with smaller operational holdings will be more likely to resort to off-farm employment to bolster household income.

Ecological theory contends that populations will respond in several ways to the pressure of population growth. One is to look outward in search of additional resources—territorial expansion (Hawley 1950). In Rwanda, this phenomenon occurred for many years, and in the 1960s and 1970s it ended in a massive resettlement (*paysannat*) program that displaced over 80,000 farmers and their families into previously unoccupied areas (Rwanda 1985). Though some spontaneous movement of households toward Kibungo continued into the early 1980s (Olson 1989), the late 1970s signaled the conclusion of this period of territorial expansion.

A second demographic response is for farm couples to have fewer children in order to limit the number of mouths to feed now and the number of future inheritors of the small family landholdings (Bilsborrow 1987; Duncan 1959). This alternative is the only long-term solution, but there are many reasons why it will not be adopted easily or quickly: (1) in Rwanda, large families are traditionally honored for their size; (2) children eventually provide their parents with labor, either on or off the farm; and (3) Rwanda's strong kinship system assures parents of support in their old age, and this safety net is strengthened with each additional child (Clay and Vander Haar, 1993).

A third response is to develop a more complex division of labor in the economy so as to deploy the existing resources of farmland and child labor to maximize farm output (Gibbs and Martin 1959; Durkheim [1893]1933). Since occupational differentiation can raise both the efficiency and the quality of production and thereby enable a fixed resource base to sustain a larger population, we center the current chapter on this third response. We argue that nonfarm employment in Rwanda restructures the traditional, undifferentiated agricultural order. It occurs spontaneously as young farmers, aware that their very survival depends on their ability to draw a livelihood outside of, or in addition to, what they squeeze from the small, fragmented landholdings inherited from their fathers, begin to experiment with alternative employment strategies.

In agrarian society, farming classes are split into agricultural entrepreneurs and agricultural wage laborers, depending on whether they have managerial control over arable land (Marx 1967). Those controlling or accessing farmable lands too small for their families' subsistence must obtain income from another source. In turn, those with excessive landholdings can employ farm labor for a set wage. Peasant farmers unified the interests of both classes, but the scarcity of farmland disrupted this unity. The "farm manager," or entrepreneur, orients toward production for a surplus and enters a competitive market where this surplus is exchanged for profit (Mendras 1970, 146). In contrast, the agricultural laborer loses his/her identity as a peasant farmer and competes in a market for the sale of his/her labor. Conversion of surplus production into increased landholdings and/or higher levels of technology distinguishes the two groups further: their landholdings and occupational roles persist across generations, but the constancy leads to the formation of two identifiable social classes.

Though differentiation in the agricultural sector is closely tied to one's ability to own or rent farmland, differentiation in the rural nonfarm sector can occur independently of control over or access to arable lands. By creating new employment opportunities for the poor and near–landless segments of agrarian society, growth in the rural nonfarm sector can compensate for inequality in land wealth within the agricultural sector.

Sociocultural Context

Rwanda is a geographically small, landlocked country in the highlands of East Africa (see figure 1). To the west, Rwanda is flanked by Lake Kivu and a volcanic mountain range that occupies much of its border with Zaire. Uganda, Tanzania, and Burundi also share borders with Rwanda. With an average altitude of roughly five thousand feet, a temperate climate prevails year–round, and is marked by two rainy periods and their associated agricultural seasons.

Over 93 percent of Rwanda's rapidly growing population (increasing by 3.7 percent per year) live in rural areas, and virtually all of these rural households are engaged in agriculture. As households operate an average of only 1.2 hectares of land, farm production in Rwanda tends to be oriented toward subsistence. Beans and sorghum are the principal staple crops, while sweet potatoes, manioc, and peas also comprise much of the diet. Nearly all households grow bananas, both for home consumption and, more commonly, for beer making. Coffee and tea are Rwanda's most

Figure 1. Republic of Rwanda

important sources of foreign exchange. The agricultural system is labor-intensive and relies on small hand implements (hoes and machetes) for most tasks.

Historical ethnic divisions initially placed land ownership in the hands of the Tutsi, cattle–herders from the north, who for centuries maintained a feudal system in which agricultural labor was provided by Hutu tenants. This system was left largely intact during periods of German and Belgian colonial rule, but at the time of independence in the early 1960s, internal social revolution successfully dismantled the traditional feudal structure and created a more equitable system of independent peasant landholders.

Data and Method

Data analyzed in this chapter were obtained through a nationwide random sample of 1,019 farm households in Rwanda as part of the 1988 Nonfarm Strategies Survey. Survey questionnaires were administered over a three–month period, beginning in July 1988, to various members of sampled households, including husbands, wives, and adult children. An experienced team of Rwanda's Agricultural Surveys and Statistics Service (SESA) field staff supervisors was engaged to carry out the interviews.

The questionnaires were designed to obtain information from various members of the households, including husbands, wives, and adult children. Topics addressed in the questionnaires included: demographic characteristics of all household members and migrant children; nonfarm and off–farm employment; permanent and temporary migration patterns of selected household members; fertility/family size behaviors, plans, and preferences of all adult household members; economic support networks between the household and members of the extended family living elsewhere; sources of household income; physical characteristics of the farm and residence; hired farm labor; and the plans, aspirations, and opinions of parents and adult children regarding nonfarm training and employment and the future for young people in farming. In all, interviews averaged approximately one-and-a-half hours and usually required multiple visits to find the various respondents from each household. Adult offspring were the most difficult to locate, though multiple callbacks generally allowed the interviewers to meet with a large number of these young people.

An unusual strength of this study is that the households selected for study are part of a longitudinal study underway since 1986. Consequently, the great volume of information already collected on these households, on topics such as farm size and fragmentation, crop and livestock production, and market transactions, can be used to enhance this analysis of nonfarm strategies. Since 1986, a small number of households in the initial sample have moved away or have otherwise been dropped from SESA's current sample. The total number of households on which data are available at all points in time is 1,019; these are the households for which data are presented in the following section.

Nonfarm employment refers to the total number of days that adult members of the farm households worked in nonagricultural activities, either on the farm or off the farm, in the last 12 months. Off–farm employment is the number of days worked off the farm, in agricultural as well as nonagricultural activities. In most cases nonfarm and off–farm work was done by the male head of household and/or his spouse, and on occasion by another member of the household. Whenever possible, this employment information was obtained directly from those engaged in such activities. To avoid potential problems due to unreliable recall over a 12–month reference period, respondents were asked about their employment only over the previous three months. Previous research has shown that nonfarm and off–farm employment varies little in Rwanda from one quarter of the year to the next (Rwanda 1986b). Employment estimates were annualized by enlarging the three–month reported figures by a factor of four.

Household income was a summated measure of all major forms of gross income received plus the value of agricultural production generated by the household over the preceding 12 months. Included in this measure were: income received from the sale of labor, livestock, and banana beer (the major source of cash income for 40 percent of all farm households), plus the market value of all crop production. Average incomes were consistent with those estimated from detailed income data collected under the 1983 Rwanda Household Budget and Consumption Survey (Rwanda 1988b).

Farm size was measured as the total amount of land operated by the household irrespective of ownership. Parcels rented in are included, as are parcels operated under special agreements (often at no cost) with local authorities, kin, or other owners. Though rental agreements have become increasingly common in Rwanda, most parcels are farmed directly by owners. Thus, differences between land owned and land operated are, on average, very small.

Findings

Patterns of Off-farm Employment

Almost half (47 percent) of the farm households in Rwanda benefit from off-farm employment, and since our reference period includes only the three months prior to the interview, this figure may underestimate the true percentage. The modal source of off-farm employment is wage labor on other farms (31 percent; table 1). The remaining sources lie in the rural nonfarm sector, notably as artisans, laborers, or in commerce—generally in small businesses. Over five percent of off-farm employment is held by government functionaries.

Those engaged in agricultural wage labor are most often hired to clear and till the soil or to weed and otherwise maintain fields of crops. Only 6.2 percent of all hired agricultural labor is used at the time of harvest. The three most important crops for which labor is hired are beans, sorghum, and sweet potatoes. Time spent off the farm in artisanal activities is heaviest in the construction industry. Brick and tile makers, masons, and carpenters account for over half of all artisanal employment. Basket weaving, tailoring, and art/embroidery, all industries in which women are heavily involved, comprise another 37 percent of the artisanal subsector.

The number of days per year that households are employed off the farm in various types of activities is presented by farm size category in table 2. The estimated average number of days worked off-farm by Rwandan households is 78, or slightly under a third of a person-year.[1] As described above, agricultural wage labor, artisanal trades, and commerce constitute

Table 1.
PERCENTAGE OF DAYS WORKED OFF-FARM BY TYPE OF EMPLOYMENT.

Type of Employment	% of Days
Agricultural labor	30.8
Artisanal	18.9
Nonagricultural labor	12.8
Commerce	16.4
Functionaries	5.6
Other salaried	12.3
Other	3.1
Total	100.0
(N)	(464)

Source: 1988 Nonfarm Strategies Survey of Rwanda.

the largest portion of this time. Households in the smallest farm–size category (<0.5 hectare) spent the greatest mean number of days in off–farm work, consistent with our initial hypothesis.

The only farm households to depart from this otherwise very supportive pattern of findings are those in the largest farm–size category (>= 2.0 ha.), where work off the farm is a relatively high 77 days per year. These large farms tend also to support a relatively large number of adults; and the more adult workers there are in a household, the greater the chance that one or more of these workers will be "freed up" to work off the farm (Clay et al. 1989). Once the number of adult workers in the household is controlled, the level of off–farm employment found among members of these households drops off radically.

The type of off–farm employment is also connected to farm size. Households with the smallest landholdings are most likely to work off their farms as agricultural wage laborers, while those with the largest holdings are most likely to work in government or commerce (table 2). Employment in the artisanal trades seems to bear little connection to farm size. One can conclude that those from large farms tend to occupy jobs that require higher levels of schooling and working capital, while those from small farms comprise the bulk of the agricultural wage labor pool.

Off-farm Employment and Characteristics of Individuals

To learn more about how and why certain households use off–farm employment to generate income, we examine some of the characteristics

Table 2.
Days Worked Off-farm by Type of Employment and Farm Size.

Farm Size (ha)	N	Type of Employment							Total
		Agri-cult.	Arti-sanal	Unskld. Labor	Comm-erce	Funct.	Other Sal.	Other	
<0.5	253	31.2	16.8	10.4	10.8	4.0	20.4	3.2	96.8
0.5–1.0	325	30.8	14.8	9.6	8.8	0.4	7.6	3.6	76.0
1.0–2.0	261	15.6	14.4	10.0	16.4	1.6	5.6	0.2	63.6
2.0+	180	12.8	14.0	10.0	16.4	17.2	4.8	1.2	76.8
Total	1,019	24.0	14.8	10.0	12.8	4.4	9.6	2.4	78.0
Sig.		.003	.093	.996	.325	.001	.056	.317	.050

Source: 1988 Nonfarm Strategies Survey of Rwanda.

of the individuals who comprise these households and who engage in off–farm employment. When households do seek employment off the farm, either in the nonfarm sector or in the agricultural labor market, 77.5 percent of the time they are represented by only one person. Less frequently, a second household member (15.9 percent), or even three or more (6.6 percent) can be so employed.

Heads of households work off the farm far more often than do other household members, as they account for over 55 percent of all off–farm employment in Rwanda (table 3). Adult offspring still living in the household are next at 34.3 percent, followed by spouses at 7 percent. Consistent with these results is the finding that nearly 80 percent of all off–farm employment is held by men. Because traditional Rwandan society places a heavy burden on women to labor both in the fields and in the home, few women are encouraged to seek specialized vocational training. The areas where women make the largest contribution off their own farms are as agricultural wage laborers, basket weavers, and seamstresses—all jobs that have great flexibility as to either when or where they are performed, thereby permitting coordination between on– and off–farm responsibilities.

Age is another important determinant of off–farm employment. Roughly 50 percent of this labor market is represented by workers in their twenties and thirties. Those in the 20–29 year age bracket average 140 days yearly in off–farm work, more than any other age grouping. There are several good reasons for why this age grouping stands out in its provision of off–farm labor. The first is that these young people are still experimenting a great deal with alternative career strategies; and because they have fewer dependents (or may still be living on their parents' farms), stability of employment is less crucial. Second, parents of these young people are in their forties and fifties and are not yet ready to pass on more than fragments of their landholdings to their children. Third, many of these young farmers are aware that they will never inherit enough land to meet the subsistence needs of their families and believe they must make a niche for themselves elsewhere. Fourth, the level of schooling and specialized vocational skills obtained by this group exceeds that of their elders, allowing them to compete for those jobs in the nonfarm sector requiring higher levels of training.

Table 3 highlights the importance of educational attainment in securing off–farm employment, as nearly a third of all such employment is held by the 17.4 percent of individuals who have completed primary school. Those who comprise this "elite" group work off–farm an average of 177 days out of an estimated annual 250 work days, or 71 percent of their

Table 3.
PERCENT OF OFF-FARM EMPLOYMENT AND MEAN DAYS WORKED PER YEAR BY CHARACTERISTICS OF INDIVIDUALS
(POPULATION = ALL INDIVIDUALS WHO WORK OFF-FARM).

Selected Characteristics	% of Off-farm Employment	Mean Days Worked per Year	Distribution of Population Age 10+ Years
Relation to head of household:			
Head	55.7	134	20.0
Spouse	7.0	78	14.8
Child	34.3	124	60.6
Other	3.0	66	4.6
Total	100.0%	124	100.0%
Sex:			
Male	79.3	140	47.0
Female	20.7	85	53.0
Total	100.0%	124	100.0%
Age:			
10 – 19	13.5	111	29.9
20 – 29	31.2	140	25.2
30 – 39	30.3	118	22.1
40+	25.0	120	22.8
Total	100.0%	124	100.0%
Education level:			
None	35.6	106	41.8
Some primary	33.2	111	40.8
Primary +	31.2	177	17.4
Total	100.0%	124	100.0
(N)	(667)	(667)	(5,084)

Source: 1988 Nonfarm Strategies Survey of Rwanda.

time. By comparison, individuals with no formal schooling at all work off their farms only 42 percent of the time. Globally, those who work off-farm do so 124 days per year on average, or "half-time."

Multivariate Analysis of Agricultural Wage Labor and Nonfarm Employment

In previous sections, bivariate relationships were examined between characteristics of households and individuals on the one hand, and off–farm employment, on the other. Table 4 reports the findings of a multivariate analysis that discerns the relative importance of these individual and household factors in explaining variations in time spent in nonfarm employment and in the sale and purchase of agricultural wage labor. The strongest predictor of households' participation in the rural nonfarm sector is the number of adult male workers in the household (*beta* = 0.26). In part, this is because a large number of workers can easily exceed the labor requirements of the farm. Rather than facing underemployment, they seek off–farm jobs. A complementary interpretation is that members of larger households tend to operate relatively large and prosperous farms and to achieve higher levels of formal education, which give them a competitive edge in the nonfarm sector. By contrast, however, an increased number of female workers does not translate into increased nonfarm employment. This finding shows that women generally lack the training necessary for nonfarm employment and, concomitantly, because they are assigned so many other household responsibilities (e.g., caring for young children and preparing meals), their absence from the household tends to disrupt established patterns of daily life (and male domination) far more than does the absence of male workers.

Education of the head of household similarly has a positive effect on household employment. As suggested earlier, this is largely a reflection of the fact that nonfarm employment so often requires higher levels of formal schooling. This is true for the independent trades and small businesses, as well as for those who are salaried by local enterprises or the government.

The zero–order correlation between farm size and nonfarm employment (r = 0.04) is slightly positive but not statistically significant. However, once other variables in the model are held constant, the hypothesized negative correlation between farm size and off–farm employment emerges (*beta* = –0.11; table 4). In other words, large farms tend to have many adult workers and their heads of households tend to have achieved relatively high levels of schooling, two characteristics that have also been shown to lead to nonfarm employment. Consequently, these two factors suppress the true inverse relationship between farm size and days of nonfarm employment.

Workers in the agricultural labor force come from households well endowed with male labor (*beta* = 0.21; table 4), but not with farmland (*beta* = –0.15). However, work on the farm tends to preclude work in the

Table 4.
MULTIPLE REGRESSION ANALYSIS OF DAYS WORKED OFF–FARM BY HOUSEHOLD MEMBERS IN THE NONAGRICULTURAL SECTOR AND IN THE AGRICULTURAL SECTOR, AND DAYS OF WAGE LABOR HIRED BY HOUSEHOLDS (N= 1,019).

Explanatory variables	Days Nonag. Employment			Days Ag. Labor Worked			Days Ag. Labor Hired		
	beta	SE	(r)	beta	SE	(r)	beta	SE	(r)
Days nonag. employment	—	—	—	-.12*	.02	.07*	.17*	.03	.19*
Days ag. labor worked	-.12*	.05	-.07*	—	—	—	.02	.05	-.07
Days ag. wage labor hired	.17*	.04	.19*	-.02	.02	-.07	—	—	—
Farm size	-.11*	.00	.04	-.15*	.00	-.10*	.19*	1.01	.20*
Male workers in household	.26*	9.22	.25*	.21*	.70	.15*	-.07	1.01	.03
Female workers in household	.03	1.22	.07	.05	.76	.06	-.01	1.07	.03
Educ. of head of household	.12*	1.22	.17*	-.01	.76	-.02	.16*	1.06	.19*
Age of head of household	-.01	.07	-.05	-.06	.05	-.08*	.05	.06	.03
R2	.12		.06	.10					

* Significant = <.01

Source: 1988 NonFarm Strategies Survey of Rwanda.

nonfarm sector (*beta* = –0.12). Households whose members seek employment as farm laborers are not, generally speaking, the same households whose members find employment in the nonfarm sector (*beta* = –0.12). This finding reinforces the notion that off–farm employment serves as an important strategy mainly for those households suffering from a surplus of male labor relative to landholdings.

The third set of regression coefficients in table 4 pertain to the amount of farm labor that households hire in. It is no surprise to find that, unlike households that engage in large amounts of off–farm labor, households that hire in labor tend to operate larger farms (*beta* = 0.19). Perhaps most revealing of all is the finding that households that hire the most agricultural labor also tend to work in the nonfarm sector (*beta* = 0.17), notably in commerce, in various trades, and as functionaries. The higher education levels attained by these farmers permits them to participate in the higher end of the nonfarm employment market, and to pay minimum wage rates to those who work their holdings.

Focus on High–Income Households

To explore further the notion that farm size, education level, nonfarm employment, and the employment of agricultural wage laborers are four variables that tend to mutually reinforce one another in the process of income generation, and implicitly, of social class formation, we have isolated the 51 (5 percent) highest income households in our sample. These households generate an average income of 253,000 Rwandan francs (Frw)[2] per year, approximately 3.6 times the average for all households outside of this high income group.

As expected, we find that many of the heads of these 51 households have achieved relatively high levels of formal schooling. More than a third have completed primary school, and many of these have gone on to even higher levels. Due in large measure to the high educational attainment, these farmers and other members of their households spend much worktime in the nonfarm sector. Over two–thirds of these households generate nonfarm income from one source or another; of these, 77 percent are employed as functionaries or small businessmen (the upper echelons of the nonfarm sector).

Though these high–income households are heavily engaged in the nonfarm sector, they also operate (manage) some of the largest farms in our broader study sample. A full third of these households operate holdings of three hectares or more, and the average for this group of 51 households is 2.6 hectares. Generally speaking, these should not be considered subsistence–oriented farms. Rather, they are market–oriented and make heavy use of hired farm labor. Of the 51 farms, 37 (73 percent) employ labor from outside of the household, and four of these employ the equivalent of three or more full–time workers.

This brief analysis of high–income households highlights the combined importance of education and landholdings as the basis for income generation in Rwanda. By applying these human and land resources to an increasingly differentiated occupational structure, these households can draw from both the high end of the nonfarm sector and from a growing pool of agricultural wage labor, to further expand their income–generating capabilities.

Nonfarm Labor and Inequality

The polarization of farms in Rwanda in terms of their ability to generate income can be seen in table 5, which shows the proportion of farms in various income categories and the proportion of total income (column 3) they generate. While the households in the highest income class comprise only 15 percent of the population, they command nearly 35 percent of the country's total rural income. This concentration of wealth is represented in a Gini coefficient of 0.34, which is comparable to many other African countries even further along in the process of rural class formation.

Table 5.
PERCENT OF HOUSEHOLDS, TOTAL INCOME, ON–FARM AND OFF–FARM BY INCOME GROUP (N = 1,019).

Income group (in FRW)	% of Households	% of Total Income	% of Ag. Income	% of Nonag. Income
Less than 33,000	15.2	4.5	4.9	1.3
33,001 – 50,000	18.6	9.5	10.4	3.9
50,001 – 70,000	19.5	14.7	15.0	12.6
70,001 – 90,000	15.6	15.4	15.6	13.8
90,001 – 125,000	15.9	21.0	21.3	19.1
125,000 and above	15.2	34.9	32.8	49.2
Total	100.0%	100.0%	100.0%	100.0%
(Gini coeff.)		(0.34)	(0.31)	(0.50)

Source: 1988 Nonfarm Strategies Survey of Rwanda

Table 6.
Percent of Households, Total Income, On-farm and Off-farm by Farm Size Group (N= 1,019).

Farm size (in Ha)	% of Households	% of Total Income	% of Agric. Income	% of Nonagri. Income
< 0.25	6.7	3.6	2.9	8.6
0.25 –0.50	19.1	12.0	10.8	19.8
0.50 – 1.0	32.0	27.5	28.3	21.1
1.0 – 2.0	24.4	28.7	30.0	21.1
2.0 – 3.0	11.1	16.4	16.4	16.2
> 3.0	6.7	11.8	11.6	13.2
Total	100.0%	100.0%	100.0%	100.0%
(Gini coeff.=)		(0.19)	(0.21)	(0.08)

Source: 1988 Nonfarm Strategies Survey of Rwanda.

For purposes of the present analysis, however, our interest is more to assess the extent to which off–farm employment helps reduce income inequality. Where column 3 of table 5 presents the distribution of total household income in Rwanda, columns 4 and 5 break out this total into subcategories—agricultural and nonagricultural income. Agricultural income is the value of all crop production, livestock, and beer sales (banana and sorghum), as well as wages earned in the agricultural sector (agricultural wage labor). As described earlier, nonagricultural income is exclusively that earned from employment in the nonfarm sector.

The Gini coefficients reported in table 5 indicate that nonagricultural income is more concentrated in the hands of high–income households (Gini = 0.50) than is agricultural income (Gini = 0.31). Where the wealthiest 15 percent of households control 33 percent of income derived from farm production and wage labor, they control nearly 50 percent of nonfarm income. Not only do these findings seem to contradict our initial expectations that nonfarm income would help equilibrate inequalities in the agricultural sector, but they suggest that income received from nonfarm employment may even compound differentials in agricultural income. Though we observed earlier in our multivariate analysis of employment patterns that the number of days worked in the nonfarm sector was inversely related (*beta* = –0.12) to days worked in agricultural wage labor (an important component of agricultural income), we did not look at the correlation between incomes generated from these two sources. This correlation shows that households generating large agricultural incomes also tend to generate higher incomes in the nonfarm sector ($r = 0.08$, $p < 0.01$).

Since farm size is highly correlated with total household income ($r = 0.46$), one might suppose that the same pattern of income distribution would hold true for farm–size categories as for income groups. Table 6 tells us that while total household income is, indeed, concentrated in the larger farms (Gini = 0.19), the distribution of nonfarm income is considerably more equitable (Gini = 0.08) than is agricultural income (Gini = 0.21), contrary to the pattern of findings in the previous table. These findings suggest that nonfarm employment can, in fact, help narrow the income gap between large and small farmers; but because a small group of large farmers tend to have higher levels of training, hold higher paying jobs in the nonfarm sector, and treat their farms as business enterprises, their incomes from this combination of sources tend to be disproportionately high. Thus, when comparing income classes (as opposed to farm-size classes), we see that the effect of nonfarm employment is to create even greater disparities in total income.

Conclusions

The inheritance and accumulation of landholdings explain much, but not all, of the income inequality observed among farm households in Rwanda. For those households whose holdings do not permit an escape from poverty, their labor endowment may—not through agricultural wage labor, but through employment in the nonfarm sector. Households that have managed to secure both land resources and the skills necessary to participate in the nonfarm sector are in an exceptional position to generate higher incomes and to accumulate wealth. Households of this type also tend to use their resources to their fullest advantage; by working off the farm themselves and hiring large amounts of farm labor, they maximize income from farm production.

At the other extreme are the near–landless farm householders with little formal education and no training for alternative employment. Though not the largest identifiable group, farmers with less than 0.5 hectares of land, no schooling, and no nonfarm income are numerous and account for 26 percent of Rwanda's rural population. Providing for these households, which, underemployed on their own farms, have begun to rely on the meager wages they earn as day laborers, will require heavy investment in the rural nonfarm sector, particularly in the development of small and micro enterprises. To that end, policies should encourage the growth of small enterprises by improving the access of small producers to information, to inputs, and to managerial and technical skills (Mead and Liedholm 1989). Yet since off–farm income currently accounts for only 12.7 percent of total income in Rwanda, its effect on reducing inequality at this stage is minor.

In the interim, young men and women in Rwanda are saying that they wish to follow in the path of their parents and become farmers themselves; yet 85 percent of these young people, and the majority of their parents, believe that they will not inherit enough land for the subsistence needs of their families (Clay et al. 1989). Among the 85 percent of young men in Rwanda who believe they will not inherit enough land to meet their families' needs, nearly a quarter expect to have no other options than to make future careers as agricultural laborers; others expect to migrate in search of employment; none believe that the strategy of saving their earnings in order to purchase additional land holds any promise for the future. Those who expect to acquire the skills necessary to participate in the nonfarm sector are few. Though most parents have an opinion about how their children should plan for the future, a surprising 26 percent indicate that their children will have to make do on their own.

In light of these findings, one must conclude that the premier challenge facing parents, communities, and government officials today will be to overcome inequalities rooted in the distribution of landholdings by providing the nation's less-endowed young men and women with the skills, access to credit, guidance, and employment opportunities necessary to build a future beyond the encroaching hedgerows of their family inheritance.

Notes

1. Estimate based on 250 workdays per year.
2. 75 Frw = $1.00 US.

References

Bilsborrow, Richard E. 1987. Population pressures and agricultural development in developing countries: A conceptual framework and recent evidence. *World Development*, 15(2): 138–203.

Clay, Daniel C., Jean Kayitsinga, Theobald Kampayana, Innocent Ngenzi, and Jennifer Olson. 1989. Strategies nonagricole au Rwanda: Rapport preliminaire. SESA Document de Travail, Service des Enquetes et des Statistiques Agricoles, Rwanda.

Clay, Daniel C., and Jane E. Vander Haar. 1993. Patterns of intergenerational support and childbearing in the Third World. *Population Studies* 47(1): 67-83.

Duncan, Otis D. 1959. Human ecology and population studies. In *The study of population*, ed. Otis D. Duncan and Philip Hauser, pp. 678-716. Chicago: University of Chicago Press.

Durkheim, Emile. [1893] 1933. *The division of labor in society*. Translated by George Simpson. New York: Free Press.

Gibbs, Jack P., and William T. Martin. 1959. Toward a theoretical system of human ecology. *Pacific Sociological Review* 2:1.

Hawley, Amos. 1950. *Human ecology: A theory of community structure*. New York: Ronald Press.

Marx, Karl. 1967. *Capital – A critique of political economy. Volume 1*. New York: International Publishers.

Mead, Donald C., and Carl Liedholm. 1989. Policies to promote industrialization, and the role of SMEs: The case of low–income African nations. Draft chapter of monograph, *Employment and enterprise policy in economic development*. Unpublished report. East Lansing, Mich.: Michigan State University, Department of Agricultural Economics.

Mendras, Henri. 1970. *The vanishing peasant*. Cambridge, Mass.: MIT Press.

Olson, Jennifer. 1989. Redistribution of the population of Rwanda due to environmental and demographic pressures. Paper presented at the Michigan Academy of Arts, Sciences, and Letters, Grand Rapids, Michigan. 1989.

Rwanda, Discours du President de la Republique. 1986a. Jeuness et developpement. Expose du General–Major Habyarimana Juvenal a l'occasion de sa visite a l'Universite Nationale du Rwanda, le 21 Mai 1986.

Rwanda, Discours du President de la Republique. 1988a. 1988: Annee pour la defense du revenu du paysan. Discours du General–Major Habyarimana Juvenal, le 4 janvier 1988.

Rwanda, Ministere de l'Agriculture. 1985. *Rapports annuels pour les annees 1960–1985*.

Rwanda, Ministere du Plan, D. G. de la Statistique. 1988b. *Enquete nationale sur le budget et la consommation: Milieu rural*, Ministere du Plan.

Rwanda, Service des Enquetes et des Statistiques Agricoles (SESA). 1984. *Description sommaire des principales caracteristiques de l'agriculture au Rwanda*. Ministere de l'Agriculture, de l'Elevage, et des Forets.

Rwanda, Service des Enquetes et des Statistiques Agricoles (SESA). 1986b. *Resultats de l'enquete nationale agricole 1984: Tableaux sur les donnees saisonnieres, Rapport 1 – Volume 3*. Ministere de l'Agriculture, de l'Elevage, et des Forets.

6

SOCIAL AND ECONOMIC TRANSFORMATION IN A GREEK FARMING VILLAGE

George A. Daoutopoulos

Introduction

Since World War II, major changes have taken place throughout the world and especially within the developing countries. Through better communication, previously isolated rural areas have come into closer contact with urban centers. As population pressure upon land has steadily increased and as rural people have gradually adopted values and patterns of behavior characteristic of urban culture, the rural economy has been pressed to become more efficient and more productive.

Greek agriculture, during this period, experienced major changes as new technology replaced traditional practices. The development path chosen by Greece was similar to that followed by many other countries; that is, increasing the level of inputs. The use of chemical fertilizers, insecticides, pesticides, new high-yielding varieties, more machinery, and new farming practices expanded tremendously.

Subsistence farming declined as a result of increased surpluses for the purchase of the necessary production inputs from the industrial sector. As a result, farming communities were increasingly incorporated into and made more dependent upon the national and international markets. During the 1960s, particularly in the plains area, production for market had become the main goal of most farmers and, in general, substantial specialization was taking place. Today one observes that certain regions of the country are almost exclusively occupied with the production of certain commodities.

The present chapter explores the major changes in the structure of agriculture in a Greek farming community during the postwar era, and especially following the introduction of burley tobacco as a new crop. The main concern is to determine how the new crop affected a reorganization of the factors of production, the system of farming, the patterns of social stratification within the farming community, and the processes of cooperation and conflict within the village. In this chapter I intend to show: how relative equality in access to production factors has been altered by the new crop and has been replaced by an emerging bifurcated farm structure dominated by large-scale tobacco operations; how the egalitarian ethos in the village has been replaced by a highly competitive atmosphere, bringing clouds of conflict between small and large farmers competing against each other for access to limited resources (land, labor, and capital); and how the increased prosperity has brought new economic and social patterns of behavior.

Study Area and Methods

The village of Aghios Loukas (Saint Luke) is located in the northwestern part of the valley of Yiannitsa (fig. 1).

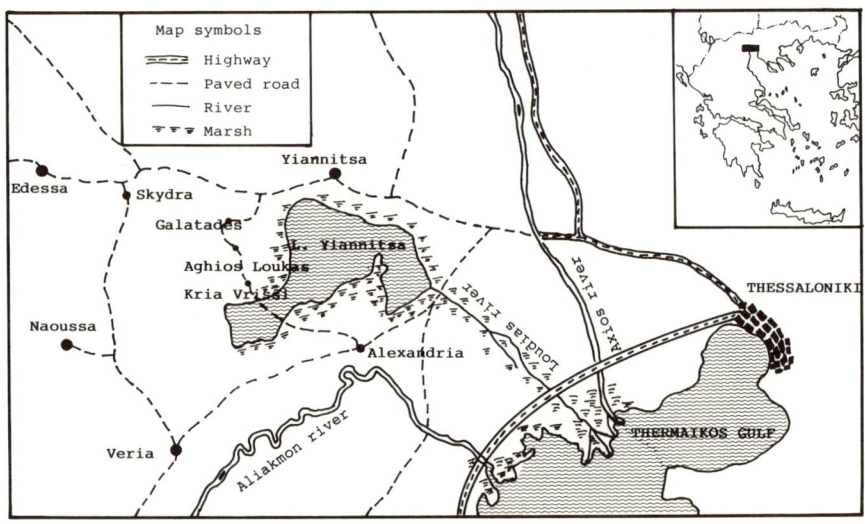

Figure 1. Map of Aghios Loukas and surrounding area with former lake Yiannitsa

Paved roads to the south and the north connect the village with the market towns of Kria Vrissi, Alexandria, Veria, Edessa, and Yiannitsa. Thessaloniki, the second-largest city of Greece, is only an hour's distance from the village (70 kilometers).

This study employs both quantitative and qualitative research techniques. Information about households, village structure, and agricultural patterns was obtained from a general household survey. Qualitative data were derived from focused interviews with selected persons and families in the village and through quasi–participant observation. Fieldwork was carried out in 1983–84, 1985–86, and 1988 (Daoutopoulos 1985; Daoutopoulos 1995).

The integration of formal survey and less-structured field interviewing procedures is intended to broaden our perspective about the changing situation. Statistical aggregations of data do not easily produce explanations of people's behavior (Greenwood 1980). Survey data can provide few clues about causes. Therefore, some combination of behavioral and statistical baseline data is needed. Sieber (1973, 1335) has also emphasized the advantages to be gained from a methodological pluralism. As he pointed out: "each method can be greatly strengthened by appealing to the unique qualities of the other."

Local and district agencies and organizations provided some unpublished data very useful to the present study. The office of the Tobacco Board at Yiannitsa provided longitudinal data on the area and production of tobacco, yields, production cost, and the number of tobacco operations in Aghios Loukas. The Irrigation Board at Kariotissa and Akrolimni proved to be a very useful source of reliable longitudinal data[1] on area planted to various crops within the boundaries of Aghios Loukas.

Data on individual farm operations enumerated during the 1981 census of agriculture were obtained from the National Statistical Service. This information was valuable in two ways. First, it was useful to expand the longitudinal data already published for the village for the 1961 and 1971 censuses of agriculture. Results of the 1981 census of agriculture were not yet available (and they were not expected to be available prior to 1985). Second, it provided detailed quantitative evidence on a farm–by–farm basis for the study of local heterogeneity (Dewalt 1979; Greenwood 1976, 1980).

Village History, Demography, and Agriculture

The village was incorporated into the modern Greek state on 18 October, 1912 (table 1). The first enumeration, taken by the Greek army in 1913, estimated the population of the village as 330 persons (table 2). About half the population at that time was of Greek origin, the rest being of Turkish and Bulgarian nationality. Immediately after annexation of the village, about a third of the non–Greek citizens left. As a result, the first census of the newly incorporated areas revealed an 18.8 percent decline for the village population and an even larger decline of 27.5 percent for the

Table 1.
MAIN HISTORICAL EVENTS AND POPULATION CHANGES IN AGHIOS LOUKAS.

Time period	Event	Population
1912	Annexation to Greek territory. Subsistence agriculture. Swamp.	330
1920	Departure of non–Greek citizens. First wave of migrants. Swamp.	268
1928	Departure of non–Greek citizens. Second wave of migrants. Swamp.	158
Mid-1930s	Drainage of swamp completed. Influx of migrants.	
1940	Influx of migrants.	613
1941–45	World War II and Nazi occupation.	
1945–48	Civil War.	
1948	Introduction of cotton as a cash crop.	
Early 1950s	Introduction of tractor, improved varieties of wheat, fertilizers, and pesticides.	866
1961	Highest population density. Outmigration to Germany started.	1,133
1966	Increased intensification of the production system. Expansion of irrigation. Introduction of burley tobacco.	
1971	New irrigation system. Land reclamation.	1,086
1981	Zero population growth.	1,053
1983	Introduction of asparagus cultivation.	
1984–88	Crisis in burley tobacco. Rapid shift to asparagus cultivation.	

Source: National Statistical Service of Greece and Field notes.

district of Yiannitsa (table 2). The village population continued to decrease, to 158 persons by 1928, an all–time low, as the last non–Greek nationals left the village in accord with the Lausanne Treaty of 1923.

Until the mid–1930s, the area northeast of the village was a large swamp. A river flowing from the mountains and the valley of Almopia

Table 2.
POPULATION TRENDS BETWEEN 1913 AND 1981 FOR AGHIOS LOUKAS, DISTRICT OF YIANNITSA, AND GREECE.

	Aghios Loukas	District of Yiannitsa	Greece
Mean Altitude (meters)	10	na	na
Area (square kilometers)	7	753	131,957
Population:			
1913	330	32,997	na
1920	268	23,916	5,016,889
1928	158[a]	36,344	6,204,684
1940	613	45,810	7,344,860
1951	866	53,071	7,632,801
1961	1,133	60,870	8,388,553
1971	1,086	57,269	8,768,641
1981	1,053	61,969	9,740,417
Annual Rate of Population Growth (%)			
1913/20	−2.9	−4.5	na
1920/28	−6.4	5.4	2.7
1928/40	12.0	1.9	1.4
1940/51	3.2	1.3	0.4
1951/61	2.7	1.4	0.9
1961/71	−0.4	−0.6	0.4
1971/81	−0.3	0.7	1.1
Density (inhabitants per square kilometer)			
1961	161.9	81.1	63.6
1971	155.1	76.1	66.5
1981	150.4	82.3	73.8

Sources: Ministry of Coordination, Regional Development Service of Central and West Macedonia. (1975); *Index of Municipalities and Communities of Macedonia and Thrace*. (1940-71); Thessaloniki; General Statistical Service of Greece (1929); *Population of Greece at the 15-16 May 1928 Census*, National Printing Office; N.S.S.G. (1982). *De Facto Population of Greece*, 5 April (1981), National Printing Office.
Note: (na) not available
[a] Only 5 persons were refugees from Turkey.

to Lake Yiannitsa (fig.1) divided into two smaller rivers just outside the settlement. Because the river beds were constantly changing due to silt deposits, the life of the people was under continuous threat, especially during the rainy season. Floods were very common, and only in late spring were fields dry enough to allow plowing. Corn and beans were the main staple crops. The swamp and the lake were the natural habitat for a great number of birds, animals, and fish. Thus, hunting and fishing provided the necessary protein for the villagers.

The thick forests of the swamp provided wood for cooking and lumber for house construction. When Minos, a retired farmer, arrived at the village in 1924 at the age of 17, only three large houses existed; they were two–storied structures made of earth bricks and covered with ceramic tiles. All other houses, about 17 to 22 of them, were huts made with bush and covered on both sides with a mixture of soil and straw or a mixture of straw and cow dung.

The swamp was a blessing as well as a curse. In Aghios Loukas and the nearby area, malaria was endemic. According to Whipple (1944, 84), the plains of Northern Greece were ". . . the principal breeding sources of mosquitoes in one of the most malarial regions of Europe." The prevalence rate, estimated by the East Mission of the Army in 1917–18, varied between 50 to 100 percent for the area around the Lake Yiannitsa (Damianakos, Nickolapoulos, and Pshychogios, 1978, 436f).

The great shortage of land in Greece following World War I and the influx of almost 1.3 million refugees from Turkey forced the Greek government to spend large sums of money for draining and reclaiming swamps and inundated and seasonally flooded land. The main objective was to provide farmland for subsistence farming to landless refugees and natives. As part of those reclamation projects, in 1935, over 31,000 hectares from the bed of Lake Yiannitsa and the Loudia Marsh were made available for cultivation.

Despite the enormous influx of refugees in the broader area, Aghios Loukas gained only five new persons. The fear of malaria prevented the influx of refugees until the mid–1930s, when the drainage work was completed. Refugees who previously had settled mainly in nearby prefectures (Nomoi) started pouring into the village. Yiannis, a retired farmer who was among the first settlers, explained the reasons for choosing to remigrate:

> We were given a plot of land but the land was very poor. We plowed and sowed the fields and we were getting nothing in return. The soil was full of stones.

The newly opened fertile lands gave yields not easily attained by farmers elsewhere. With the concomitant eradication of malarial mosquitoes, the first migrants wrote glowing accounts back to their relatives and friends. As a result, the population of the village quadrupled between

1928 and 1940 (12.0 percent annual rate of growth). But later, a growing fear of being taken over by the newcomers led the earlier settlers to express hostility against them.

When the Land Distribution Committee visited the village to decide the allocation of land, in cooperation with local people, they complained that the distribution of more land would attract more outsiders. They would be satisfied, they said, if they could retain the land they already farmed. Thus, land allocated to the village to be held as communal property was very limited and was insufficient to accommodate people in the future, as the population expanded. Persons who entered farming in successive generations received systematically smaller plots from the commons.

Social relations between the natives and the new settlers were not good at the beginning. They would not even greet each other in the streets. The village was divided into two opposing groups.[2] Marriage (a very serious family business controlled and arranged by the parents) would never cross the lines of the two groupings. Gradually, as the village was drawn into the larger society, those differences and the old antagonisms lost their salience but formed a basis for social competition.

Newcomers were ambitious, hard-working people and open to new ideas. They were the first to try new crops and farming practices. Through their success in farming, they gradually gained respect from the native people. Alekos, narrating the story of his family during the early years of their struggle to settle in the village, emphasized the initial hostile environment and the respect that his father was able to attain from native people through his success in farming:

> Here in the village we were considered by the natives as poor and useless people. When in 1938 my father produced 12,000 okades[3] of wheat (15,360 kg.) from his 4.8 hectares of family farm allotted to him in 1937, it was considered a very big success. The majority of the farmers in the village produced 5.1 to 9.0 tons of wheat. One night my father coming back home from the coffee house said to my mother with pride: "You know what happened today Despina? Paulos (a native shopkeeper) greeted me as I was passing his store with, 'Good morning, Mister Abraham.'"

While the village was experiencing an improved life for the first time in its history, the Greek–Italian war erupted. The invasion of Nazi armed forces, six months later, brought the economy to a standstill. Although the village was not the scene of battles or major guerrilla activity, its economy as part of the national economy was still affected by the high–risk conditions created and the tremendous inflation rates.

The end of World War II was followed by an equally disruptive civil war that lasted for four years (1945–48). Massive reconstruction efforts started immediately after the end of the civil war through significant financial and technical assistance from the United States. The population of the village continued to increase from 1940–51 at an annual rate of 3.2 percent, as compared to 1.3 percent for the District of Yiannitsa and only 0.4 percent for the country as a whole (table 2), for migration continued, although at a slower pace.

Cotton was introduced to the village in 1948 and in the 1960s became the main cash crop for the farmers (fig. 2). Introduction of cotton is a significant turning point in the agricultural history of the village, as it marks the end of subsistence farming and the beginning of an agriculture increasingly oriented toward the national and international markets. Credit and technical assistance soon became available to farmers through the Agricultural Bank and the Agricultural Extension Service (established in 1953). During the early 1950s, the first privately owned tractor began to operate in the village. The demand for its services was so great that farmers had to place their names on a waiting list. During the same period, new, improved varieties of wheat began to replace the native varieties. Fertilizers and pesticides became available through the Agricultural Bank, and a program to improve the local strains of cows through artificial

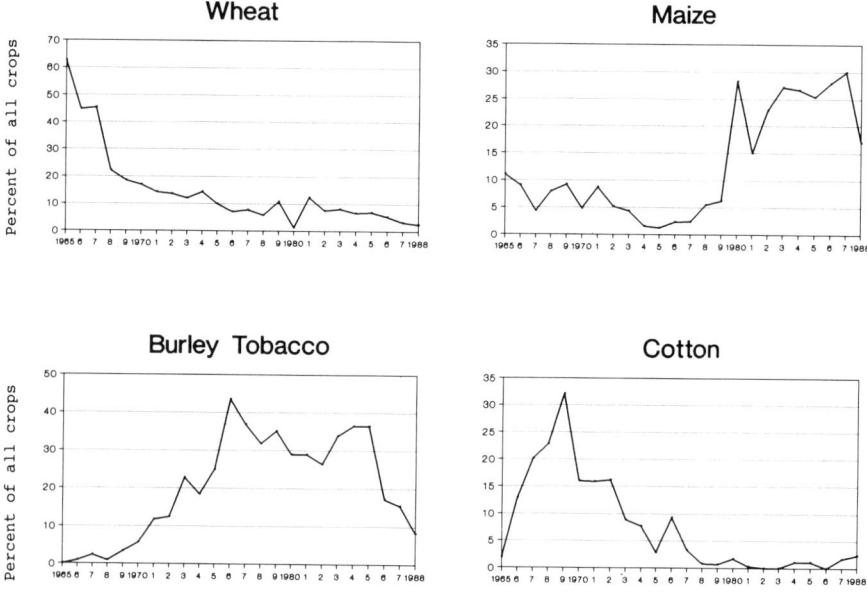

Figure 2. Trends in the area of wheat, maize, burley tobacco, and cotton planted in the village farmland, 1965-88

insemination was set forth. Also, farmers started building new houses, using bricks and ceramic roof tiles to replace the old houses made of earthen bricks and covered with rye straw.

Sugar beets were introduced in 1962 by farmers who were not satisfied with the production of cotton. Early rainy seasons had ruined several cotton crops because farmers were unable to harvest. Sugar beets never gained a dominant position in the production system of the village, however. Yields and prices paid according to the sugar content of the crop were very rarely considered by farmers as satisfactory. Sugar beets presently account for 5 percent of the total cropland (fig. 3).

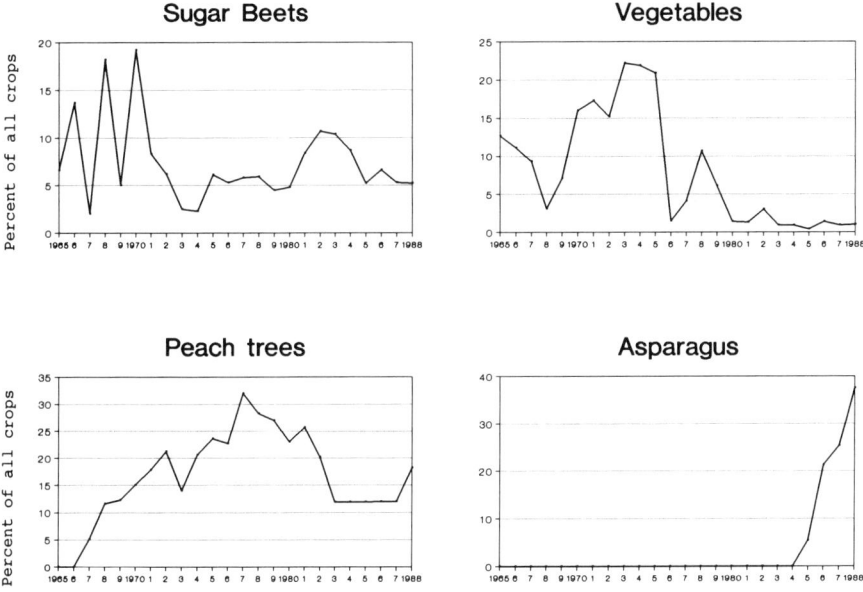

Figure 3. Trends in the area of sugar beets, vegetables, peach trees, and asparagus planted in the village farmland, 1965-88

Tree crops, mainly peaches, were planted by several farmers during the 1960s. Peaches are now the main crop in an area west of the village, which produces about 90 percent of the total Greek peach crop. But tree fruits did not become very popular in the village. They reached a peak at about 29 percent of the total farming area in the village between 1977 and 1979, and thereafter started dropping off as a result of low prices due to unsuccessful marketing of the huge surpluses. New plantings in 1988 reversed the downward trend of 1978-87 (fig. 3).

The period of increased intensification of the production system of the village (1951–65) coincides with increased population pressure upon the land. By 1961, the population density reached an all-time high of 162 inhabitants per square kilometer, twice that of the District (81.1 inhabitants per square kilometer) and 2.5 times that of the nation (63.6 inhabitants per square kilometer; table 2). This was the last decade of population increase, however. Pressure upon the land became great, and opportunities opened up in other areas of the country and abroad (United States, Germany, Australia, and Belgium). Over the next 20 years, there were slight population decreases (although the district of Yiannitsa and several other rural areas of the country experienced an 0.7 percent annual rate of population growth).

Data derived from the 1961 and 1971 population censuses reveal that outmigration from the village increased during the 1960s. In 1961, 106 persons, or 8.9 percent of the "de jure" population[4] of the village, were living in other parts of the country and 0.4 percent were living abroad. By 1971 those who migrated to other parts of the country and abroad comprised 12.2 percent and 3.1 percent, respectively, of the population of that year.

More recent data on migration of families compiled from the Registry Book (table 3) indicates higher migration rates for the entire period of

Table 3.
PRESENT PLACE OF RESIDENCE OF THE FAMILIES LISTED IN THE POPULATION REGISTER, AGHIOS LOUKAS, DECEMBER 1984.

Place of Residence	Number of Families	%
1. Village	321	62.3
2. Other places in Greece	78	15.2
Total Greece	399	77.5
3. Germany	30	5.8
4. Belgium	2	0.4
5. United States	80	15.5
6. Canada	1	0.2
7. Australia	3	0.6
Total abroad	116	22.5
All Places	515	100.0

Source: Village Population Register, analysis by the author

1955–84. Of the 515 families recorded in December 1984 in the Registry Book, 321 families (62.3 percent) lived in the village, 78 families (15.2 percent) lived elsewhere in Greece, and the remaining 116 families (22.5 percent) lived abroad, mostly in the United States (80 families, or 15.5 percent) or Germany (30 families, or 5.8 percent).

Population decrease also resulted from lower fertility rates. Data on the median number of children born to women of various cohorts revealed a dramatic shift in the fertility behavior of women in Aghios Loukas.[5] While women born between 1900 and 1920 gave birth to a median of five children, those born between 1921 and 1940 gave birth to a median of only three children. A further reduction by one child is indicated for younger cohorts, but this evidence is inconclusive since those cohorts are still of reproductive age.

During the 1970s, a new irrigation system brought abundant water to the fields and expanded tremendously the crop choices of the farmers. This project was followed by a redistribution of the land. As a result, the number of farmland parcels dropped from 1,003 in 1961 to 559 in 1981. Although water was made available in large quantities through U–shaped concrete channels, irrigation still required the use of additional power (tractors, diesel pumps) in order to properly apply the water in the fields. During the same decade, electricity and drinking water were brought to nearly every home in the village. New and better homes were constructed during this period.

The Tobacco Era

Various tobacco-exporting companies visited the village in 1966 and persuaded six or seven farmers to plant burley tobacco that year. Burley tobacco is a land–demanding crop, for it must be rotated every other year with other crops or moved to a new field. Before a first crop can be harvested, heavy outlays in cash or short–term credit are necessary for purchases of machinery and buildings (for soil preparation, weed control, mist irrigation and spraying, and a curing barn) and for rents and wages.

Cultivation of burley tobacco is labor–demanding despite the adoption of labor–saving technologies. It requires substantial technical skill on the part of the farmer and especially managerial skill when the scale of operation is beyond the labor capacity of his/her farm family. However, since burley tobacco offers very high returns to investments in both land and labor, other farmers who were financially able to adopt it did so quickly. Thus, burley tobacco became the major cash crop of Aghios Loukas over the next decade (figs. 2 and 5).

Figure 4. Outside View of a Tobacco-curing Barn in Aghios Loukas, Greece.

Burley tobacco changed the social and economic structure of agriculture in this farming community. For example, the number of farmers from Aghios Loukas growing burley tobacco doubled between 1981 and 1984, but the initial costs of its adoption favored those who could set up large-scale operations (figs. 2 and 5). One mode of expansion was to rent cropland from other villages, since the average farm in Aghios Loukas was not large enough to accommodate the need for field rotation. Hence, the owners of large-scale farm operations (termed *farm businessmen* by the local people) owned twice the amount of land and rented 21.5 times the amount of land so as to farm a total of five times the amount of cropland as did the small-scale owners (termed *farmers*[6] by the local people). In keeping with the superior scale of operations, *farm businesses* owned and operated a larger number of high-powered tractors than did *farms*.

A second mode of expanding the scale of farm production was to hire a nonfamilial workforce. Some farm businessmen expanded the scale of their farm so much that their own family laborers became a fraction of those needed to run the farm. Similarly, some farm businessmen freed themselves from direct involvement in fieldwork by employing a full-time farm manager. The regular fieldwork was done by the manager, who

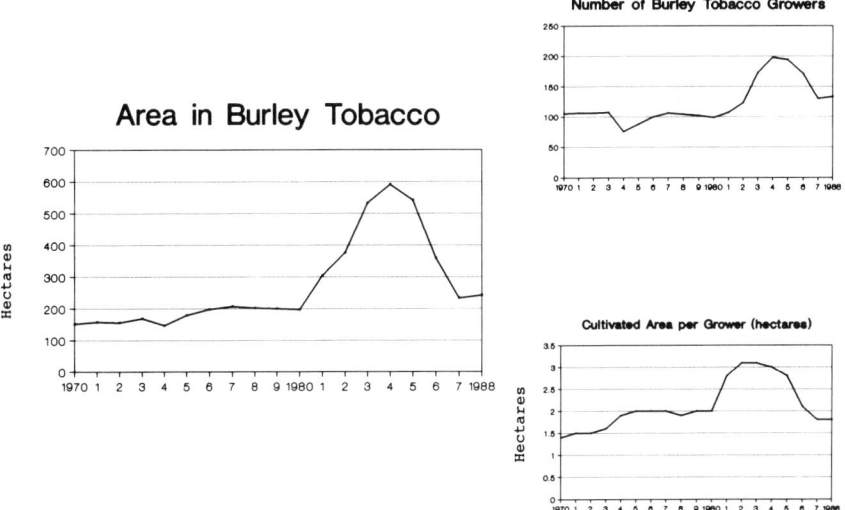

Figure 5. Area in burley tobacco, number of growers and average area per grower for Aghios Loukas, 1970-88.

supervised temporary migrant workers hired for specific seasonal tasks. At the same time, most household relatives of the farm businessman placed themselves under his control by working more on their family farm than on other farms or in off–farm jobs.

A contrast comes from the householders in small–scale operations, who not only do most of their family's farmwork, but also allocate their labor time equally among their own farm, other farms, and off–farm activities. Seasonal labor deficits have been mostly handled by labor exchange arrangements in the form of *sinergasia, parea*,[7] or *danika*.[8] The traditionally supportive networks of helping obligations and expectations are now being threatened by large tobacco growers, whose monetary calculus of time and energy may overturn traditional community relations (Poole 1981). As such, the new way of engaging familial and hired agricultural laborers in large–scale operations may signal the onset of *industrial agriculture* or *commercial agriculture* in Greece, as it did in other Western societies.[9]

A third difference between large–scale and small–scale farms is in the diversity of the crops. Tobacco occupies the largest share (41.4 percent) of the land operated by the large–scale farm businessmen, followed by corn (20.0 percent). In contrast, small–scale farmers grow mainly fruit

Figure 6. Two Tractors and a Four-Row Planting Machine Ready for Tobacco Planting.

trees (29.4 percent), wheat (17.6 percent), and generally a small amount of corn, vegetables, and tobacco. Fortunately, the diversity of crops on small-scale farm operations minimizes financial risk; unfortunately, it also minimizes profit.

The strong momentum behind these changes in the structure of agriculture intensified in the 1970s. The marginal value to opportunity–cost ratios increased for all factors of production: for land from 3.10 to 4.11; for labor from 0.53 to 1.36; and for capital from 0.53 to 0.73 (Kitsopanidis and Martika 1982, 35). These numbers demonstrate that productivity of land and labor increased faster than rents and wages paid, respectively, from 1965–68 to 1978–80.

While the productivity of capital increased, its dividend stayed below the initial cost of a share of investment. This fact highlights the small farmer's dilemma of whether or not to mechanize. Not to mechanize but to plan on growing tobacco requires the small farmer to rely on contract crews and their machinery. This dependency is infeasible in the present system of farming in Aghios Loukas. With increased tobacco monoculture, owners of machinery are busy tending their own fields. Even in times of leisure, these owners are uninterested in the marginal monies to be earned through these contractual activities. On the other hand, mechanization

Figure 7. Tobacco Planting in Aghios Loukas, Greece.

without increasing the scale of operation leads gradually to financial ruin. Labor savings are minimal, and costs of operating the machinery are above the returns. Therefore, those who decide to buy machinery (tractors and various implements) have no other option but to expand their amount of land operated. Expansion lowers the cost of machinery, as fixed costs can then be distributed over a larger productive base. Also, renting more land and hiring more labor benefits them by a greater return from both land and labor, as compared to the investment.

At the same time, mechanization and expansion of the scale of operation helps the average farm family to save a lot on hiring labor by employing a greater percentage of its own labor than can a family operation with the same degree of mechanization but of smaller scale. Therefore, when tobacco quotas did not apply, tobacco growers had every reason to expand their scale of operation if they had the machinery, the curing facilities, and the cash or credit needed.

While present incomes from tobacco production can sustain the tractorization of farms, increased mechanization has deprived farmers of some disposable income from tobacco production. Most of them, especially small farmers, must consider the depreciation for buildings and machinery, which amounts to 19.1 percent of all expenses. If some profit is not saved annually over a period of 15 years to cover eventual replacement costs, mechanization can bring financial ruin.

Despite a substantial decline in the number of agricultural workers between 1970 and 1981 and a significant increase in the cultivation of labor–intensive crops, the work load of the average self–employed agricultural worker in Aghios Loukas did not increase (Daoutopoulos 1985, 128–32). In 1970, a total of 675,404 man–hours was required to farm the 752.6 hectares of crops in Aghios Loukas; in 1981, 672,073 man–hours were required to cultivate the crops in production at that time. The decline was due to labor–saving technology (machinery, chemicals, etc.), and to more use of nonvillage farm labor.

The village is no longer an autonomous unit. It is entirely incorporated[10] into the international product market and the international labor market, as described by Wallerstein (1980). These tobacco markets are controlled by the handful of multinational corporations that brought burley tobacco into Greece and into other developing countries throughout the world, in order to avail of the cheap labor. The future economic prosperity of Aghios Loukas thus depends heavily on decisions reached in Athens, Brussels, and other European and international decision–making centers. The present Common Agricultural Policy of the European Economic Community (EEC) and the continued devaluation of the Greek currency have favored the prices paid to tobacco growers. But this policy (the only common policy of the EEC) is presently under revision, mainly as a result of pressures from its northern industrialized members, who no longer want to pay most of the costs of supporting the agricultural products of the southern EEC member–states. Also, since cured tobacco is not perishable, the multinational tobacco companies can stockpile enough leaves to manipulate the foreign market advantageously.

Another important aspect of the dependence of the village on northern European markets is that 90 percent of the burley tobacco crop is exported "raw" for processing in the plants of multinational tobacco corporations in Europe and elsewhere. A recent report by the U.S. Department of Agriculture (1984, 27) estimates that "only about 8 percent of the price of a pack of cigarettes reflects the leaf in the cigarette." Therefore, the added value is maximal in both America and Europe, and Aghios Loukas in particular and Greece in general are deprived of the profits that would be created by the local manufacture of cigarettes and cigars.

Expansion of tobacco production has raised the demand for short–term capital to defray seasonal costs. Credit available to farmers is generally insufficient, since it covers only half of what is needed. Small tobacco growers willing to expand their acreage are especially limited by the lack of credit. Therefore, the present credit policy favors large growers and, in the long run, concentrates production in their hands.

Furthermore, entry into farming has become extremely difficult for aspiring young people. With no communal land left for distribution to the landless, inheritance is the only means of access to farmland. But because of normative and legal restrictions on the concept of property rights and equity among heirs, the land share in the parental estate for most aspiring farmers is less than a hectare. In addition, capital requirements are an insurmountable obstacle for most young persons seeking entry into farming. Capital of 3.5 million drachmas (U.S. $25,000) was required in 1984 for machines, curing barns, and so on.

Big capital like that is unlikely to be raised by any aspiring farmer. As a result, many brothers continue working together with their father, hoping to accumulate the capital needed to finance adequately the new farms to be formed after the division of the parental family farm. The delays in the division of the parental farm increase tension within the family and might explain some of the present intergenerational conflicts in the village.

With the tremendous expansion of burley tobacco in 1981–84, production was increasingly pushed to less fertile soil, with a much lower humus content and inadequate irrigation and drainage. Chemical fertilizers are increasingly being used to bring yields to normal levels (at least 3 metric tons per hectare). In this race to acquire land, of ever–lower fertility, with inadequate irrigation, far from the village, and at ever-higher rents (and wages for labor), small farmers are becoming less competitive vis–à–vis the larger farmers. Indubitably, expansion in the scale of operation and bifurcation in the social structure of agriculture will only increase in the near future.

Clearly, too, the cooperative movement in Aghios Loukas has not progressed during the period of increased tobacco production. Individuality and self–reliance have been further enhanced, and currently, with increased inequality of wealth among farmers, the prospects for cooperation in other spheres (production, marketing) beyond simple distribution of credit, seem very limited.

The traditional suspicion of others' motives, the strong feeling of helplessness, the mistrust of local leaders, and the belief that everyone should put his or her own personal interests before group interests, all point the way to a cognitive orientation that is best understood through the "image of limited good."[11] Tobacco dealers successfully exploit this image and, through sales by the barn door rather than by auction, squelch any effort by local cooperatives to control the tobacco market. Partisan politics have further retarded any possibilities for significant progress, in terms of farmers gaining more control over their productive activities.

The high incomes from tobacco production have changed the economic and social patterns of behavior of the local community. Consumption patterns for most farmers' households are similar to urban ones. Most tobacco farmers' houses are new and replete with modern furniture and appliances—including color televisions. About half of the homes (a very high percentage for a Greek village) have telephones. During the last decade, consumption has been pushed beyond necessities to luxuries, and approaches an epidemic scale that McNall (1976, 41) termed "commodity fetishism."[12] A prime indicator of the consumption of new luxuries is the 30 passenger cars—among them six BMWs that only wealthier Greeks can afford—owned by farmers in Aghios Loukas.

Also, the increased affluence from tobacco production resulted in large expenditures by men in the numerous nightclubs that sprouted like mushrooms along the main rural roads. This extravagance burgeoned in the early 1980s, but has recently been curbed somewhat by pressure from women and by the tobacco crisis of 1985–88. This trend bespeaks the greater influence of females and of the tobacco economy on the familial power structure.

A major change in the village is the restructuring of the family. The decline in the head–of–household's position, more in relation to his children than to his wife, is the most profound change. With jobs available outside the family unit as a result of tobacco expansion, the village boys have become less economically dependent on their father; and his hold over them has weakened. The elderly, too, have been disempowered.

The cafeteria as the challenging open club to the control exerted by the coffeehouse is a prime indicator of the changes brought about in intergenerational relations. Girls, too, are not restricted to home anymore and have the opportunity to visit a cafeteria without parental permission. One can hear the elderly grumbling together in the parks or the coffeehouses about the "immoral" and "incomprehensible" behavior of the youths, yet their opinions do not count so much now.

The Meta–tobacco Era

Burley tobacco cultivation expanded until 1984 (fig. 5). Unfavorable prices paid for that year's crop and long delays in selling the cured tobacco spelled disaster for farmers in Aghios Loukas. The small drop in tobacco–planted cropland in 1985 was followed by a big drop in the next two years. As a result, tobacco production fell to the pre–expansion levels of 1980, and local informants expect more decline in the future.

Farmers have begun replacing tobacco with asparagus. Asparagus cultivation has expanded tremendously since 1981 in the next village of

Galatades, which has become the main export center of asparagus from Greece, with direct exports mainly to Germany. Asparagus cultivation is also expanding rapidly in Aghios Loukas. Presently it accounts for 37.5 percent of the cultivated area, and more expansion is expected in the future, although at a lower pace (fig. 3). The local cooperative has constructed a warehouse for asparagus packaging and has tried to expand its role in the marketing and processing of the crop.

Shifting to the new crop is not easy. The high initial investment for seedlings and the absence of profit during the first two years handicap small farmers. The new crop comes to full production in the fourth year and remains in the field for fourteen years. The perennial character of the new crop prohibits its cultivation in rented fields, a disadvantage for the large-scale farmers. The latter have started asking for extended rental contracts (at least ten years).

Farmers now worry if they will get trapped with the new crop of asparagus, as with burley tobacco. Asparagus, like burley tobacco, is an export completely out of local control. Fear of repeating the tobacco story is expressed in discussions among farmers in the coffeehouses.

Policy Implications and Considerations for Future Research

Through the field research in Aghios Loukas, it became evident that burley tobacco had a significant impact in the organization of the factors of production, the system of farming, the patterns of social stratification, and the processes of cooperation and conflict within the village. The development of large-scale farming redefined the social relationships among farmers. Conflicts were frequent between small-scale and large-scale farmers and were related to the continuation of traditional forms of cooperation, to equality in access to input and output markets, and to the functioning of the local cooperative. Large farmers, called *farm businessmen*, held themselves apart from the traditional farmers, who had very little social prestige.

Fifty years after the peasant land reform that restored social equality among peasants in Greece and a farm policy that protected small farmers, inequalities are becoming increasingly evident. In due course, those inequalities can even become the grounds for the creation of new social strata within the village. Therefore, the results of the present study contradict the assertion of Lambiri–Dimaki (1986, 45) that there are no inequalities within rural society in Greece and that thus it should be characterized as a "democratic society." Instead, our study provided evidence that is in line with Burgel's (1978, 213) statement on the penetration of the market forces in the Greek countryside and the gradual increase of inequality among farmers. Those inequalities, depending on the farm policy, might be aggravated and might have far-reaching social impacts.

A related issue concerns the replacement of burley tobacco with asparagus. Recent trends in new plantings (fig. 3) suggest that asparagus will become the dominant crop in Aghios Loukas in the 1990s. Because asparagus places different demands on land, labor, and capital, it should "make different kinds of demands on the people who grow them" (Wolf 1956, 58). For example, since asparagus is a perennial plant, it is preferable to plant it on owned rather than rented land. Large farmers will find it difficult to expand their scale of operation by buying more land in this land–scarce village. Also, since asparagus does not yield cash returns until the third year of growth, small–scale farmers will find it difficult to obtain credit allowing them to wait that long. It is likely, then, that economic stratification will not lessen in this village (see Burgel 1965). A future study of the village will show whether large–scale or small–scale farmers benefited more from the introduction of asparagus into the farming system of Aghios Loukas.

Some preliminary research has provided evidence of a positive effect of the new crop on the development of the local agricultural cooperative as a result of another characteristic of the crop. Asparagus is a very perishable crop. Spears, once harvested, must be cooled immediately to 32° to 36° F. Cooling preserves the sugar content, which is important in quality. Local growers, in order to meet those demands, have successfully persuaded the cooperative to build a cooling and packaging facility where harvested spears are prepared for the market by grading, sizing, and bunching. In addition, the cooperative has managed to organize the export of the produce directly to European markets and therefore has more control over the earnings of the new crop.

Another issue concerns the destruction of local institutions and local culture in general, as a result of the penetration of market forces and urban or national and international cultural elements. The local culture lost its ability to provide guidance for local people. As was also the case with the small town of Stavroupolis (Photiadis 1976, 29–36), social control in Aghios Loukas is today less effective, and norms are less clear and more diverse than before.

Farmers in Aghios Loukas are increasingly comparing themselves in terms of income and level of living with urban people. The traditional values of hard work and thrift have been replaced by an orientation that McNall (1976, 41), in his study of two Greek villages (Varnavas and Milessi), termed *commodity fetishism*. This orientation is equally strong among farmers in Aghios Loukas. Farmers are not saving as much as they could for farm improvements and expansion. Consumption of luxurious items allows farmers in Aghios Loukas to participate in the modern world, but at the same time undermines the viability of their farms as they are deprived of savings. Restrictions in the credit available to farmers and an increase in the interest rates paid for farm loans—changes that are more likely to be adopted in future Greek farm policy—will have tremendous impacts on farmers in Aghios Loukas.

While farming is not appealing to the younger generation, and entry into farming is becoming increasingly difficult for aspiring youngsters in Aghios Loukas, we do not yet have the rejection of village life and farming that was evidenced in Aschenbrenner's study in the village of Karpofora, despite its abundant and fertile resources (Aschenbrenner 1976, 220). Whether that will happen in Aghios Loukas in due time is another future research question.

Acknowledgments

The author gratefully acknowledges the suggestions and comments of Nan Johnson, Harry Schwarzweller, and Ching-Li Wang.

Notes

1. According to Korsching (1982, 22), in studies dealing with changes in the structure of agriculture, "longitudinal data are necessary primarily to determine what is changing, consistencies—through time—in the variables that are changing, and causal relationship among the variables."
2. McNeill (1957, 95–107) provided similar accounts for the social relations between old settlers and refugees in the village of Neo Eleftherohori (Prefecture of Pieria): "The two groups (old settlers and refugees) stood more or less apart, especially at the beginning. Many of the Caucasus people seemed wild and barbarous to the old settlers, farmers, and poor housekeepers."
3. One *oka* (plural *okades*) is equal to 1.28 kilograms.
4. The *de jure* population refers to all persons legally included in the registry book of the village, irrespective of where they might happen to reside at the day of the enumeration.
5. The median number of children born is defined as the value that divides the distribution into two equal parts, one–half the cases falling below this value and one half above.
6. The term *farmers* refers to "full–time small farmers."
7. *Sinergasia* or *parea* is a form of labor exchange practiced among small tobacco growers who plant approximately the same area of tobacco. According to this arrangement, occurring mainly among relatives and neighbors and centered primarily on tobacco transplanting, hoeing, and harvesting, the participating parties join their working crews and execute work schedules in each one of the two or three farms participating in the arrangement.

8. *Danika* is a form of labor exchange arrangement whereby farm households with surplus labor in a particular period help others for a number of days in anticipation of reciprocal help at a later period in time.
9. Burgel (1978, 213) also notes that the penetration of the market in the Greek countryside is detrimental to the survival of the small family farms and might have far-reaching social impacts if it favors a small number of farmers who have easy access to credit, managerial abilities, and large land ownership.
10. Andrew Pearse used the concept of incorporation in his study of the Latin American peasantry (1975, 251–64). In a later article (1978, 198) he provided the following definition of the concept: ". . . the persistent outward expansion of the great industrial powers and their compulsion to incorporate peripheral human groups and resources in their communication and transport systems, their international market structure (including the manpower market) and their institutions and cultural forms."
11. Of course, although the behavior patterns of the present farmers in Aghios Loukas can be explained to a large extent through Foster's "image of the limited good" or Banfield's "amoral familism," we still do not line up entirely with those who believe that all the people of individual communities everywhere are all alike—homogeneous in cultural and psychological characteristics. We believe, and our research has provided evidence, that significant heterogeneity exists. There is a "pool of behavioral possibilities" (Pelto and Pelto 1975, 14) in the village from which new behaviors can be selected.
12. McNall (1976) sees *commodity fetishism* as a manifestation of the desire of Greeks for participation in the modern world. As he pointed out: "the Greek villager exchanges his slim savings for transistor radios, German umbrellas, and Italian shoes." Unfortunately, in the case of Aghios Loukas, savings spent for consumer goods are far greater than those spent by villagers in Varnavas and Milessi and therefore have more far–reaching implications for the farmers themselves and the local and national economy.

References

Aschenbrenner, E. Stanley. 1976. Karpofora: Reluctant farmers on a fertile land. In *Regional variation in modern Greece and Cyprus: Toward a perspective on the ethnography of Greece*, ed. Muriel Dimen and Ernestine Friedl, 207–21. Annals of the New York Academy of Sciences, vol. 268.

Banfield, Edward C. 1958. *The moral basis of a backward society*. New York: Free Press.

Burgel, Guy. 1965. *Pobia: Etude geographique d' un village cretois*. Athens: National Center of Social Research.

———. 1978. Agrotikes erevnes stin Hellada (Agricultural studies in Greece) *Greek Social Review* 33/34: 190–213. Translated into Greek by Dr. M. D. Theofilou. Originally published in Memoires et Documents, vol. 13 (1972), Paris: CNRS.

Damianakos, Stathis, Elias Nickolakopoulos, and Dimitris Pshychogios. 1978. Vergina: Agricultural modernization and social change in a village in central Macedonia. *Greek Review of Social Research* 33/34: 432–78 (in Greek).

Daoutopoulos, George. 1985. Burley tobacco and the changing structure of agriculture in a Greek village. Ph.D. diss., Michigan State University, East Lansing.

———. 1995. Georgi ke Epichirimaties: h peri–ptosi enos choriou ston kampo ton yiannitson (Farmers and businessmen: The case of a village in the valley of Yiannitsa). *Greek Social Review* 88 (in Greek).

DeWalt, Billie R. 1979. *Modernization in a Mexican ejido: A study in economic adaptation*. Cambridge: Cambridge University Press.

Foster, George M. 1965. Peasant society and the image of limited good. *American Anthropologist* 67: 293–315.

General Statistical Service of Greece. 1929. Population of Greece at the 15–16 May 1928. Census. Pp. 267. Athens, Greece: National Printing Office.

Greenwood, Davydd. 1976. *Unrewarding wealth: The commercialization and collapse of agriculture in a Spanish Basque town*. Cambridge: Cambridge University Press.

———. 1980. Community–level research, local–regional governmental interactions, and development planning: A strategy for baseline studies. Rural Development Occasional Paper No.9. Ithaca, N.Y.: Cornell University Center for International Studies.

Kitsopanidis, George, and Marieta Martika. 1982. Evolution of economics and productivity of various crop and livestock enterprises during the 25-year period 1955–80. Thessaloniki, Greece: Department of Agricultural Economics Research, Aristotelian University of Thessaloniki.

Korsching, Peter F. 1982. Measuring the relationship between changes in agricultural structure and community viability. *The Rural Sociologist* 2(1): 20–27.

Lambiri–Dimaki, Ioanna. 1986. H agrotiki kinonia (Rural society). In *H Domi tis Hellinikis kinonias* (Structure of Greek society), ed. M. N. Antonopoulou and I. Lambiri–Dimaki, 23–62. Athens: Kentavros (In Greek).

McNall, Scott G. 1976. Barriers to development and modernization in Greece. In *Regional variation in modern Greece and Cyprus: Toward a perspective on the ethnography of Greece*, ed. Muriel Dimen and Ernestine Friedl, 28–42. New York: Annals of the New York Academy of Sciences, vol. 268.

McNeill, William H. 1957. *Greece: American aid in action 1947–1956*. New York: Twentieth Century Fund, Inc.

Ministry of Coordination. 1975. *Regional development service of central and west Macedonia. Index of municipalities and communities of Macedonia and Thrace, years 1940–71*. Thessaloniki 57:124 (in Greek).

National Statistical Service of Greece (N.S.S.G.). 1982. *De Facto Population of Greece, April 5, 1981 Census*. Athens: National Printing Office. Pp.154.

Pearse, Andrew. 1975. *The Latin American peasant.* London: Frank Cass and Co. Ltd.

———. 1978. Technology and peasant production: Reflections on a global study. In *International Perspectives in Rural Sociology*, ed. Howard Newby, 183–211. London: John Wiley and Sons.

Pelto, Pertti J., and Gretel Pelto. 1975. Intra–cultural diversity: Some theoretical issues. *American Ethnologist* 2: 1–18.

Photiadis, John. 1976. Changes in the social organization of a Greek village. *Sociologia Ruralis* 16(1): 25–40.

Poole, Dennis L. 1981. Farm scale, family life, and community participation. *Rural Sociology* 46: 112–27.

Shryock, Henry S., and Jacob S. Siegel. 1976. *The methods and materials of demography.* New York: Academic Press.

Sieber, Sam D. 1973. The integration of fieldwork and survey methods. *American Journal of Sociology* 78(6): 1335–59.

U.S. Department of Agriculture. 1984. *Tobacco: Background for 1985 farm legislation.* Washington, DC: Economic Research Service, Agriculture Information Bulletin No. 468.

Wallerstein, Immanuel. 1980. *The modern world system II: Mercantilism and the consolidation of the European world economy.* New York: Academic Press.

Whipple, C. E. 1944. The agriculture of Greece. *Foreign Agriculture* 8(4): 75–96.

Wolf, Eric R. 1956. San Jose: Subcultures of a "traditional" coffee municipality. In *The People of Puerto Rico*, ed. Julian Steward, chap. 7. Urbana: University of Illinois Press.

PART 3

Demographic Adaptation

7

RECENT POPULATION CHANGE IN MICHIGAN'S METROPOLITAN AND NONMETROPOLITAN AREAS[1]

Ching–li Wang

Introduction

Population change in the nonmetropolitan areas of the United States turned from historical decline to sudden growth in the early 1970s. Not only did the growth rate in nonmetropolitan counties outstrip that in metropolitan counties, but its strength derived from the faster increase in rural than in urban populations (Lichter, Fuguitt, and Heaton 1985). The well-publicized "rural revival" surprised many people and inspired a large body of literature to document, analyze, and explain this unexpected development (Beale 1975; Fuguitt and Beale 1978; Wardwell 1977; Voss and Fuguitt 1979). In the late 1970s, however, the rate of nonmetropolitan growth slackened; and its difference from the metropolitan rate narrowed. Researchers wondered whether the rural revival would soon be over (Richter 1985).

The 1990 United States Census (U.S. Bureau of the Census 1991) showed that it was over at the national level. The nation's 284 metropolitan areas had 192.7 million residents on 1 April 1990, an increase of 11.6 percent during the 1980s, while nonmetropolitan territory, with 56 million residents, grew by only 3.9 percent. The larger metropolitan areas (more than 1,000,000 people) grew faster than the smaller ones in the 1980s, and these smaller metro areas grew faster than the nonmetropolitan areas (Frey and Speare 1991). This pattern of growth became even more evident in the second half of the 1980s. It so resembled the pattern of the 1960s that *The Number News* speculated: ". . . music of the 1960s drifts over the airwaves, bringing back memories of where we used to be" (*The Number News*, May 1991). To wit, nostalgia might explain the trend of returning to metropolitan lifestyles. The *National Journal* even labeled the "rural renaissance" of the 1970s as a mysterious fad that had failed (Stanfield 1991, 2328). In other words, the rural revival in the 1970s may have been just a temporary interruption of the ongoing population concentration of urban and metropolitan areas of the United States.

To understand why the rural revival ended in the 1980s, we must first know why it began in the 1970s. Many researchers explained the novel migration pattern of the 1970s as the migrant's attempt to attain certain amenities at the place of residence (Fuguitt and Zuiches 1975). In this vein, some analysts (DeJong 1977) stressed noneconomic features such as access to meaningful social ties and the natural beauty of rural settings. On the other hand, Fuguitt, Brown, and Beale (1989, 29) cited several important economic and technological pulls. For example, the exodus of laborers from agricultural to nonagricultural jobs slackened in the 1970s because most underemployed farm laborers had left before the decade began. Likewise, the expansion of manufacturing and recreational industries into nonmetropolitan settings during the 1970s drew adults of both labor–force and retirement ages. Also, an extension of the electronic technologies of communication into the remote hinterlands reduced disparities in lifestyles between metro and nonmetro residents. Finally, more efficient technologies of transportation enabled a greater sprawl of workers traveling to jobs in the metropoles.

Then why did the rural revival of the 1970s stop in the 1980s in many parts of the United States? Did these economic and technological inducements to nonmetropolitan inmigration suddenly weaken or disappear, or is the American public fickle? The individual's capacity to enact a residential preference is conditioned by the social and economic structures in the community of origin and potential destination. Thus, one's reasons for preferring a nonmetropolitan residence may have continued to outweigh desires for a metropolitan setting, but their fulfillment may have become harder to achieve in the 1980s.

It is in the structures of urban and rural social systems that I shall seek answers to the questions posed in the preceding paragraph. My test case shall be Michigan. I must first show that before the 1980s, its nonmetro and metro patterns of population growth mirrored those of the United States: slower nonmetro than metro growth before the 1970s and faster nonmetro than metro growth during the 1970s. I shall then show that in the 1980s, Michigan did not follow the nation's reversion to the pre–1970s pattern. I shall explain Michigan's departure from the national trend as structured by the state's rural and urban economies. My interpretation will suggest how and when the nation will be poised to return to a rural revival.

Population Growth in Michigan's Metro and Nonmetro Areas

Before I begin my analysis, I must explain the difference between metropolitan and nonmetropolitan populations and clarify their substitutability for urban and rural designations. A Metropolitan Statistical Area (MSA, formerly termed "SMSA" until 1983) is a geographic area consisting of a large population center together with adjacent communities that have a high degree of economic and social integration with that center. An area qualifies as an MSA if it includes a city of at least 50,000 population, or else has an urbanized part of at least 50,000 with a total county population of at least 100,000. Adjacent county(ies) having strong commuting ties to the central county may be included in the MSA. Metropolitan counties may have some rural people (i.e., persons living in places of less than 2,500 population or outside urbanized areas) and nonmetropolitan counties may have some urban people (i.e., persons living in places of more than 2,500 population). Generally, however, urban people predominate in metropolitan counties and rural people in nonmetropolitan counties. Therefore, it makes our analysis easier if we use the metropolitan/nonmetropolitan designations of counties to represent urban/rural areas.

A methodological problem is that a particular county's designation as metro/nonmetro may vary over time if its population's size or commuting patterns change a lot. For example, on the basis of the Censuses of Population in Michigan, the number of metro counties fluctuated from 17 in 1970 to 26 in 1980 to 22 in 1990. Then, should I use the same designation for a given Michigan county for all decades in the analysis? If not, then should I use the census at the beginning or the ending of the decade to classify a county as metro/nonmetro? The simplest solution would be to require a particular county to carry the same label in every decade under study.

I shall allow a county's label to vary according to Census–measured changes, however, for I want to know how four possible methods of classification affect the conclusions of my study. Method 1 uses the current definition as of the 1990 Census to stick the same MSA designation on a county for all five decades shown in the table. Method 2 allows a county's MSA status to change every decade by using the two censuses bracketing the decade as the referents. Methods 3 and 4 force a county to keep the same status over a whole decade, but Method 3 depends on the designation at the start of the decade and Method 4 depends on the designation at the end.[2] Table 1 shows the number of metropolitan and nonmetropolitan counties and the percentage of decadal population change implied by the four methods of defining metro/nonmetro counties.

Table 1.
Percent Change of Population in Metropolitan and Nonmetropolitan Areas in Michigan between Two Censuses.

Year	Constant as of the 1990		Designation as of the Census Year		Constant as of the Beginning of Decade		Constant as of End of Decade	
	#counties	% change	#counties	% change	#counties	% change	#counties	% change
Metropolitan Areas								
1990	22	−0.5	22	−2.2	26	−0.9	22	−0.6
1980	22	1.6	26	11.8	17	0.7	26	1.9
1970	22	14.2	17	19.0	14	13.8	17	13.5
1960	22	25.7	14	35.4	10	25.7	14	36.8
1950	22	25.8	10	28.1	9	25.4	10	21.2
1940	22	–	9	–	9	–	9	–
Nonmetropolitan Areas								
1990	61	3.8	61	12.1	57	6.0	61	4.4
1980	61	17.1	57	−20.5	66	16.0	57	17.0
1970	61	10.6	66	−1.3	69	12.9	66	11.6
1960	61	10.6	69	−2.1	73	17.0	69	15.6
1950	61	5.3	73	9.7	74	34.9	73	14.1
1940	61	–	74	–	74	–	74	–

Source: U.S. Bureau of the Census: Census of Population, 1940, 1950, 1960, 1970, 1980, and 1990.

Regardless of the method used, the rate of population growth was lower for nonmetro than for metro counties of Michigan in the 1950s and the 1960s (table 1). But this occurred because a number of counties branded "nonmetropolitan" at the beginnings of those decades were reclassified at the ends as a result of significant population growth. Note that the rates of nonmetro growth in the 1950s and the 1960s appeared higher when so labeled by Method 3 (which lets a county defined as nonmetro at the beginning of a decade keep that definition through the end) than by Method 4 (which labels a nonmetro county as metro for the whole decade if it achieves metropolitan status on the basis of the census at the end of the decade). As such, the difference between nonmetro and metro growth rates in the population of Michigan based on Methods 3 and 4 paralleled that of Method 1.

Population growth in more sparsely populated areas remained so dramatic in Michigan in the 1970s that nine counties classified as nonmetro in 1970 were reclassified as metro in 1980. This reclassification shifted 758,000 people (31.5 percent of the nonmetropolitan population of 1970) into the metropolitan category. Plausibly, only Method 2 for defining metro and nonmetro counties made it seem that the rural revival of population growth was absent from Michigan in the 1970s. However, it really meant that there was tremendous growth in nonmetropolitan Michigan. Consequently, the differential pattern of nonmetro and metro rates of population growth in Michigan reflected that of the United States at large in the 1970s.

Population Growth within Michigan during the 1980s: What Happened and Why?

Despite the method used to distinguish metro from nonmetro populations, the inescapable conclusion from table 1 is that the more rapid population growth in nonmetropolitan than in metropolitan counties endured in Michigan in the 1980s, while faltering in the nation as a whole. Hence, the findings from table 1 support my rationale for treating Michigan as a test case to isolate the structural causes for the maintenance of a rural population revival in a state and for its demise elsewhere in the United States.

To simplify the rest of the analysis, Method 1 is used in defining metro and nonmetro counties. Except for four counties, all the nonmetro counties have never been metro counties. Even so, nonmetro counties differ from each other depending on where they are located. It is reasonable to distinguish the nonmetro counties according to whether they are in the Upper or Lower Peninsula and to subdivide the latter into southern and northern tiers by drawing a line across the northern border of Bay, Midland, Isabella, Mecosta, Newaygo, and Oceana counties. Almost all nonmetropolitan counties in the Southern Lower Peninsula (SLP) are adjacent to metropolitan areas, which are all located in the southern half of the Lower Peninsula. All the counties in the Northern Lower Peninsula (NLP) and Upper Peninsula (UP) are nonmetropolitan counties. The Northern Lower Peninsula is mostly rural, with recreation and retirement communities. The Upper Peninsula is a remote rural area, far away from metropolitan areas. In the order mentioned here, the three groups of counties form a scale of decreasing proximity to metropolitan areas in Michigan.

Due to a severe economic recession at the beginning of the 1980s, population growth in Michigan during that decade was the slowest since the 1930s era of the Great Depression. In fact, the size of the state's population fell due to a net outmigration of 510,000 people between 1980 - 85. In metro counties, the growth rate of the population fell from the 1.6 percent level of the 1970s to -0.5 percent for the 1980s (table 2). This happened because net outmigration from the metro counties was so strong in the first half of the decade that a return to net inmigration in the metro fringe counties in the last half of the decade could not reverse the negative-growth trend for the whole decade (table 3).

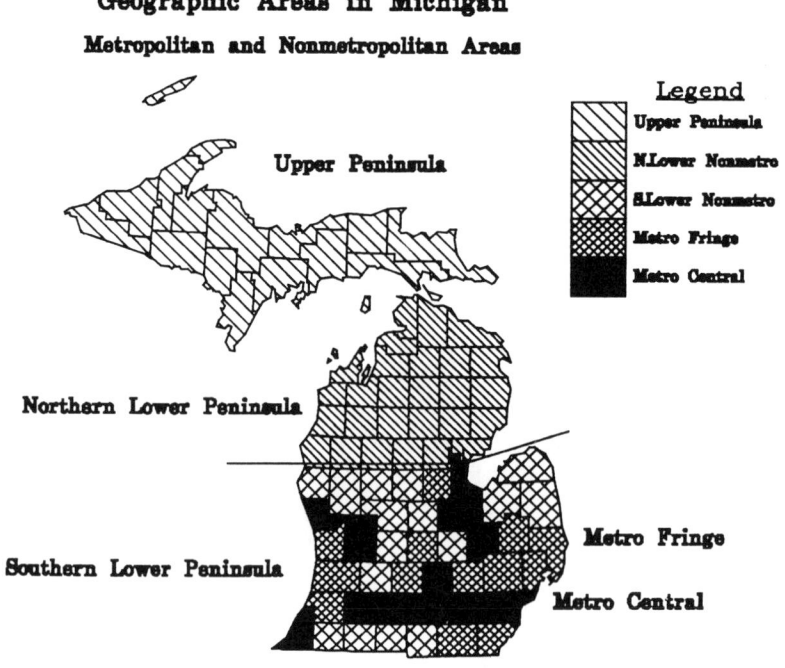

Unlike in metro counties, the population continued to grow in nonmetro counties in the 1980s but at a much weaker pace than in the 1970s (3.8 percent vs. 17.1 percent; table 2). Net inmigration continued to add people to nonmetro counties in the NLP and secured nonmetro population growth in the region in the 1980s (table 3). Population growth struggled ahead of zero in the nonmetro counties of the SLP only because an excess of births over deaths (i.e., net natural increase) overcompensated for net outmigration there. In the UP, the rate of population change swung from positive to negative because net natural increase was insufficient to replace population losses from net outmigration. But despite the net migration loss in two of the three groups of nonmetro counties (i.e., those in the SLP and the UP), the nonmetro counties grew at a rate of 3.8 percent in the 1980s, which was approximately the same rate (3.9 percent) for the nation.

Since the trends in population growth varied so much across nonmetro counties of Michigan in the 1980s, let us inspect these trends more closely across the MSAs. The Detroit MSA, the largest one in Michigan, lost 2.4% of its original 1980 population before 1990, while the other 10 MSAs gained 2.4% (table 2). Five of these other 10 MSAs registered losses, and five marked gains (table 4). But we see from table 2 that the end - result spelled metro population growth in Michigan well below that in the nonmetro counties and qualified Michigan as a "deviant" State of the Union in that respect for the 1980s. The questions before us now are: (1) Why was there a big slump in the 1980s in the positive rate of nonmetro population growth that had abided since the 1950s? (2) Why did negative population growth strengthen in such MSAs as Detroit, Flint, and Bay City-Saginaw-Midland in the 1980s?

Structural Changes in the Rural and Urban Economies of Michigan during the 1980s

Michigan's deviancy in the 1980s can be explained by changes in the economic structures of its rural and urban environments. The greater overall growth of population in nonmetro than in metro Michigan in the 1980s implies that rural lifestyles continued to be an important magnet attaching people to nonmetro counties. However, this attachment was loosened by the economic recession in the early 1980s. The state unemployment rate rose to 15.5 percent of the labor force, the highest in the nation. That percentage cannot reflect the true proportion of households disadvantaged by such a prolonged recession, because it excludes unemployed persons searching for work who became discouraged and stopped.

Under such economic stress, many households could not afford to move to a new place of preferred residence, because the high mortgage

Table 2.
PERCENT POPULATION CHANGE IN METRO AND NONMETRO AREAS IN MICHIGAN.

Metro/Nonmetro as of 1990	1950–60	1960–70	1970–80	1980–90	1980–85	1985–90
Michigan	22.8	13.5	4.3	0.4	-2.0	2.4
Metropolitan Areas	25.7	14.2	1.6	-0.5	-2.7	2.3
Central area	16.7	7.1	-4.1	-3.9	-4.4	0.5
Fringe area	63.6	35.2	15.1	6.3	0.5	5.8
Detroit MSA	24.8	12.4	-1.5	-2.4	-3.8	1.5
Central area	9.5	0.2	-12.5	-9.7	-7.3	-2.5
Fringe area	70.8	36.1	14.1	5.6	0.1	5.5
Other MSAs	27.4	17.1	6.6	2.4	-1.2	3.6
Central area	26.9	15.6	4.8	1.2	-1.7	3.0
Fringe area	31.7	30.1	21.2	10.5	2.9	7.4
Nonmetropolitan Areas	10.6	10.6	17.1	3.8	1.1	2.7
Southern Lower Peninsula	15.9	12.5	15.9	3.3	0.6	2.7
Northern Lower Peninsula	8.7	16.9	29.4	8.4	4.0	4.3
Upper Peninsula	1.2	-0.5	5.1	-1.8	-1.8	0.0

Source: U.S. Bureau of the Census: Census of Population, 1950, 1960, 1970, 1980, and Federal-State Cooperative Program for Population Estimates for 1985.

Notes: 1. Central metropolitan counties are the counties that contain central cities of the Metropolitan Statistical Area defined as of 1990.

2. Fringe metropolitan counties are the counties not containing central cities.

3. Southern and Northern Lower nonmetropolitan areas are divided by the northern border of Bay, Midland, Isabella, Mecosta, Newaygo, and Oceana counties in the lower peninsula.

Table 3.
Net Migration Rates in Metro and Nonmetro Areas in Michigan.

Metro/Nonmetro as of 1990	1950–60	1960–70	1970–80	1980–90	1980–85	1985–90
Michigan	2.7	0.6	–3.4	–6.3	–5.3	–1.0
Metropolitan Areas	4.2	0.5	–6.2	–7.4	–6.2	–1.3
Central area	–3.2	–5.3	–11.5	–10.8	–7.8	–3.2
Fringe area	35.0	17.9	6.3	–0.8	–3.0	2.2
Detroit MSA	3.5	–0.3	–8.4	–8.3	–6.6	–1.8
Central area	–8.8	–10.1	–18.3	–15.0	–9.8	–5.6
Fringe area	40.8	18.6	5.6	–1.1	–3.1	2.0
Other MSAs	5.2	1.9	–2.6	–6.1	–5.5	–0.7
Central area	4.8	0.6	–4.3	–7.1	–6.0	–1.2
Fringe area	9.0	13.8	10.7	0.8	–2.1	2.8
Nonmetropolitan Areas	–3.2	1.1	10.3	–1.7	–2.0	0.3
Southern Lower Peninsula	0.9	1.9	7.8	–3.3	–3.0	–0.3
Northern Lower Peninsula	–4.9	8.0	23.7	3.7	1.2	2.4
Upper Peninsula	–10.4	–8.3	0.3	–5.1	–4.0	–1.1

Source: Michigan Department of Management and Budget, calculated from the United States Census of Population in 1950, 1960, 1970, 1980, and 1990; the 1985 population estimates from the Federal–State Cooperative Program for Population Estimates; and birth and death statistics from The Office of the State Registrar, Michigan Department of Community Health.

Note: Net Migration rates are calculated as percent net migration of the population at the beginning of decade.

rate (18.5 percent in the last quarter of 1981) hampered the sale of their houses and because the high price of gasoline ($1.353 per gallon for regular unleaded gasoline in the last quarter of 1981) blocked many from moving to rural homes and commuting to urban jobs. Thus, the internal migration from metro to nonmetro counties was reduced greatly in the early 1980s. At the same time, the severe recession must have driven both nonmetro and metro peoples out of state in search of better economic opportunities—those so driven must have disproportionately been persons lacking property to sell and jobs to quit. Indeed, from 1980 to 1983, Michigan had a net outmigration of 400,000 people, exceeding the net outmigration of 300,000 from the state for the whole decade of the 1970s.

What industries were most at fault for Michigan's net exportation of people in the 1980s? Because the nonmetro and metro economies of the state are integrated, change in a single industry affects both; nevertheless, the strength of the effect depends on its locus. For example, the dramatic growth in numbers of persons employed in agriculturally related jobs in nonmetro counties during the 1970s (13.7 percent) slowed significantly during the 1980s (to 0.6 percent; see table 5) and actually declined in the nonmetro counties of the SLP, where these jobs had been most heavily concentrated for the last three decades. Somewhat surprisingly, agriculturally related jobs grew more rapidly in metropolitan than in nonmetropolitan counties in the 1980s (27.3 percent vs. 0.6 percent, table 5). This probably reflects an expansion of agribusinesses rather than an inauguration of new farms in the metropolitan environment. It is noteworthy that persons working in agriculturally related jobs composed a paltry 1.2 percent of the metropolitan labor force by the end of the 1980s. Apparently, these transitions in agriculture were more detrimental to nonmetropolitan counties in the 1980s than in the 1970s, and more so to nonmetropolitan than to metropolitan counties. In short, the slow growth of the population in nonmetro counties of Michigan in the 1980s could not be attributed to a surge in farm employment.

Another industry that deeply affected nonmetro and metro population growth in the 1980s was manufacturing. The exportation of manufacturing jobs from metropolitan to nonmetropolitan settings was evident as far back as the 1960s, during which the growth in numbers of persons employed in manufacturing was higher in nonmetro than in metro counties (23.7 percent vs. 11.3 percent; table 6). That growth switched to decline in metro counties as a whole in the 1970s (–5.1 percent), but remained positive in the nonmetro counties (11.8 percent). It appeared that manufacturing jobs were moving out of the Detroit MSA, particularly from its core of Wayne County (which posted losses of –9.3 percent and

Table 4.
Percent Population Change in Michigan's Metropolitan Areas.

Metropolitan Statistical Area	Percent Change					
	(10-Year Rate)				(5 Year Rate)	
	1950–60	1960–70	1970–80	1980–90	1980–85	1985–90
Ann Arbor PMSA	28.1	35.8	13.1	6.9	-2.2	9.2
Battle Creek MSA	14.9	2.2	-0.3	-4.0	-3.4	-0.5
Benton Harbor MSA	29.5	9.4	4.5	-5.8	-4.1	-1.7
Detroit PMSA	24.8	12.4	-1.5	-2.4	-3.8	1.5
Flint MSA	38.1	19.0	1.1	-4.4	-4.0	-0.4
Grand Rapids MSA	27.6	16.7	11.6	14.4	4.9	9.1
Jackson MSA	22.3	8.5	5.7	-1.1	-4.7	3.7
Lansing–E.Lansing MSA	22.4	26.6	10.9	3.1	-1.3	4.4
Kalamazoo MSA	33.9	18.8	5.4	5.2	0.1	5.1
Muskegon MSA	23.4	5.0	0.1	0.9	-0.1	1.0
Bay–Saginaw–Midland MSA	25.8	14.8	5.2	-5.3	-3.8	-1.5
Total Metropolitan	25.7	14.2	1.6	-0.5	-2.7	2.3
Total Nonmetropolitan	10.6	10.6	17.1	3.8	1.1	2.7
Michigan Total	22.8	13.5	4.3	0.4	-2.0	2.4

Source: U.S. Census of Population, 1950, 1960, 1970, 1980, and 1990.
Note: Metropolitan definition is held constant as of 1990, not changed since 1983. Ann Arbor PMSA (Primary Metropolitan Statistical Area) and Detroit PMSA together form Detroit CMSA (Consolidated Metropolitan Statistical Area).

Table 5.
Employment in Agriculture in Michigan's Metro/Nonmetro Areas.

Metro/Nonmetro As of 1990	Percent Change			Percent Total Employed			
	1960–70	1970–80	1980–90	1960	1970	1980	1990
Michigan	−37.3	8.2	14.1	3.4	1.8	1.7	1.7
Metropolitan Areas	−29.6	3.4	27.3	1.9	1.1	1.0	1.2
Central Counties	−27.3	−1.9	26.0	1.5	1.0	0.9	1.1
Fringe Counties	−32.8	11.3	28.9	3.4	1.6	1.3	1.3
Nonmetropolitan Areas	−44.3	13.7	0.6	11.1	5.5	4.8	4.1
Southern Lower	−43.8	15.0	−2.5	13.5	6.5	5.9	5.0
Northern Lower	−45.3	13.6	11.1	10.2	4.8	3.8	3.5
Upper Peninsula	−45.1	4.5	0.5	5.4	2.9	2.5	2.3

Source: U. S. Bureau of the Census: Census of Population, 1960, 1970, 1980, 1990.
Notes: 1. Central metropolitan counties are the counties that contain central cities of the Metropolitan Statistical Area defined as of 1990.
2. Fringe metropolitan counties are the counties not containing central cities.
3. Southern and Northern Lower nonmetropolitan areas are divided by the northern border of Bay, Midland, Isabella, Mecosta, Newaygo, and Oceana counties in the Lower Peninsula.

Table 6.
PERCENTAGE CHANGE IN TOTAL EMPLOYMENT AND IN MANUFACTURING EMPLOYMENT IN MICHIGAN'S METRO/NONMETRO AREAS.

Metro/Nonmetro As of 1990	% Change in Total Employment			% Change in Manufacturing			% of Total Employment
	1960–70	1970–80	1980–90	1960–70	1970–80	1980–90	1990
Michigan	19.3	15.3	11.1	12.8	-2.8	-9.7	24.6
Metropolitan Areas	20.4	12.7	9.9	11.3	-5.1	-12.0	24.7
Detroit MSA	18.9	7.8	8.1	10.3	-9.3	-14.7	24.9
Other MSAs	22.9	20.6	12.5	12.9	2.1	-7.9	24.6
Metro–Central	12.1	2.5	4.1	4.0	-13.8	-18.4	24.0
Wayne	4.6	-11.8	-4.2	-1.5	-25.7	-27.9	23.7
Other Central	21.2	17.5	10.7	11.1	-0.5	-10.3	24.1
Metro–Fringe	46.7	37.4	20.4	32.7	15.3	-1.0	25.9
Nonmetropolitan Areas	13.5	29.3	16.5	23.7	11.8	2.8	24.1
Southern Lower	16.4	26.4	15.3	30.3	10.0	1.7	29.6
Northern Lower	16.6	41.9	23.1	24.3	15.3	5.1	18.2
Upper Peninsula	1.5	22.0	10.1	-11.7	17.6	5.9	15.0

Source: U.S. Bureau of the Census: Census of Population 1960, 1970, 1980, 1990.
Notes: 1. Central metropolitan counties are the counties that contain central cities of the Metropolitan Statistical Area defined as of 1990.
2. Fringe metropolitan counties are the counties not containing central cities.
3. Southern and Northern Lower nonmetropolitan areas are divided by the northern border of Bay, Midland, Isabella, Mecosta, Newaygo, and Oceana counties in the Lower Peninsula.

–25.7 percent, respectively), to nonmetropolitan counties. Even the nonmetro counties of the UP saw a change in the number of people employed in manufacturing reverse from a loss in the 1960s (–11.7 percent) to a gain in the 1970s (17.6 percent).

The severity of the recession in the automotive industry in the early 1980s halted these patterns. The decline in numbers of persons employed in manufacturing in the metro counties accelerated from –5.1 percent in the 1970s to –12.0 percent in the 1980s and spread out of the Detroit MSA to both the central and fringe counties of other MSAs in the state (table 6). The nonmetropolitan counties continued to gain manufacturing jobs in the 1980s, but the rate of this growth was only a quarter of what it had been in the 1970s (2.8 percent vs. 11.8 percent; table 6). This suggests that the loss of metropolitan jobs in the 1980s did not simply mean a shift of those jobs over to Michigan's nonmetropolitan counties.

Discussion

In the 1980s, population growth in Michigan's nonmetropolitan counties continued to exceed that in metropolitan counties, as had been true in the 1970s. This pattern made Michigan a "deviant" from the national trend, which saw a return in the 1980s to faster population growth in metro than in nonmetro counties. An important reason for Michigan's deviancy was that net migration still favored the nonmetro counties in the Northern Lower Peninsula (NLP). However, nonmetro counties outside the NLP began to experience net outmigration again. The fact that the rate of population growth in Michigan's nonmetro population as a whole almost matched the national rate (3.8 percent and 3.9 percent, respectively) meant that Michigan's departure from the national trend was due to the net loss of population from metropolitan counties through outmigration.

Since 1970, Michigan has been losing population through outmigration to other states. In the 1970s, this loss reflected a decentralization of manufacturing industries from Michigan's metropolitan counties to its nonmetropolitan counties and to other states. However, in the 1980s, this decentralization process crossed United States boundaries into other countries and cost the state a net loss of people through the outmigration of those in the labor force. This loss came not only from the metropolitan counties, but also from the adjacent nonmetropolitan counties in the Southern Lower Peninsula and from the nonadjacent nonmetropolitan counties in the Upper Peninsula. Somewhat surprisingly, employment in agricultural occupations grew in metro counties of Michigan during the 1980s (27.3 percent), but the growth was not enough to stanch the net outmigration precipitated by the loss of manufacturing jobs.

The interrelationship of population redistribution with alterations in the urban and rural economies of Michigan suggests what demographic trends we might expect in the last decade of the twentieth century. If automobile manufacturing continues to be the state's largest employer, and if more new jobs created by the Michigan headquarters of this industry continue to leave than to stay in the state, net outmigration will likely continue to drain the metropolitan population from the state in the 1990s, as it has done for the past two decades. This trend could be revoked by a net retention of these jobs within the state or by a diversification in Michigan's base of metropolitan employment.

Long (1988) found that recovery from the economic recession of the early 1980s happened more slowly in rural and small–town America and discouraged population growth there, even when population began to grow again in metropolitan centers. Thus, Michigan's nonmetro counties might continue to grow at a positive rate and sustain Michigan's deviant pattern from the rest of the nation if they continue to receive manufacturing jobs from the metropolitan centers of decisionmaking. However, this continuity is not assured in the 1990s. As foreign competition against United States automakers has intensified, many factors that have allowed decentralization of industries to rural areas have also facilitated the continued migration of jobs overseas (Long 1988).

On the other hand, several factors may stimulate population growth in nonmetro Michigan in the 1990s. While the economic recession was deepest in this state in the early 1980s, a return to economic expansion, combined with increasingly sophisticated technologies for communication, could enable the population of Michigan to grow through inmigration and could empower persons with metropolitan employment to act on a preference to purchase nonmetropolitan residences without a need to commute. Therefore, stronger population growth in nonmetro Michigan can be expected in the 1990s.

The woods and lakes of the Northern Lower Peninsula will probably continue to attract tourists and retirees and encourage the expansion of leisure industries there. This trend may gain momentum in the 1990s, as the aging of the population produces returning retirees who had left their native Michigan or had moved to its cities in the previous decades. The aging of the population not only in the state but also in the United States at large guarantees that leisure industries will remain an important part of the rural economy of the Northern Lower Peninsula. If this potential is realized, the ensuing population growth will probably not soon transform these nonmetropolitan counties into metropolitan ones, as this transformation has occurred in Michigan only in nonmetropolitan counties that are adjacent to metropolitan counties.

Notes

1. Revised version of a paper presented at the session on Some Aspects of Demographic Trends in the Great Lakes Region at the 10th Conference on the Small City and Regional Community, Western Michigan University, Kalamazoo, Michigan, 2–3 April 1992.
2. The designation of new core metropolitan counties occurs throughout the decade whenever the new census counts become available or new population sizes are estimated. However, the adjacent counties ("fringe metro counties") become part of a Metropolitan Statistical Area only when the census shows a significant commuting flow to the core metropolitan county. Thus, the designation of metropolitan counties is more census–dependent when those counties are fringe counties, and is reflective of the commuting patterns as reported in that census.

References

Ballard, Patricia L., and Glenn V. Fuguitt. 1985. The changing small town settlement structure in the United States, 1900–1980. *Rural Sociology* 50(1): 99–113.

Beale, Calvin L. 1975. The revival of population growth in nonmetropolitan America. Washington, D.C.: USDA Economic Research Service ERS–605.

DeJong, Gordon F. 1977. Residential preferences and migration. *Demography* 4(2): 169–78.

Frey, William H., and Alden Speare, Jr. 1988. *Regional and metropolitan growth and decline in the U.S.* New York: Russell Sage Foundation for the National Committee for Research on the 1980 Census.

———. 1991. U.S. metropolitan area growth in the 1980s: Do the old explanations hold for new patterns? Paper presented at the 1991 Annual Meeting of the Population Association of America, Washington, D.C., 22 March 1991.

Fuguitt, Glenn V., and Calvin Beale. 1978. Population trends of nonmetropolitan cities and villages in subregions of the United States. *Demography* 15(4): 605–20.

Fuguitt, Glenn V., and David L. Brown. 1990. Residential preferences and population redistribution, 1972–1988. *Demography* 27(4): 589–600.

Fuguitt, Glenn, David L. Brown, and Calvin L. Beale. 1989. *Rural and small town America*. New York: Russell Sage Foundation for the National Committee for Research on the 1980 Census.

Fuguitt, Glenn V., and James J. Zuiches. 1975. Residential preferences and population redistribution. *Demography* 12(3): 491–504.

Lichter, Daniel T., Glenn V. Fuguitt, and Tim B. Heaton. 1985. Components of nonmetropolitan population change: The contribution of rural areas. *Rural Sociology* 50(1): 88–98.

Long, Larry. 1988. Population shifts in urban and rural America. Paper presented to Subcommittee on Census and Population, 13 June 1988. St. Paul, Minnesota.

The Number News. 1991. "Return to the Sixties." 11(5): 3.

Richter, Kerry. 1985. Nonmetropolitan growth in the late 1970s: The end of the turnaround. *Rural Sociology* 22(2): 245–64.

Stanfield, Rochelle L. 1991. Strains in the family. *National Journal,* 28 September 1991, 2316–33.

U.S. Bureau of the Census. 1991. Metropolitan areas and cities. 1990 Census profile, No. 3, September 1991.

———. 1992. Residents for farm and rural areas: 1990. Current Population Reports P-20, No. 457.

Voss, Paul R., and Glenn V. Fuguitt. 1979. Turnaround migrations in the Upper Great Lakes Region. Madison, Wisc.: Applied Population Laboratory, University of Wisconsin–Extension, Population Series 70–12.

Wardwell, John M. 1977. Equilibrium and change in nonmetropolitan growth. 42(2): 156–79.

Wardwell, John M., and C. Jack Gilchrist. 1987. Nonmetropolitan migration: Facts of the 1980s—theories of the 1970s. Paper presented at Rural Sociological Society annual meetings, Madison, Wisconsin, 11-15 Aug.

8

THE TRANSMISSION OF INFORMATION REGARDING POPULATION CHANGE IN A RURAL COUNTY

Richard W. Rathge

The decade of the 1970s was a dynamic period for many rural areas in the United States. An unprecedented number of nonmetropolitan counties (more than 80 percent) experienced population growth, a situation unparalleled since the turn of the century (Long and DeAre 1982). For some counties, the resurgence ended a long history of steady outmigration. The *population turnaround*, as it was aptly labeled, also signaled a shift in migration patterns that favored counties rich in recreational and retirement amenities (McCarthy and Morrison 1978; Beale 1976). Residential expansion in the scenic areas of rural America illustrated an important change in motivations on the part of this new contingent of migrants. Quality–of–life concerns outweighed traditional economic incentives as the leading catalyst for residential relocation (Sofranko and Williams 1980; Voss and Fuguitt 1979).

The unexpected turnaround migration patterns of the 1970s, however, were not continued uniformly throughout the 1980s (see Engels 1986; Beale and Fuguitt 1986). Preliminary population counts from the 1990 census confirm the reappearance of an old and time–honored pattern of rural–to–urban net movement. Rural growth once again seems to be most prevalent in counties adjacent to metropolitan centers. Nearly three in four nonadjacent nonmetropolitan counties registered net outmigration during the first half of the 1980s, in part a reflection of the downturn in agriculture (Johnson 1987).

The slowdown or reversal of the population turnaround poses a variety of important issues. At the forefront are questions regarding the consequences of the current trend and the response by residents and decision–makers to mitigate impacts. An intriguing concern that has received limited attention is the process by which information regarding community impacts is disseminated. In particular, what role does the rural media play in providing policymakers and residents insight into demographic changes and their related consequences?

This case study explores the transmission of information regarding the effects of population growth on a rural county system. An appropriate starting point for examining information exchange is the rural press because residents largely rely on it for information concerning local affairs (Shaw and Riffe 1979) or for cross–checking the validity of news gained from personal contacts (Fry and McCain 1983). My aim is to detail the amount and type of coverage given to issues associated with population change in a rural turnaround county over a nine–year period. The analysis offers insight into the knowledge base residents and decisionmakers develop from issues and events articulated in the rural newspaper.

Previous Research

Two theoretical perspectives have guided much of the research regarding the role and influence of printed news media in rural social systems. The first views the interplay between the press and its public from a structural vantage point. The thrust of investigations from this perspective links the complexity of the rural social system to the corresponding role and influence of the local media in community affairs. A key tenet of this perspective is that structural characteristics of the social system condition the outlook of residents and editors concerning the function of the press. A somewhat different perspective is the social maintenance model. Researchers using this approach tend to focus on the media's ability to maintain the status quo. The central theme of this perspective is grounded in Marxist philosophy and suggests that local printed media reflect the concerns of local power brokers. A brief literature review summarizes some of the important findings from these two perspectives, exposes various shortcomings of previous research, and provides the foundation from which I formulate the research design.

Structural Approach

The news media is influenced by a diverse assortment of forces. One notable element is the environment in which it operates. Various studies indicate that the focus of the media shifts with the complexity of the social system. In the case of small homogeneous communities, the flavor of printed news is typically geared toward parochial interests that highlight social and civic events. This is perhaps due to the feeling among many rural editors that their newspaper should establish and nourish the area's

Figure 1. This former church in rural Michigan was converted into a residence for an urban-to-rural migrant. (Photo by Nan E. Johnson)

identity (Greenberg 1964; Stone and Morrison 1976). Editors convey this unifying theme through their emphasis on social consensus and their strong support for existing institutions (Paletz, Reichert, and McIntyre 1971). One consequence of this editorial philosophy is an increased likelihood of an uncritical perspective toward local events. Important issues that cast a negative light on social institutions, events, or situations may be overlooked. For example, editors, in their eagerness to promote unity during chaotic periods of population flux, may neglect to investigate or discuss the ramifications of change. A large inflow of population may be lauded by the local press and viewed as beneficial to the area's economy, while information concerning potentially harmful side effects (e.g., strip businesses, environmental concerns) receive limited exposure. The documented tendency of rural newspapers to avoid or downplay controversy (see Paletz, Reichert, and McIntyre 1971; Tichenor, Donohue, and Olien 1980), although admirable in intent, may retard the ability of both readers and policymakers to recognize and effectively adjust to change.

The tone and detail of the local paper also appear to be influenced by regional or community characteristics. Small rural villages tend to maintain a generally conservative philosophy that is paralleled, and perhaps perpetuated by, the conservative slant typically found in rural weekly or semiweekly newspapers (Hynds and Martin 1979). Along similar lines, the information base of rural newspapers usually is more narrow than that of metropolitan daily newspapers. This fact most likely reflects the limited resources, information retrieval systems, and data-gathering capabilities of small newspapers. Nonetheless, an important implication is an increased likelihood that residents in rural areas who rely solely on information from weekly or semiweekly newspapers may be inadequately informed about local and extralocal (i.e., national or world) issues, a contention that has received some empirical support (see Tichenor, Donohue, and Olien 1987).

This notion raises important policy concerns, especially in the context of the population turnaround. For example, how well informed were rural residents and decisionmakers in turnaround counties regarding changes in the structure and character of their communities and surrounding areas? More precisely, how accurate and comprehensive was the information they received through their local press? Answers to these questions may improve our understanding of communities' adaptation to rapid population redistribution.

Social Maintenance

Content and type of news reporting is also influenced by various power brokers. Community leaders and editors can be particularly persuasive in establishing the tone of the local media. There is some support for the notion that community leaders, through the establishment and maintenance of specific norms, set guidelines for what should be printed in the local press (see Donohue, Olien, and Tichenor 1985). Ironically, these same studies suggest that community leaders frequently perceive that the newspaper's agenda reflects the relationship of the newspaper to external organizations and groups (e.g., government agencies, school boards, corporations). Nonetheless, a common feeling among community leaders is that the press's role is one of social maintenance. In brief, the belief in many rural communities is that the news media should promote community cohesion at the expense of confrontation (Edelstein and Schultz 1964). Not surprisingly, this attitude is often shared by small–community residents (see Janowitz 1952). In contrast, metropolitan readers tend to encourage open debate in the printed media (Tichenor, Donohue, and Olien 1980).

Editors, on the other hand, are more likely than community leaders to believe that the reporting of controversies is an important function of news (Donohue, Olien, and Tichenor 1985). Editors often also perceive their role as including that of community "watchdog." The contrasting views of community leaders and editors illustrate the potential variation in information transmitted via the rural press. More importantly, such variation underscores the need for a more adequate understanding of the reliance of rural communities on the press as an information source.

These two theoretical perspectives, although not mutually exclusive, lead to distinctly different predictions about the content of information within rural newspapers. From the structural perspective, one would expect to find coverage of social institutions dominating the news. This would reflect the editor's attempt to promote interest in parochial events while simultaneously showing support for existing institutions. The narrative, according to this viewpoint, should lack a critical tone, thereby minimizing conflict in order to foster unity. In contrast, from a social maintenance perspective, articles concerning general community affairs will overshadow those pertaining to social institutions. By concentrating on general issues (e.g., crime, public service needs, environmental concerns) that have broad ramifications, the editor enhances his/her ability to promote the status quo by emphasizing a particular political or economic viewpoint. The editorial style, therefore, would most likely be conflictive from this perspective.

The different theoretical perspectives also lead to distinctly different predictions regarding the location of articles within the newspaper. Stories regarding institutional issues of population growth are front–page news from a structural perspective. Such visibility helps nourish the area's identity, when positively reported. In contrast, the editor acting as "watchdog" and spokesperson for the status quo is more likely to publish political and economic issues of population growth as editorials. This format allows the most flexibility for persuasive reporting.

The divergent positions of these two theoretical perspectives served as guideposts for structuring the content analysis. I realized that both content and location of population-related stories were important dimensions to explore. More importantly, I recognized the need to augment the analysis with personal interviews in order to establish a comparative base for examining the transmission of information regarding population change.

Methods

Study Site

The site for my analysis was a typical rural turnaround county in the scenic Upper Great Lakes area. Pine Tree County[1] (a pseudonym) is located about 75 miles from the nearest metropolitan center. It is heavily forested, with numerous lakes dotting the wooded landscape. Various rivers and streams bisect the county and add to its scenic beauty. Pine Tree County is easily accessible, with three major highways cutting through its rolling hills.

Overall, the population of Pine Tree County grew by more than 27 percent between 1970 and 1980. The increase of nearly 3,000 residents came after four decades of population loss. The residential expansion primarily occurred outside the county's six population centers, the county's towns and villages accounting for only 6 percent of the growth. Most newcomers to the area settled along the lakes and rivers of the county. As a result, growth was not physically conspicuous.

Data

Data for this study were derived from two sources. First, a nine–year content analysis was carried out using the county weekly, *The Herald*. A total of 634 newspaper items, directly or indirectly related to residential change, were coded for analysis. My aim was to explore what issues, directly or indirectly related to population growth, were most often reported during the county's dramatic turnaround growth period. This approach expands previous knowledge by focusing on subject matter (e.g., population change), as opposed to type of issues (e.g., conflict). Because a nine–year period was examined, I could track the relationship between the rate of population change during the decade and the way it and its impacts were reported.

This approach addresses serious shortcomings of previous cross–sectional studies by examining shifts in the pattern of news coverage. I included the location of the story within the analysis by coding items that appeared on the front page, on the editorial page, and as letters to the editor. The underlying assumption is that both readers and editor give more attention to items appearing on the front page, as compared to those buried in the middle of the newspaper. Likewise, from the editor's standpoint, editorials focus on the critical issues that require commentary (Hynds and Martin 1979). Alternatively, letters to the editor cover issues that readers view with concern. Coder reliability was checked to insure accurate recount.

Second, in–depth interviews were conducted during the summers of 1979 and 1981 with over 100 local residents and key informants representing four major institutional sectors—education, government, economy, and health and social services. This qualitative dimension afforded interpretive insight into issues omitted from the press.

Limitations

It is important to recognize the limitations of this study before discussing the findings. One must keep in mind that the data represent a single case study of one rural county. It is limited to a single rural weekly paper and encompasses several editors over the nine years of observation. The county is mainly recreational in nature, thus it may be atypical from those linked to agricultural or industrial activities.

Findings

Pine Tree County sustained residential growth throughout the decade of the 1970s. Population estimates shown in table 1 indicate that the greatest gains were at the beginning of the decade, when annual growth exceeded 7 percent. A second population spurt appeared at mid–decade, with an annual increase above 4 percent. When one considers the relatively small base population of the county, combined with its historical record of outmigration, the implications of rapid growth are more apparent. In brief, net growth between 1970 and 1980 exceeded the county's combined experience since the turn of the century. A growth of 3,889 residents, although meager in most other contexts, generated numerous social, political, and economic impacts.

There was no discernible relationship between annual population growth and the overall number of articles published concerning growth (see table 1). However, of the 634 stories analyzed, the largest proportion was published during the first half of the decade, a period that corresponds with the county's most rapid growth.

Type of Articles

I classified articles concerning population growth into two major groupings, those relating to social institutions (e.g., education, economy, health and social services, and government) and those pertaining to general community affairs (e.g., quality of life, crime, and public services) (see table 1). This general dichotomy allowed me to isolate the relative importance of institutional issues, compared with broader, more holistic concerns such as crime, environmental problems, or public safety.

Articles relating to education and population growth maintained the highest profile in *The Herald* of all the institutional sectors. Over 100 stories were coded in the nine-year period (see table 1). The trend in educational coverage paralleled fluctuations in population (see table 1). News coverage of educational issues increased as population growth began to

Table 1.
Population Change and Corresponding Distribution of Articles Related to Population Change Published in *The Herald* by Type and Year.

Year	% Change During Year	Total Pop.	Total	Institutions					General Community Affairs		
				Education	Gov.	Econ.	Health/ Soc. Ser.	Crime and Public Ser. Needs	Quality of Life	Other
1970	7.18	14,838	81	15	7	12	4	13	26	4
1971	4.42	15,903	67	5	6	3	11	18	18	6
1972	1.22	16,606	56	10	10	6	4	8	13	5
1973	1.81	16,809	99	17	18	15	2	28	15	5
1974	2.35	17,114	91	26	6	16	10	19	9	4
1975	4.01	17,516	89	17	9	5	24	29	5	—
1976	2.77	18,218	44	6	6	8	5	18	1	—
1977	0.56	18,722	52	1	17	7	1	18	8	—
1978	−0.53	18,827	55	6	15	9	3	14	8	—
1979	1.07	18,727	—	—	—	—	—	—	—	—
Total	27.56	—	634	103	94	81	64	165	103	24

accelerate. The population spurt in 1970–71 strained the small educational systems serving the county and made them very sensitive to further growth. Articles regarding education increased in number from 1972 to 1975 and highlighted the accelerated population expansion between 1973 and 1976.

The consequences of population expansion on education within the county were given relatively high visibility in the press. The paper documented most of the major issues articulated by school administrators and teachers in our interviews. For example, several articles described the chronic overcrowding of the county's schools, the short–term solutions used (e.g., portable facilities and subdivided classrooms), and their resulting consequences (e.g., program cuts, such as in Head Start, and partial curtailment of various electives such as art, music, shop, and gym). Attempts by the editor to encourage support for education, the county's major social institution, are consistent with the social structural perspective. The coverage of two additional issues (i.e., millage levies/school bonds and transient families) that impacted education were also consistent with the social structural perspective, in that controversial aspects were downplayed.

Limited debate in the press was given to various millage levies and school bond issues proposed to finance expansion or improvement of facilities. The press generally favored such issues; voters, however, consistently rejected these school bonds and millage levies, a situation that had not occurred for a least a quarter of a century prior to 1972.

A second issue impacting education that was infrequently noted in the paper revolved around students from transient families. The substantial contingent of highly mobile newcomers to Pine Tree County created a highly fluid student body, particularly at the high school level. One high school principal commented: "There is a hell of a turnover . . . about 30 percent are mobile, very mobile." This situation accelerated the dropout rate, increased tension in the schools, and heightened delinquency. However, sentiments among residents were that newcomers were not necessarily the "troublemakers." As one student aptly explained in a letter to the editor, "[our schools] have been swept by a wave of city kids. This has led to some dissension among the student body, yet a vast majority causing the problem [vandalism] are not city kids but those who were born and raised in the area."

News stories about government as related to population growth maintained the second–highest profile (see table 1). Ninety–four items were published on government issues during the nine–year period. Problems regarding increased taxes, soaring property valuations, and the demand for improved services (e.g., road repair and snow removal) were often aired in the paper. For example, numerous articles described the explosion of resort and retirement homes, a fact that severely inflated land values and raised property taxes. During the nine–year period, real property values more than doubled for the county and quadrupled in 16 townships. Various stories also discussed battles over road improvements and snow removal, a persistent impact of the rural residential growth. Increased use of thoroughfares, in combination with diminished state highway funds, forced townships to assume rising road–maintenance costs. Conspicuously missing from the newspaper, however, was the bitter resentment between township and county administrators concerning issues of financial assistance. In interviews with township supervisors, the hostility that existed between the townships and the county was frequently mentioned. Limited coverage of this clash by the press may mean that the editor wanted to downplay controversy. However, this is inconsistent with the paper's coverage of other governmental issues, especially zoning.

In general, stories concerning government increased as annual population growth decreased relative to the previous year (see table 1.) One possible explanation for this pattern may be that local and county government tended to react to population growth, instead of planning in advance. Given the county's history of depopulation, few would argue against such a strategy. Nonetheless, the hindsight philosophy of the policymakers severely limited their effectiveness in mitigating various negative growth impacts. For example, zoning that could have controlled much of the riverfront and lakeshore development received strong support in the press but had limited support from policymakers and residents. As one county official noted, "they think it's a Communist plot." Although the issue was first discussed and well documented in the press in 1970, the county commission delayed nine years before voting on the issue. It was ultimately defeated in 1979. The press taunted the county's inaction and highly publicized the resulting consequences, such as lots sold without proper authorization, groundwater quality problems due to overbuilt riverfront and lakeshore areas, and diminished scenic appeal because of large mobile home developments. This form of press coverage reflects more the "community watchdog" quality of the social maintenance perspective. The editor elected to debate county leaders' decisions regarding zoning and environmental issues. However, the paper's attempt to sway public opinion into an active political lobby was unsuccessful. Few ordinances were passed that were aimed at regulating growth.

Articles covering the economy as impacted by growth maintained a moderately low profile (see table 1). Economic issues mainly focused on shifts in various small manufacturing industries in the county. The editor, consistent with the social maintenance perspective, did not hesitate to take stands on various economic issues that directly opposed the views of local and county administrators. For example, the editor cautioned policymakers not to oversell tourism, urged lawmakers to reconsider zoning ordinances, and condemned county commissioners for reacting, instead of acting, on sanitary landfill and building code issues. Clearly, the editor once again used the press as "community watchdog."

Health issues centered mainly on the severe shortage of services produced by the population influx. Topics most frequently reported included the need for elderly housing, expanded social services, additional medical care personnel and facilities, and teen recreation. Interviews with key health and social service providers offered insight not found in the press regarding the magnitude and variety of impacts resulting from population growth. For example, medical staff in the county nearly doubled in the nine–year span, along with significant expansion of hospital facilities. Mental health clinic loads nearly tripled between 1970 and 1979. Three new subsidized housing complexes were built for the elderly, yet long waiting lists persisted throughout the decade. Also, the number of recipients of public assistance increased 155 percent between 1972 and 1980, a rate exceeding all other rural counties in the state. One interpretation of the coverage of health and social service issues is that the paper attempted to downplay the controversy surrounding social service needs, thereby attempting to enhance community unity. Alternatively, one might suggest that limited attention to the issue was intended to maintain the status quo.

More than one in four stories dealt with crime or public services as related to the population influx, the most prevalent among the seven categories (see table 1). The precipitous rise in criminal offenses in the county, 86 percent between 1971 and 1977, generated widespread public concern within the county. Reports of vandalism and theft were common stories reported in *The Herald* throughout the decade. Increased levels of unemployment and the large number of unoccupied seasonal homes inflated the crime rate. Similarly, the influx of youth heightened the incidence of student shoplifting to the extent that various stores barred students during lunch hours. Recreational facilities were threatened by acute levels of vandalism and malicious destruction, especially during summer months.

Stories involving crime and public services maintained the highest profile of all the population growth related stories in *The Herald* (see table 1). Their numbers closely reflected the ebb and flow of the county's population. One possible explanation for this close association is that crime and public service needs are repercussions immediately felt, thus quickly articulated in the press. On the other hand, these findings may also suggest that issues of crime and public service are topics perceived by the editor as more important than institutional impacts, a perspective consistent with the social maintenance model.

Quality–of–life items mainly revolved around the environment. Various stories illustrated how the scenic beauty of the county was diminished by the rapid and uncontrolled riverfront and lakeshore developments, as well as by the expanded number of mobile home parks. The issue of zoning ordinances frequently appeared in the press during the first part of the decade. These included greenbelt ordinances to restrict overdevelopment of riverfronts and lakeshores, snowmobiling ordinances to reduce property damage, agricultural development ordinances to limit farm losses to development, and solid waste disposal ordinances to insure groundwater quality. However, the issue of zoning was bitterly contested by local and county officials; thus, few townships adopted such ordinances.

The pattern of stories regarding quality of life throughout the period studied is intriguing. They have the highest incidence early in the decade, then systematically diminish in frequency (see table 1). One possible explanation for this pattern may be that quality-of-life concerns are the first to be resolved, but a more probable explanation is that the zeal over quality of life is only temporary and short–lived.

Location of Stories

The front–page articles regarding population change were dominated by those relating to crime or public services. In six of the nine years studied, crime or public service stories were the most prevalent news topics (see table 2). This visibility suggests that crime and public service concerns were viewed, at least by the editor, as the most important issues related to population redistribution. With front-page story lines such as "Local Merchants Seek More Police Patrols," "Crime in County Keeps up with Nation," and "City Threatens to Close Parks," the message of social disruption was clearly articulated to readers. An article concerning crime or public services appeared on the front page of almost every weekly issue of *The Herald* for the first six years covered by the study.

In contrast, letters to the editor about population growth were seldom found in *The Herald* (see table 2). Rather, institutional concerns predominated. Residents were concerned about schools, especially bond issues or millage levies for expansion of school facilities. As one resident wrote, "in the past 4 years the tax assessor has increased the valuation over 100 percent. Are we, after all these years of paying taxes, going to be forced to leave our home? We are not against the new school, but we are definitely against the size and kind that is proposed."

Table 2.
CATEGORY OF ARTICLES MOST FREQUENTLY PUBLISHED ON THE FRONT PAGE, AS A LETTER TO THE EDITOR, OR AS AN EDITORIAL IN *THE HERALD*, BY YEAR.

Year	Front Page		Editorial		Letter to the Editor	
	Number	Category	Number	Category	Number	Category
1970	40	Education (30%)	13	Economy (54%)	6	Quality of Life (83%)
1971	49	Crime (32%)	11	Quality of Life (64%)	—	—
1972	30	Government (30%)	7	Education (43%)	3	Education (67%)
1973	64	Crime (27%)	10	Quality of Life (40%)	3	Education (67%)
1974	46	Education (37%)	7	Government (29%)	7	Education (42%)
1975	53	Crime (63%)	14	Health/Social Svc. (29%)	6	Health/Soc.Svc. (83%)
1976	19	Crime (63%)	4	(No category with more than one story)	—	—
1977	31	Crime (39%)	—	—	4	Government (50%)
1978	36	Crime (22%)	6	Crime (50%)	—	—
Total	368		34		72	

Note: Number in parenthesis indicates the proportion that category represented of all other coded stories appearing in that section of the paper for that year.

Additionally, residents voiced disappointment with county and local officials for their lack of planning or protection of the area's environment and scenic beauty. For example, speaking in regard to landfill regulations, zoning, and building codes, one resident wrote: "The county should act, not react." Finally, residents' criticisms of county and local policies were apparent, as illustrated by one person who wrote: "The county should not be subsidizing year–round vacation sites for a few;" or another who commented: "The city is not applying for money to expand our recreational facilities." In sum, residents utilized the paper to express concerns, especially those regarding institutional impacts. However, this expression was limited and infrequent.

The editor, on the other hand, commonly used the editorial page as a medium for debating various viewpoints. During the first half of the 1970s, nearly one in five editorials focused on a topic relating to population change (see table 2). The economy was first targeted by the editor, who raised concerns about overselling tourism at the expense of land and recreational quality. In following years, the editor's criticism turned to quality-of-life issues. Commentaries were written prodding officials to consider the "merits of greenbelt zoning," an ordinance that would restrict lakeshore and riverfront development. Subsequent to the passage of some zoning legislation along with funding measures for a new senior citizen facility and low–income housing projects, the editor praised the "progressive leadership" of local officials. Later in the decade, the editor focused more on issues relating to health and social services, government, and crime. In general, the broad array of controversial issues that were targeted in editorials suggested the editor assumed a "watchdog" role. However, editorial commentaries concerning residential change were infrequently seen during the latter half of the decade.

Summary and Conclusion

This study explored the transmission of information via the local press regarding the consequences of inmigration. My analysis of Pine Tree County suggests that the rural weekly newspaper provides a reasonably detailed account of institutional impacts, as well as of broader quality–of–life concerns, and shifting public service demands as related to population influx. Although little information was provided regarding the actual amount of residential growth, the editor addressed a surprisingly full array of impact concerns.

Issues that received most attention in the press seemed to be those with the most visible consequences. For example, crime received most notoriety in *The Herald*, both in total number of stories printed and in the amount of front page coverage. Additionally, institutional impacts that were most easily noticed also gained more press. Consequences of growth for the school system, such as chronic overcrowding and curtailments of various programs and course offerings, were frequently mentioned in the paper. In contrast, the impact of residential growth on social services was infrequently mentioned.

Controversy was not avoided in *The Herald*, contrary to expectations. The literature suggests that rural papers tend to downplay conflictual issues in an attempt to promote social cohesion. Results from this case study did not support that claim. The editor, for example, frequently played the watchdog role by challenging various policies and stances made by local or county officials. Nearly one in five editorials addressed an issue related to population change, many critical of the inaction of leaders or their policy directions. Ironically, limited coverage of the animosity between county and township governments surfaced in the press.

Residents, on the other hand, seldom used the press as a forum for their opinions. Only a handful of letters to the editor concerned population change. Of those, the majority focused on institutional concerns, especially education.

My research poses an intriguing question. While *The Herald* provided readers with a fairly accurate account of demographic changes occurring in the county, interviews with residents and policymakers indicated that many were unaware that a substantial increase in population had occurred. When asked, county residents typically underestimated the magnitude of residential growth, even though they were cognizant of the county's increasing size. Even many county officials perceived the expansion to be only modest and of no great significance. In contrast, township administrators viewed the influx as substantial. The differing perceptions of these two groups fostered clashes and delays in planning, conditions that underscore the need for a more comprehensive understanding of how information is diffused within rural social systems. The consequences of this lack of recognition are best illustrated in the scenic and environmental problems the county faced as a result of inadequate planning.

The question that still remains is why residents and officials underestimated their county's expansion. Perhaps the information provided by the paper was viewed as parochial or biased. Or maybe the issue was simply not viewed as important. This area of uncertainty has important implications for those who use the rural press as a vehicle for community development. For example, what information is most effectively relayed through the rural press and what topics should be communicated via an alternative medium?

The two theoretical perspectives used to guide this research offer important insight. Evidence from this case study suggests that different forces are at work that impact the quality of information relayed via the rural press, and these forces are topic specific. For example, reports of institutional issues seemed to follow a social structural perspective by avoiding controversy and promoting support for the institutions. In contrast, issues regarding general community affairs were presented in a manner more in line with a social maintenance perspective. The paper assumed a "community watchdog" role and tended to debate policy decisions of local and county leaders.

The degree to which these findings reflect a general pattern assumed by the rural press may indicate the degree to which rural residents and policymakers are adequately informed about consequences regarding population dynamics. Policymakers in rural areas may not be acting from a broad information base and may be delaying community preparations for emerging structural problems. This would be especially true regarding social institutional issues. Ironically, the informational deficit would not be due to a lack of exposure to appropriate news. Rather, the lack of necessary insight would be a function of the manner in which the information is relayed via the press. The challenge that researchers face, therefore, is to determine the accuracy of the base of information that rural policymakers use and to decide how this base can be improved.

Notes

1. This chapter is part of a larger study of Pine Tree County. Previous analyses focused on the impact of residential growth on the county's social institutions. One article entitled, "The Impact of Growth on a Rural Michigan County," appeared in the September–October, 1984 issue of *Small Town*. A related article, entitled, "The Consequences of Population Growth for Pine Tree County, Michigan," is a chapter in *Research in Rural Sociology and Development*, vol. 2, Harry K. Schwarzweller and Frank Fear, eds. (Greenwich, Conn.: JAI Press, 1985).

References

Beale, Calvin L. 1976. A further look at nonmetropolitan population growth since 1970. *American Journal of Agricultural Economics* 58(5): 953–58.

Beale, Calvin L., and Glenn V. Fuguitt. 1986. Changing patterns of nonmetropolitan population distribution. Paper presented at the annual meeting of the Association of American Geographers. May, 1986, Minneapolis, Minn.

Donohue, George A., C. N. Olien, and Philip J. Tichenor. 1985. Leader and editor views of role of press in community development. *Journalism Quarterly* 62(2): 367–72.

Edelstein, Alex, and J. Blaine Schultz. 1964. The leadership role of the weekly newspaper as seen by community leaders: A sociological perspective. In *People, Society and Mass Communications*, ed. Lewis A. Dexter and Davis M. White. New York: Macmillan.

Engels, Richard A. 1986. The metropolitan/nonmetropolitan population at mid–decade. Paper presented at the annual meeting of the Population Association of America. April 1986, San Francisco.

Frankena, Frederick. 1980. *Community impacts of rapid growth in nonmetropolitan areas*. Rural Sociology Series No. 9, Department of Sociology, Michigan State University, East Lansing.

Fry, Donald, and Thomas A. McCain. 1983. Community influences media dependence in dealing with controversial local issue. *Journalism Quarterly* 60(3): 458–63.

Greenberg, Bradley S. 1964. Person–to–person communication in the diffusion of news events. *Journalism Quarterly* 41: 489–94.

Hynds, Ernest C., and Charles H. Martin. 1979. How non–daily editors describe status and function of editorial pages. *Journalism Quarterly* 56(2): 318–23.

Janowitz, Morris. 1952. *The Community Press in an Urban Setting*. New York: Macmillan.

Johnson, Kenneth M. 1987. Population redistribution trends in nonmetropolitan America. Paper presented at the annual meeting of the Rural Sociological Society. August 1987, Madison, Wisc.

Long, Larry, and Diana DeAre. 1982. Repopulating the countryside: A 1980 census trend. *Science* 217(4565): 1111–15.

McCarthy, Kevin F., and Peter A. Morrison. 1978. *The changing demographic and economic structure of nonmetropolitan areas in the 1970s*. Santa Monica, Calif.: Rand Corporation.

Paletz, David, Peggy Reichert, and Barbara McIntyre. 1971. How the media support local government authority. *Public Opinion Quarterly* 35: 80–92.

Shaw, Eugene F., and Daniel Riffe. 1979. Newspaper reading in two towns. *Journalism Quarterly* 36(3): 477–87.

Sofranko, Andrew J., and James D. Williams, eds. 1980. *Rebirth of rural America: Rural migration in the midwest*. Ames: North Central Regional Center for Rural Development, Iowa State University.

Stone, Gerald, and Janet Morrison. 1976. Content as a key to the purpose of community newspapers. *Journalism Quarterly* 53(autumn): 494–98.

Tichenor, Philip J., George A. Donohue, and Clarice N. Olien. 1980. *Community Conflict and the Press*. Beverly Hills, Calif.: Sage Publications.

Tichenor, Philip J., Clarice N. Olien, and George A. Donohue. 1987. Effect of use of metro dailies on knowledge gap in small towns. *Journalism Quarterly* 64(2–3): 329–36.

Voss, Paul R., and Glenn V. Fuguitt. 1979. *Turnaround migration in the Upper Great Lakes Region.* Population Series 70–12, Applied Population Laboratory, Madison, Wisc.: University of Wisconsin–Extension.

9

FATAL FARM ACCIDENTS IN MICHIGAN: IMPLICATIONS FOR RESEARCH AND POLICY[1]

Nan E. Johnson

Introduction

Farming, along with mining, construction, and transportation, is one of the deadliest occupations in the United States (see Baker et al., 1992; Bernhardt and Langley 1992; Heyer et al., 1992; Wilk 1993). Therefore, the U.S. Public Health Service (USPHS 1991) has called for a reduction in fatal farm accidents from an average of 14 such deaths per 100,000 farmworkers in 1983-87 to no more than 9.5 per 100,000 farmworkers by the Year 2000.

From our view, accidents are never haphazard events but are outcomes of risky behaviors. Social pressures recruit the risk takers by rewarding certain people (e.g., males in special age groups) for physical bravery or by hindering their capacities to make less dangerous choices (e.g., through a financial inability to buy farm equipment with safety devices). Using this perspective, we review recent literature on fatal farm injuries in the U.S. and then use it as a guide to analyze death certificates registered from 1989-91 in Michigan. Three socially constructed risk factors emphasized below are gender, ages too young or too old to be in the labor force, and status within the farm labor force (farm operators or managers vs. other farm laborers). In the last section, we use the results to recommend public-health policies and future studies promoting farm safety.

Background

Between 1930-80, the death rate from farm machinery jumped 44 percent in the U.S. while that from nonfarm machinery fell by 79 percent (Baker et al., 1992, 128). Thus, in 1981, the National Safety Council (NSC) began a year-long survey of fatal and nonfatal farm accidents with

31 states participating voluntarily. The report showed that the stereotypical victims of farm accidents were males who suffered cuts, fractures, or sprains during farm chores (NSC, 1982). Few injuries were fatal (0.6 percent), but most (65 percent) were severe because of the time needed off from work to recover. Yet the study may have painted an obsolete picture because it was conducted 15 years ago.

More recent studies on farm safety have focused on specific states and have taken two approaches. One approach, exemplified by Bernhardt and Langley's (1992) work in North Carolina, has described the identities of those killed in farm accidents and detailed the nature of their injuries. To these ends, Bernhardt and Langley (1992) obtained a computer printout of certificates of deaths occurring in 1984-88 whereon the cause was listed as an injury sustained on a "farm and surrounds" or from an agricultural machine. It concentrated on 123 deaths to farmers injured in farmwork. The Reports of the Investigation of the Medical Examiner (RIME) were used to clarify the means of death.[2] The availability of two differently phrased questions on the occupation of the decedents (from the RIME and from the Medical Examiner's (ME's) certificates of death) provided Bernhardt and Langley with a way of deciding whether the decedents had been full-time or part-time farmers.

All accident victims were males, and 35 percent were categorized as part-time farmers. Yet regardless of part-time or full-time status, the majority were injured by machines (mainly tractors) which caused them to die at the scene of the accident. The deaths disproportionately befell farmers who were black and/or elderly, groups tending to have lower incomes. Hence, the findings implied that the victims may have been using old tractors that they could not afford to retrofit with the new Roll-Over Protective Structures (ROPS).

Dunn and Runyan (1993) reviewed the RIME data from North Carolina on all on-the-job fatalities to a younger group of farmworkers: those under age 20. A motorized vehicle caused 36 of the 71 deaths, and 15 vehicles were tractors. Thus, tractors contributed unevenly to fatalities among children and youths working on farms in North Carolina. In contrast with older farmers (Bernhardt and Langley, 1992), these young farmworkers may have faced the additional risk of inexperience in operating tractors.

Tractors injured half the patients dying after admission to a Wisconsin referral trauma center (Cogbill et al., 1991), and most of the decedents were aged 65+. Farm animals caused no deaths but traumatically injured more patients than tractors did, although the means of injury varied by age. Children aged 16 or less were more often hurt in falls from horses; adults, more often from animal assaults. These hospital cases could not

Figure 1. The crush–proof posts supporting the roof of this tractor will shield the driver in case of a roll–over. (Photo by Nan E. Johnson)

represent all severe farm injuries since they omitted deaths at the scene of the accident. But consistently with the two studies in North Carolina, the Wisconsin study stressed the need to include children and elders in analyses of severe farm injuries.

Because the prominence of tractors in such injuries has been shown above, it is noteworthy that run-overs occur typically when passengers fall off a tractor, and children are more often passengers than drivers of farm machinery. For example, Stallones's (1989) study of fatal farm accidents among children in Kentucky found that run-overs were more threatening than roll-overs by tractors. Also, girls died more often than boys from accidents due to farm machines and farm animals; boys more often than girls from the discharge of firearms. Hence, gender is important in placing children (and adults) in different environments of physical risk on the farm.

The second category of farm-safety study has looked exclusively at non-lethal farm injuries, since prevention of these more common farm mishaps can reduce both fatalities and disabilities. The only study of on-farm injuries in Michigan in the past decade was conducted in Sanilac and Tuscola counties in the "thumb" of the Lower Peninsula. It reaffirmed findings from North Carolina, Wisconsin, and Kentucky on the great risks posed by agricultural machines and farm animals (Michigan Department of Public Health (MDPH), 1989). The Michigan study showed that the main sources of wounds to the 114 people injured in 1987 on the farms in this analysis were farm animals (12.3 percent) or farm machines other than tractors (27.2 percent). The relative absence of tractors may have reflected the nonfatal nature of all the mishaps. The injured did not differ much by age but were overwhelmingly male (92.1 percent). About 75 percent of the injuries were suffered by members of the farm family; and the other 25 percent, by hired laborers, who nonetheless comprised just 13.4 percent of the work force. This study did not explore the reasons why hired laborers were injured disproportionately often, but one may be that farm operators substituted the time they would have spent operating heavy farm equipment or handling animals by hiring laborers to perform these risky tasks.

In some cases, the substitution might replace the farm proprietor's own farmwork completely enough to allow him/her to hold a nonfarm occupation. Since nonfarm job opportunities are generally greater in metropolitan (metro) counties, one might expect more hired laborers per farm and thus higher rates of fatal and nonfatal farmwork injuries on farms in metro than in nonmetro counties.[3] The study of Sanilac and Tuscola counties in Michigan could not explore these possibilities since both counties are nonmetro. Hence, the current study will use data from death certificates and agricultural and population censuses collected in Michigan to contrast the rate of *lethal* accidents on nonmetro vs. metro farms in both non-work-related and occupational contexts.

Data and Methods

In Michigan, the physician who pronounces a body dead must certify all relevant medical causes. The Michigan death certificate contains four lines for sequential medical causes, starting with the immediate medical cause of death (line 1) and working backwards to the underlying cause (UC) which triggered the whole chain of moribund events (line 2, 3, or 4, according to the medical complexity of the case). If the UC was an injury, then it must be declared an accident, suicide, or homicide. From the International Classification of Diseases, Injuries, and Causes of Death, Ninth Revision (ICD9), implemented by the World Health Organization (1977) in January, 1979, these three respective sources of injury on the Michigan death certificate were coded as E800.0-E949.9, E950.0-E959, and E960.0-E978. The ranges allowed for details on how the accident, suicide, or homicide/legal intervention took place. Only a few deaths were from an "injury undetermined whether accidentally or purposely inflicted" (E980.0-E989).

In addition, the place of the occurrence of the injury was classified on the Michigan death certificate as a: farm, home, street, factory, office building, or other. The present analysis is based on all death certificates for those who were pronounced dead in Michigan in 1989-91 and whose deaths were precipitated by an injury from an accident on a farm (N=73). This broad rule includes accidental deaths despite the age, sex, or usual occupation of the decedent or the work/leisure context of the mishap on the farm.

The relationship of the injury on the farm to the job of farming was determined from two items on the death certificate. One item was whether the injury occurred at work (answered "yes" or "no" by the certifying physician). The other item was the usual occupation, the "kind of work done during most of [the decedent's] working life." Only one usual occupation is allowed to be reported, and "retiree" is not a permissible response. We defined a "part-time farmer" as anyone whose death was reported to be from an accident during farmwork but whose usual occupation was in the nonfarm sector.[4] Also, we labeled a "part-time farmer" as anyone whose usual occupation was in farming but whose death resulted from a farmwork injury at ages 75 or older. Since the death certificate does not specify whether an elderly farmer killed in the line of duty was already retired and thus farming only part-time, we chose 75 as the arbitrary cut-off age for retirement. All others who reportedly died from a farmwork injury (i.e., decedents under age 75 whose usual occupation during most of the worklife was in farming) were termed "other farmers."[5] These conservative rules must have undercounted fatal occupational injuries to part-time farmers: the one elderly farmer who died performing farm chores at an age between 65-74 years may have already retired, and the other 10 younger farmers not classified as "part-timers" may have received some wages from the nonfarm sector (table 1).

Findings

Who Died Accidentally and How

Between 1989-91, 73 people died in Michigan from farm accidents. Forty-eight (calculable from table 1) of these accident victims were *not* wounded at work, since farms are places of residence and recreation, as well. Because males are more likely than females and young children are more likely than adults to venture physical risks, it is not surprising that 12 of the 48 non-occupational fatalities were children under age 16; and 38 of the 48 were males (table 1). The most common causes of deaths were agricultural machines (N = 16) even outside the context of farmwork; but other causes were drownings (N = 4), firearms (N = 4), a plane crash (N

Table 1.
WHO DIED IN MICHIGAN FROM ALL ACCIDENTS ON FARMS AND FROM WORK-RELATED FARM ACCIDENTS IN 1989-91.

			Work-Related Accidents (N=25)			
	All (N=73)		Part-Time Farmers (N=14)		Other Farmers (N=11)	
Characteristic	N	%	N	%	N	%
Race						
White	72	98.6	14	100	11	100
Other	1	1.4	0	0	0	0
Sex						
Males	61	83.6	12	85.7	11	100
Females	12	16.4	2	14.3	0	0
Ave. Age (yrs)	42.4	NA	49.2	NA	44.6	NA
< 16	12	16.4	0	0	0	0
16-64	47	64.4	9	64.3	10	90.9
65-74	7	9.6	2	14.3	1	9.1
75+	7	9.6	3	21.4	0	0
Ave. Education (yrs.)	10.1	NA	11.1	NA	10.9	NA
Marital Status						
Single	26	35.6	5	35.7	4	36.4
Married	40	54.8	4	28.6	7	63.6
Widowed	2	2.7	2	14.3	0	0
Divorced	5	6.8	3	21.4	0	0
State of residence						
Michigan	68	93.2	13	92.9	11	100
Other	5	6.8	1	7.1	0	0
Michigan Co. of injury:						
Metro	39	53.4	7	50.0	7	63.6
Nonmetro	32	43.8	7	50.0	4	36.4

Note: Percentages may not sum to 100 due to rounding error. Computations for each variable are based on 73 cases, except for education, which is based on 72 cases with valid scores, and county of injury, which excludes two injuries occurring on farms outside Michigan.

= 3), animal assaults (N = 3), and falls (N = 5; table 2). Those who died from drowning or interacting with animals were much younger on average than the other farm accident victims. As such, if studies of farm safety are confined to on-the-job accidents to people of labor-force ages (16-64), they will miss most of the fatal accidents and many machine accidents on Michigan farms today.

The majority (=14) of the 25 people fatally injured in the line of farm duty were part-time farmers (table 1). This outcome contradicts the results of the study in North Carolina, where a majority of on-the-job fatalities occurred to full-time farmers (Bernhardt and Langley 1992).

Location of the farm also mattered, as the number of, and the annualized rate of, all fatal work accidents on Michigan farms were somewhat higher in metro than in nonmetro counties (table 3, lines 12 and 13).[6] At first glance, it is puzzling why metro farms would pose somewhat more dangers, especially to those working: census figures show that metro farms averaged 58 fewer acres as compared to nonmetro farms (table 3, line 3). However, note that farm workers and related farm employees outnumbered farm operators and managers by a factor of more than 2:1 on metro farms while farm operators and managers outnumbered other farm employees on nonmetro farms (table 3, cf. lines 5 and 6). Hired farmworkers may confront greater risks than farm owners or managers if the former are hired to replace the latter as machine drivers or animal caretakers. The tendency of laborers to do farmwork seasonally may be one reason why most of the people killed in the line of agricultural duties farmed only part-time.

Twenty of the 25 fatal farmwork injuries were inflicted by agricultural machinery (ICD9 code E919.0)(table 2). Tractors caused 12 of these 20 deaths. In addition, the power take-off, tiller, and cornpicker proved fatal to three part-time farmers. A fall into an auger (3) or by a hay elevator (1) claimed the lives of four other farmers, who may have been farming full-time (table 4). The traumatic injury inflicted by heavy farm equipment may explain why 18 of the 25 people injured in farmwork died instantly or within a few minutes at the scene of the accident.

When They Died

Because the most common sources of terminal injuries were met in outdoor activities on farms, such deaths showed monthly patterns (table 5). There were no fatal accidents on a farm in January, the coldest month in Michigan. Congruently with the earlier study of nonlethal farm injuries in the state (MDPH 1989), about one-third of the deadly farm injuries occurred in the summer months of June - August. This seasonal pattern

Table 2.
CAUSES OF DEATH, MEAN AGE, AND NUMBERS OF FATALITIES ON FARMS BY WORK STATUS.

Cause of Accident	All Deaths		Work-Related Deaths			
			Part-time Farmers		Other Farmers	
	Mean Age	N	Mean Age	N	Mean Age	N
Motor Vehicle, nontraffic	15.0	1				
Fall from horse	36.0	1				
Plane crash	48.0	3				
Vehicle, not otherwise stated	10.0	1				
Poisoning, other than by drugs	42.5	2				
Fall, other than from horse	51.6	7	41.0	2	23.0	1
Hypothermia	53.5	2				
Animal assault	38.0	3				
Drowning	37.0	4				
Struck by falling obj.	52.6	7			40.0	1
Agricultural machine	41.2	36	51.8	11	47.6	9
Mining/earth drilling machine	50.0	1				
Firearm	40.8	4				
Electrocution	19.0	1	19.0	1		
Total	42.4	73	49.2	14	44.6	11

Note: For categories with only 1 case, the age is not a mean but that of the victim.

Table 3.
CHARACTERISTICS OF FARMS IN MICHIGAN BY TYPE OF COUNTY.

Characteristic	Metro	Nonmetro
1. No. of farms [a]	26,542	24,630
2. No. acres in farmland [a]	4,606,769	5,710,092
3. Ave. no. acres/farm (Line 2 ÷ Line 1)	173.57	231.83
4. Total no. employed persons aged 16+ in farm occupations (Line 5 + Line 6):	34,884	26,473
5. Farm operators and farm managers [b]	10,358	13,352
6. Farm workers and related occupations [b]	24,526	13,121
7. Ave. no. employed persons aged 16+ in farm occupations per farm (Line 4 ÷ Line 1)	1.31	1.07
8. Ave. no. farm operators or managers/farm (Line 5 ÷ Line 1)	0.39	0.54
9. Ave. no. farm & related workers/farm (Line 6 ÷ Line 1)	0.92	0.53
10. Number of all fatal accidents on Michigan farms, 1989-91 [c]	39	32
11. Annualized rate of all fatal accidents on Michigan farms per 10,000 farms ((Line 10 ÷ Line 1) ÷ 3) X 10,000)	4.90	4.33
12. Number of fatal work accidents on Michigan farms, 1989-91	14	11
13. Annualized rate of fatal work accidents on Michigan farms per 10,000 farms (((Line 12 ÷ Line 1) ÷ 3) X 10,000)	1.76	1.49
14. Annualized rate of farmwork fatalities per 100,000 members of farmwork force (((Line 12 ÷ Line 4) ÷ 3) X 100,000)	13.38	13.85

[a] From the 1987 Census of Agriculture, Michigan, Table 10.
[b] From the 1990 Census of Population. Social and Economic Characteristics. Michigan. Section 1 of 2, Table 39.
[c] Of the 73 farm-accident victims pronounced dead in Michigan, two had suffered their non-work-related farm accidents in Ohio.

Table 4.
FATAL ACCIDENTS CAUSED ON FARMS BY AGRICULTURAL MACHINES (ICD9 E919.0) AND BY WORK STATUS.

Type of Machine	All Deaths	Work-Related Deaths	
		Part-time Farmer	Other Farmer
Tractor roll-over on the ground	11	5	1
Tractor roll-over into pool/ditch	2	1	1
Tractor run-over	1	1	0
Tractor crushed victim vs. sprayer.	1	0	1
Tractor, other crushing	4	1	1
Tractor, unspec. mode	1	0	0
Run over by:			
farm wagon	2	0	0
farm truck	1	0	0
farm trailer	1	0	0
Fall into auger at:			
feed wagon	1	0	1
grain elevator	1	0	1
silo	1	0	1
Fall into combine	1	0	0
Power take-off	2	1	0
Fall by hay elevator	1	0	1
Tilling machine, entrapment	1	1	0
Cornpicker, entanglement	1	1	0
Machine unspecified	3	0	1
Total	36	11	9

was more pronounced for part-time farmers, 64 percent of whom were killed in the summer months (table 5).

If the daily pattern of farm - accident deaths were random, about one-seventh (14.29 percent) of all such deaths should happen each day of the week. Consequently, the strikingly lower proportion of work-related deaths to part-time and other farmers on Sunday may reflect the traditional taboo against working on the Christian Sabbath (7 percent and 9 percent, respectively, table 5). One fifth of all the deaths happened on Monday. Maybe a jump in both work-related and other activities on a farm on Monday increased the odds of a fatal accident.

Table 5.
TIMING OF DEATHS IN MICHIGAN FROM FARM ACCIDENTS, BY WORK STATUS.

| | All Cases (N=73) | | Work-Related Deaths (N=25) | | | |
| | | | Part-Time Farmers (N=14) | | Other Farmers (N=11) | |
Time Unit	N	%	N	%	N	%
Year: 1989	25	34	4	29	2	18
1990	26	36	4	29	3	27
1991	22	30	6	43	6	55
Mo.: Jan.	0	0	0	0	0	0
Feb.	3	4	0	0	2	18
Mar.	4	5	0	0	0	0
Apr.	7	10	1	7	2	18
May	7	10	1	7	1	9
Jun.	9	12	5	36	1	9
Jul.	11	15	3	21	2	18
Aug.	5	7	1	7	0	0
Sep.	4	5	0	0	2	18
Oct.	7	10	2	14	1	9
Nov.	12	16	1	7	0	0
Dec.	4	5	0	0	0	0
Day: Mon.	15	20	5	36	0	0
Tue.	12	16	3	21	3	27
Wed.	10	14	1	7	2	18
Thu.	10	14	3	21	2	18
Fri.	10	14	0	0	1	9
Sat.	7	10	1	7	2	18
Sun.	9	12	1	7	1	9

Note: Percentages may not sum to 100 due to rounding error.

A small annual number of cases and a short, three-year period make it hard to discern a trend in accidental farm deaths. However, it is worth remarking that the number of farmwork-related deaths was greatest in the most recent of the three years (table 5). If this signifies a trendlet, it is consistent with the secular rise in U. S. deaths from farm machinery between 1930-80 (Baker et al., 1992).

Discussion

Because farming is one of the most hazardous jobs in the U. S., this study analyzed death certificates registered in 1989-91 on persons who were injured in an accident on a farm and declared dead in the State of Michigan. Michigan is an especially appropriate study site due to the importance of agriculture in the state's economy.[7] However, most of the fatal accidents on a farm did *not* wound people in the course of farm chores, for farms are residences and playgrounds, as well as work sites.

Contrary to the results from North Carolina (Bernhardt and Langley 1992), part-time farmers outnumbered others killed in the line of farm duty in Michigan. The somewhat higher rate of work-related fatalities on metro than nonmetro farms in Michigan was associated with differences in the social structure of agriculture. Metro farms were more likely to be worked by those who did not operate or manage a farm, and this category of farmworker had the highest rate of labor accidents (Michigan Department of Public Health 1989). Nevertheless, if the fatality rate for all categories of farmworkers is to be lowered to the goal of 9.5 deaths annually per 100,000 farmworkers (set by the U. S. Public Health Service for the Year 2000), both metro and nonmetro farms in Michigan have a long way to go (annualized rates for 1989-91 were 13.38 and 13.85, respectively; table 3).

The modal cause of fatal accidents to part-time farmers in the current study was a tractor roll-over. The Occupational Safety and Health Administration (OSHA) requires farmers to upgrade their old tractors with Roll-Over Protective Structures (ROPS) if at least 11 people receive income from work on the land. This rule now applies to fewer than 5 percent of U. S. farms (Purschwitz and Field 1990: 179); and in Michigan, there is an average of fewer than two farm-wage recipients per farm (table 3). For these reasons, fewer than half of the 4.6 million tractors in use in the U. S. today have ROPS (Centers for Disease Control and Prevention 1993, 57). As a remedy, a special grant program might be initiated by a major foundation (e.g., the U. S. Farm Bureau) or a subsidy program by the U. S. Department of Agriculture to help farms with small workforces to retrofit tractors with ROPS. In addition, the OSHA rule could be tightened to include farms with fewer than 11 employees. Inspections to monitor compliance with the OSHA rule should take place before the summer months of June - August, when two-thirds of the part-time farmers were killed in the course of farm duties (table 5).

Several limitations of the present research are shared by other analyses of U. S. death certificates on fatal farm accidents (e.g., Bernhardt and Langley 1992). For example, there was probably an undercount of farms as places of injury in Michigan. In several cases, the hand-written answer to the place-of-injury item on the death certificate was "field," "barnyard," or "woodlot;" but it was not coded as a "farm" on the computer-readable file since it was unclear whether this physical space was part of an operation yielding agricultural income (it could have been only a residence). In addition, the place-of-injury item on the Michigan death certificate offers "home" and "farm" as discrete choices; but these are not mutually exclusive if farmers live on the farm they operate (over 80 percent of Michigan farmers do). The tendency in such cases to prefer "home" over "farm" was probably stronger if the sale of agricultural products from the land was not the principal means of the residents' support. In addition, the item on the "usual occupation" during most of the decedent's working life may not reflect his/her current occupation at the time of death if he/she had switched from full-time to part-time farming shortly before the fatal farm accident. But these problems would invite an undercount of those killed while farming on a part-time basis on the day of the fatal farm injury. Stated otherwise, these diverse sources of error inherent to the format of the death certificate make it plausible that this study of recent death certificates in Michigan underestimated the prominence of part-time farming in fatal occupational injuries in agriculture.

One reader pointed out that studies based on death certificates overcount the number of deaths from "accidents" as the underlying cause (UC). For example, to avoid embarrassing the close relatives of decedents, physicians certifying the underlying cause of death on the death certificates may choose to call some deadly farm injuries "accidents" even when these disasters look suspiciously suicidal. Referral of the case by the family physician to a Medical Examiner (ME) as the certifier-of-last-resort cannot defeat this source of bias in overstating accidents (Copeland 1995) and thus must compromise the validity of any research on farm "accidents" based on reports by MEs (e.g., Bernhardt and Langley 1992; Dunn and Runyan 1993). Despite this fact, the upward bias introduced into counts of farm "accidents" should be more serious in nonmetro than metro counties of Michigan, since the rate of suicide is higher in sparsely populated areas of the state and since the greater visibility of death in small communities creates pressures to minimize shame to the next-of-kin (Houser and Beegle 1951; Schroeder and Beegle 1953; Dennis 1967). As such, the somewhat lower reported rate of fatal farm accidents observed for nonmetro than metro counties in the current study (4.33 vs. 4.90 per 10,000 farms) is not likely to be an artifact of poor data.

The results of this analysis point to several lines for further inquiry. Future work might clarify whether severe injuries or deaths are more common in certain farm commodity systems than in others or are related to the scale of farming. The Sanilac-Tuscola study in Michigan found that the number of nonlethal work injuries was directly related to the number of acres on field-crop farms but not on dairy farms (Michigan Department of Public Health 1989). Rather, permanently disabling or deadly injuries may be more closely associated with the size of animal herds on dairy farms; but answers to that question must await future investigation. Also, the present analysis could not discriminate between deaths to farm operators/managers vs. farm laborers. But if future research can make this distinction, it will refine our understanding of how the social structure of agriculture creates differential environments of risk on farms.

Notes

1. George Van Amburg, State Registrar, Michigan Department of Community Health, granted access to microfilmed copies of the Michigan death certificates analyzed in this chapter. Glenn Copeland and Kathy Humphries provided valuable discussions about the methods used by MDCH to collect and record these death certificates into computer-readable format. Drafts of this report were presented at the 1994 annual meetings of the Southern Demographic Association and the 1996 annual meetings of the Rural Sociological Society. Janet Bokemeier, Bruce Christenson, Glenn Copeland, Kenneth Kochanek, Felicia Le Clere, Diane McLaughlin, Brendan Mullan, and Denise Reiling constructively commented on earlier drafts. This research was funded by grants from the Michigan Agricultural Experiment Station (#3350), the All-University Research Initiation support (#61-6663), and the Institute for Public Policy and Social Research (#34229).
2. North Carolina requires that unattended or violent deaths be investigated and certified through the State Medical Examiner System.
3. The U. S. Census Bureau classifies a county as metropolitan if it contains a city of at least 50,000 residents or is economically integrated with such a county (as shown by employment and commuting patterns). A nonmetropolitan county is one not classifiable as metropolitan.
4. By application of these rules, "part-time farmers" included a 65-year-old man for whom two usual occupations (one farm and one nonfarm) were listed (against the rules of death certification) and a housewife and two adult students who died while reportedly doing farmwork.
5. The label "full-time farmers" was avoided because the simultaneous existence of their own nonfarm earnings could not be determined from these death certificates, which allowed mention of only one usual pre-mortem occupation.
6. The 1987 Census of Agriculture in Michigan enumerated 51,172 farms. Thus, the average annual accidental death rate due to farm injuries was 4.75 per 10,000 farms.
7. Agriculture is second only to automotive manufacture as a source of state revenue.

References

Baker, Susan P., Brian O'Neill, Marvin J. Ginsburg, and Guohua Li. 1992. *The injury fact book.* New York: Oxford University Press, second edition.

Bernhardt, Judy Hays, and Ricky L. Langley. 1992. Accidental occupational farm fatalities in North Carolina: 1984 to 1988. *Journal of Rural Health* 8(1): 60-69.

Centers for Disease Control and Prevention. 1993. Public health focus: Effectiveness of rollover protective structures for preventing injuries associated with agricultural tractors. *Morbidity and Mortality Weekly Report* 42(3): 57-59.

Cogbill, Thomas H., Eric S. Steenlage, Jeffrey Landercasper, and Pamela J. Strutt. 1991. Death and disability from agricultural injuries in Wisconsin: A 12-year experience with 739 patients. *The Journal of Trauma* 31(12): 1632-7.

Copeland, Glenn, Assistant State Registrar at the Michigan Department of Community Health. 1995. Personal interview with author on May 2.

Dennis, Ruth. 1967. Suicide differentials in Michigan: A replication. Unpublished Master's thesis. East Lansing: Department of Sociology, Michigan State University.

Dunn, Kathleen A., and Carol W. Runyan. 1993. Deaths at work among children and adolescents. *American Journal of Diseases of Children* 147(Oct.): 1044-6.

Heyer, Nicholas J., Gary Franklin, Frederick P. Rivara, Paul Parker, and Joanna A. Haug. 1992. Occupational injuries among minors doing farmwork in Washington State: 1986 to 1989. *American Journal of Public Health* 82(4): 557-60.

Houser, Paul M., and J. Allan Beegle. 1951. Mortality differentials in Michigan. East Lansing: *Michigan Agricultural Experiment Station Bulletin* #367.

Michigan Department of Public Health. 1989. *Farm injury surveillance in Michigan: The 1987 Sanilac-Tuscola Project.* Lansing.

National Safety Council. 1982. *Farm accident safety report.* Chicago.

Purschwitz, Mark A., and William E. Field. 1990. Scope and magnitude of injuries in the agricultural workplace. *American Journal of Industrial Medicine* 18: 179-92.

Schroeder, W. Widick, and J. Allan Beegle. 1953. Suicide: An instance of high rural rates. *Rural Sociology* 18 (Mar.): 45-52.

Stallones, Lorann. 1989. Fatal unintentional injuries among Kentucky farm children: 1979 to 1985. *The Journal of Rural Health* 5(3): 246-56.

U.S. Bureau of the Census. 1989. *1987 Census of Agriculture. Volume 1, Geographic Area Series. Part 22, Michigan: State and County Data.* Washington, D.C.: U.S. Government Printing Office.

U.S. Public Health Service. 1991. *Healthy People 2000.* Washington, D.C.: U.S. Government Printing Office. DHHS publication number (PHS) 91-50212.

Wilk, Valerie A. 1993. Health hazards to children in agriculture. *American Journal of Industrial Medicine* 24: 283-90.

World Health Organization. 1977. *Manual of the International Statistical Classification of Diseases, Injuries, and Causes of Death, based on recommendations of the Ninth Revision Conference, 1975.* Geneva: World Health Organization.

10

IRISH RURAL–URBAN MIGRATION: POST-1960 CHANGES

Damian F. Hannan

Introduction

In the 1960s, Ireland's economic growth recovered from a serious 1950s recession. Nevertheless, there continued to be substantial rural–to–urban migration, which had started in the midnineteenth century (Kennedy 1973). Since Irish industrial and urban growth was very sluggish, most rural–to–urban migrants emigrated. However, economic recovery had started, so that from the mid–1960s onward, cumulating economic growth led gradually to national population growth, with rapidly declining emigration rates (Kennedy 1975; Bacon, Durkan, and O'Leary 1982). Even in this early period of economic recovery, however, significant rural–urban migration was still occurring—though increasingly within Ireland itself. Economic growth accelerated during the 1970s, however, so that most rural districts started to grow in population—some very rapidly, as the industrial world trend toward "nonmetropolitan population turnaround" began to affect Ireland (Johansen and Fuguitt 1984).

Hannan's (1970) 1965–68 study of migration decisionmaking by rural youth from one of the poorest and least industrialized counties in a time of very high outmigration provides a baseline from which to examine changes in migration patterns over the following 20 years. Part of the fuel for rapid economic growth in Ireland in these two decades was large-scale deficit spending, geared to counteract the worst effects of the 1974 and 1979 oil crises (Conniffe and Kennedy 1985). As a result of general European recessionary trends, as well as severe cutbacks in government expenditures to correct the spiraling borrowing requirement, the Irish economy suffered from very severe recessionary trends over the 1980s. As a result, high levels of unemployment and emigration again became characteristic of Ireland—strongly reminiscent of the severe 1950s recessionary period.

A comparative restudy of rural–urban migration in the mid–1980s from the most remote and least industrialized counties would, therefore, be especially valuable. It would particularly illuminate the extent to which migration decisionmaking and the resultant clear social differentials in migration propensity observed in the 1960s show an equally *clear pattern* in the 1980s. Given the extent of economic and social change over 20 years and in the institutional and cultural environment, one would expect substantial change in migration patterns. The educational system, especially, grew enormously in coverage and importance in the mediating role it played between individuals' social background and their occupational placement. As a result, it was likely to have much more significant effects on migration in the 1980s than in the 1960s. Whether its equalizing effect on class, regional, and gender differentials was as great as was envisaged in the late 1960s, when free postprimary education was first introduced, is open to doubt (Breen 1984a, 1984b). Nevertheless, its current dominance in occupational placement should have brought substantial changes in migration differentials since the mid–1960s, when only a minority of youths completed postprimary education and strong differences in migration existed by sex, farm origin, social class, and remoteness from an urban area (Hannan 1970, 65–76).

The chapter, therefore has four objectives: (1) it reviews the pattern and process of Irish rural–urban migration in the 1960s; (2) it briefly describes the extent and nature of change in the economic and social structure of Ireland since the mid–1960s; (3) it analyzes the labor market and migration experience of current rural second–level school leavers; and (4) finally, it evaluates the nature and causes of change in rural outmigration patterns from the 1960s to the 1980s.

The Underlying Motives, and Differentials in Migration Planning and Behavior: The 1960s to the 1980s.

One study of migration decisionmaking found that over 80 percent of a cohort of rural Irish youths considered migrating during a three–year interval (1965–68), and almost half actually migrated (Hannan 1970, 182–88). Two push factors were: no expectation to inherit the family farm, and a perception that their occupational aspirations (and desired consumption patterns) could not be satisfied locally.

These push factors structured migration differences according to sex, social class of origin, educational attainment, and remoteness of the community of origin. The local rural economy offered few nonfarm occupations, and the nonfarm jobs that existed were concentrated in the semiskilled and skilled manual trades and in service employment, not in unskilled or lower skilled industrial employment. Hence, the rural–urban migration stream was dominated by females (who rarely inherited the family farm), by those from local middle–class or large–farm backgrounds (who disproportionately received higher second–level educations), by those reaching higher second–level education (who usually aspired to higher–level nonfarm occupations), and by rural youths living closer to urban centers. Also, since nonfarm jobs in the rural economy were generally acquired by those from local upper working class and middle–sized farm backgrounds having intermediate levels of education (particularly "vocational" education; Hannan 1970, 216–35), noninheriting youths with very poor educational levels were disproportionately excluded from the local economy and were highly likely to migrate—mainly to emigrate.

Subsequent studies, either of a particular rural community (Kelly 1971) or of a number of rural communities throughout Ireland (Walsh 1984), document the remarkable stability in the rate of, motives for, and differentials in rural–urban migration. Roughly the same proportions intended to migrate or stay in the 1980s as in the 1960s. The frustration of occupational and consumption aspirations in one's home community remained the principal motivations to leave, with over 80 percent citing either or both reasons as the main factor involved in the decision. Equally, if these basic occupational status and mobility motives could be satisfied locally, most potential migrants would stay. What still appears to explain both the rate of migration and the clear–cut migration differentials evident between the sexes and among social classes or occupational groups is mainly the differential nature of their educational achievement and their occupational decisionmaking and placement (Walsh 1984, 7–21).

However, the fieldwork for Walsh's (1984) study was carried out in 1981–82, before the return of high rates of emigration in the mid–1980s. Net emigration is estimated to have been only 1,000 persons per year in 1981–82, whereas it is estimated to have grown to 28,000 persons per year in 1986. (Census of Population of Ireland 1986a). Besides this recent dramatic growth in emigration rates, Walsh's study also may not be generalizable to the rural population at large. It was restricted to those completing the Leaving Certificate examination (roughly equivalent to a U.S. high school diploma) and so left out about one–third of each local cohort who had dropped out of school previously. It was also restricted to very specific local case studies. The highly unexpected stability of both migration motives and social differentials in propensity to migrate over a 15–year period of very rapid economic and social change cannot then be taken as a model for explaining modern rural–urban migration patterns. Before we finalize our model of migration decisionmaking, we need to consider the nature and extent of the changes that have occurred, and attempt to estimate what the likely effects of these changes have been on migration differentials. This is attempted in the following section.

Economic, Social, and Migration Changes: 1961–86

Between 1961 and 1986, the population of Ireland grew from 2.8 to 3.5 million. Because emigrants outnumbered immigrants except during the 1970s, the main cause of population growth was the excess of births over deaths. During the 1970s, however, there was a historically unique appearance of net immigration due to the return from abroad of previous emigrants. In fact, net immigration accounted for over 15 percent of the total population growth for the decade.

The 1970s witnessed population growth in both rural and urban populations in a fashion similar to the "rural renaissance" observed in the United States during the same decade (see chaps. 7 and 8 in this volume). In fact, the open country areas contiguous to the larger urban areas grew faster than the urban population itself (Commins, Cox, and Curry 1978; Hannan 1986). And of the total 155 rural districts (areas of small towns and open country) in the Republic of Ireland, only one–sixth showed any population decline. These were the least densely populated, the most remote, and those in which income depended mainly on a small farm economy (Commins, Cox, and Curry 1978).

The rural renaissance responded to important changes in the structure of the national economy, but, as in the U.S. case, it did not signify an expansion in the farm labor force. Over the whole period from 1961 to 1986, agricultural employment declined from 36 to 15 percent of total employment. The declining significance of agriculture for youths' employment can perhaps best be illustrated by the drop in the employment category "relatives assisting"—mostly farmers' sons working on the home farms—in the census employment statistics: from 28 percent of all 15–19 year-old-males in 1961, to 14 percent in 1971, to 6 percent in 1981 (C.P.I. 1961, 1971, and 1981); for 20–24 year–olds, from 22 to 5 percent over that 20–year period. On the other hand, those remaining in agriculture benefited from a substantial improvement in agricultural prices (particularly from 1974 to 1980) following Ireland's accession to the European Economic Community in 1974; this had a trickle–up effect on families in the rural nonfarm economy. Moreover, a national policy of dispersed industrialization resulted in sizable growth in jobs in the value–added agricultural processing, manufacturing, and construction industries in most of the rural counties.

These substantial changes in the structure of the rural and national economy coincided with equally dramatic changes in education.

Postprimary education became free in 1967, when the state began paying all teachers' salaries and school expenses. As a result, attendance at the second level grew very rapidly. In 1961, for instance, less than half of Irish 15-year-olds were in school—a proportion that had increased to almost 95 percent by 1985 (Hannan 1986). Likewise, the proportion of each youth cohort completing second-level education (receiving the equivalent of a U.S. high school diploma) by taking the national "Leaving Certificate" examination (usually between ages 17 and 18) increased from less than 10 percent in 1961 to almost 70 percent by 1986 (Hannan 1986). Third-level educational participation has shown an even greater proportionate increase—from around 4 percent of the cohort in 1961–62 (*Investment in Education* 1966, 120) to 25 percent in the mid-1980s (Clancy 1982). What is surprising about the Irish figures is that rural and farm participation rates at second and third levels are higher—for some rural areas substantially higher—than for the larger urban areas (Clancy 1982; Hannan 1986).

Statement of Hypotheses

The structural changes in the economic and educational systems of Ireland in the 1970s should have altered the selectivity of rural–urban migration in the following ways. Differential tendencies to migrate from rural to urban areas according to sex and farm origin should have weakened because of the substantial decline in the importance of farming inheritance for retaining males in rural locations and because of the growing universalism of second-level education for males. Likewise, since remoteness from urban centers is less important in preserving unequal access to educational opportunities than it was in the 1960s (Hannan 1970, 72–76), its selective influence on migration should have waned. However, educational reform has been less successful in reducing inequalities in educational attainment by social class of origin (Rottman et al. 1982; Breen 1984a). Given the increased importance of educational credentials in occupational achievement (Breen 1984b; Whelan and Whelan 1984), class inequalities in rural–urban migration are hypothesized to be as significant now as in the late 1960s. As indicated in fig. 1, these hypothesized relationships should be mediated by the level of education achieved and the occupational status achieved or desired.

Data and Methods

The analysis is based on the combined 1986 and 1987 national School Leavers Surveys, which were done for the Department of Labor by the Economic and Social Research Institute, Dublin, Ireland. These annual

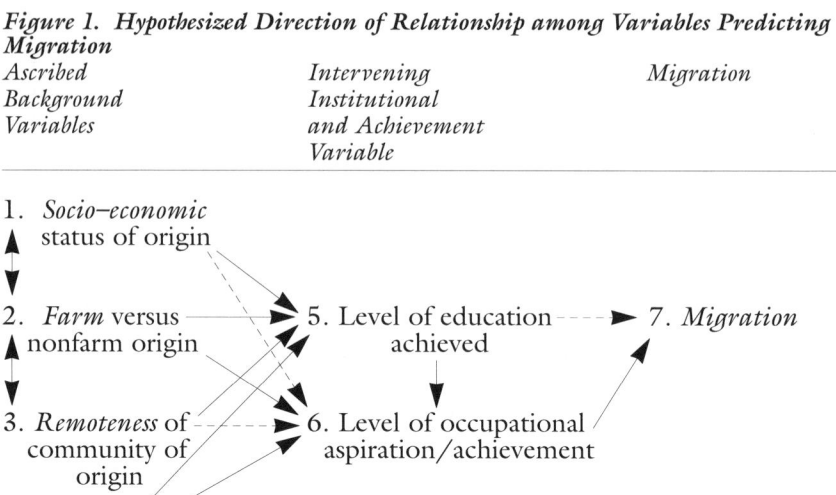

Figure 1. Hypothesized Direction of Relationship among Variables Predicting Migration

surveys are based on interviews with a national sample of school leavers aged 15–19 who have been out of school for at least 11 months. Each year, a two-stage stratified random sample of schools and of their preceding year's school leavers nets about 2,000 respondents. They are interviewed at their residence about their employment and further education since leaving school, as well as about their basic familial, occupational, and school background characteristics. The home and school addresses of respondents when they left school and their home addresses at the time of the survey are recorded. Thus, I could calculate residential changes and estimate intracounty, intercounty and emigration movements of individual school leavers. Then I could compare their migratory and social characteristics in order to test my hypotheses.

I restricted the present study to the 1,083 respondents leaving schools in the 12 "rural" counties, defined as those with no more than 30 percent of the whole population residing in towns of more than 1,500 people. These highly rural counties included County Cavan and mirrored most of its economic and sociodemographic characteristics. The similarity was important, since Co. Cavan was the focus of my earlier (1970) study and since I wished now to make as close a comparison as possible of socially selective factors in migration in the 1980s as implied by Co. Cavan for the 1960s.

I operationalized the study variables as follows. The dependent variable was measured dichotomously to show whether the respondent had migrated from the rural county between the time of school leaving and the date of the survey: 0 = no; 1 = yes. Since the distribution of respondents across these two categories was skewed (32 percent were negatives and 68 percent were affirmatives), the assumptions necessary for OLS regressions did not hold. Thus, I performed logit regressions with the SHAZAM software package.

The factors hypothesized to cull individuals into migratory streams were measured in the following ways. Sex was dichotomized as: 0 = males; 1 = females. Likewise, farm origin was indicated by whether or not the respondent's father's main job was farming: 0 = no; 1 = yes.

The formula for the distance (D) of the respondent's community of origin from an urban center was:

$$D = \frac{1}{\sqrt{p_1}} + \frac{d_2}{\sqrt{p_2}} + \frac{d_3}{\sqrt{p_3}}, \text{ where}$$

p_1 = the size of the population in the town in which R's last school was located; p_2 = population of the nearest town of at least 3,000 residents; p_3 = population of the nearest town of at least 25,000 residents (a regional center); d_2 = road distance to nearest town of 3,000+; and d_3 = road distance to the nearest regional center. The square roots of the population sizes were used because they yielded a more reliable estimate of the urban dominance of contiguous large centers of population than using total population itself. Note that D has a very low value where the population of the "hometown" is large or where distance to nearest town (3,000–25,000) is small, and a very high value where the local community's population is small or where distance to nearest urban center is far.

Social class of origin was tapped by the occupational status of the father's occupation. Fathers whose main occupation was nonfarm were ranked inversely from high to low, the six ranks being: 1 = professional, upper managerial, large proprietorial, etc.; 2 = semiprofessional, middle managerial, upper technical, etc.; 3 = intermediate and lower nonmanual, clerical, etc.; 4 = skilled manual; 5 = semiskilled manual; and 6 = unskilled manual. Fathers who were mainly farmers were ranked inversely from high to low according to the relative size of the farm: 1 = 200 acres and over; 2 = 100 to 200 acres; 3 = 50 to 100 acres; 4 = 30 to 50 acres; 5 = less than 30 acres (Census of Population 1986, Classification of Occupations).

It was more difficult to rank the respondent's own occupational achievement, because some were enrolled in tertiary schooling and some were unemployed. If the respondent was currently working in a job, it was ranked in the same manner as the paternal occupation. I assigned all tertiary–level students an occupational score of 1 and all technical–college students an occupational score of 2. In addition, I assigned all those who were unemployed or in short–term training courses the rank of the occupation to which they reportedly aspired.

The respondent's education was ranked such that higher scores meant more school completed. The scores were: 1 = left school without taking any examination and usually before completing the third year of second–level; 2 = left after completing the Group Certificate examination—taken by some "vocational stream" students after two or three years of second–level schooling; 3 = left after completing the Intermediate Certificate examination—done after having completed three of four years of secondary school; 4 = left school after completing the Leaving Certificate; 5 = completed second level by passing the Leaving Certificate examination and is now in third level.

Results

Model 1 (table 1) estimates how the odds of migrating from the home county are affected by sex, farm origin, paternal social status, and remoteness from an urban center. The logic regression provided a close fit between observed and predicted values, as is indicated by the large likelihood ratio chi–square (41.7, which was statistically significant at 4 degrees of freedom). Females, respondents from middle–class origins, and persons schooled distantly from urban centers were significantly more migratory than others, ceteris paribus. However, farm origin did not predict the odds of being a migrant from the home county.

Model 2 added the respondent's educational and own achieved/aspired occupational rankings to the list of predictors and significantly increased the likelihood ratio chi–square by 127.12 (168.82 – 41.70) and the degrees of freedom by 2 (6 – 4). Respondents with more education or with middle–class occupational achievements/aspirations had greater odds of migrating from the home county (t = -2.307 and -8.22, respectively). While gender and remoteness from an urban center remained statistically significant in Model 2, as in Model 1, paternal social status was no longer statistically significant (t = -0.137). This result suggests that the influence of paternal social class on the propensity to migrate operates by structuring the educational attainment and occupational achievements/aspirations of rural youths in Ireland.

Conclusions

In the late 1960s and early 1970s, several structural changes with implications for the national economy took place in the Republic of Ireland. First, the abolition of tuition fees at secondary schools in 1967 made education more accessible to the masses. Also, entry of the Republic into the European Economic Community (EEC) in 1974 led to a substantial improvement in agricultural prices. In addition, a national policy of dispersed industrialization resulted in a sizable increase in industrial jobs in

Table 1.
LOGIT REGRESSIONS OF MIGRATION FROM HOME COUNTY (1 = YES) ON STUDY VARIABLES: 1986–87 SCHOOL LEAVING SURVEYS OF THE REPUBLIC OF IRELAND.

Variable	Estimated Coefficient	Standard Error	T-Ratio
Equation 1			
Social status of origin	−0.18	0.053	−3.423
Farm origin	0.23	0.154	1.470
Sex	0.47	0.146	3.241
Remoteness	1.60	0.368	4.078
Intercept	−1.20	0.299	−3.958
Equation 2			
Social status of origin	−0.01	0.059	−0.137
Farm origin	0.21	0.166	1.256
Sex	0.38	0.159	2.361
Remoteness	1.78	0.419	4.246
Educational achievement	−0.21	0.091	−2.307
Occupation achievement/ aspiration	−0.52	0.063	−8.222
Intercept	0.23	0.340	0.671

most rural areas. In response to economic growth in the rural nonfarm sector, net emigration from Ireland turned to net immigration, and the open countryside contiguous to the urban centers began growing more rapidly than the centers themselves. A severe recession felt in the EEC nations during the 1980s led to a reversion to the earlier pattern of rural (and national) net outmigration. Thus, this study assessed whether the social factors selecting young labor–force entrants into migration streams might have changed substantially after 1967, as one would expect, given the major economic and educational changes that had occurred. The purpose of this analysis was to examine this question with a national probability sample of school leavers drawn in 1985–86.

The results showed important continuities and discontinuities. While the educational policy objective of removing regional and rural differences in educational access has been remarkably successful, the other main social objective of equalizing access by social class of origin has not (Breen 1984a). Although class differences in educational opportunity have been slightly reduced since the 1960s, educational attainment itself now plays a much more central role in occupational aspirations/attainment (Rottman et al. 1982; Breen 1984a, 363-86). As a result, the underlying importance of socioeconomic background factors in educational selectivity and occupational attainment, and consequently on migration, have become more central than they were before the 1970s. However, father's social class appears to affect the young adult's odds of migration solely through influencing his/her total level of schooling. Therefore, despite the growing universalism of *entering* the secondary school level, the effects of *completing* educational attainment on the tendency to migrate from the home county appear to have become stronger rather than weaker.

Gender differences in migration remain very important, though somewhat different in their nature and causes from the 1960s. Females do reach higher levels of educational completion than males do and partly for that reason are still more prone to migrate. Historically, rural males have been less migratory because the eldest son could expect to inherit the family farm and his younger brothers could expect their keep so long as they worked on the land. The decline in agricultural occupations has removed this anchor against male migration. But the rural nonfarm economy still retains its pro–male biases in occupational opportunity and thus offers heavier anchors to male youths than to their sisters.

Above–cited studies from the 1960s showed that distance from an urban center was associated with a reduced propensity to migrate. The present analysis for the mid–1980s shows quite the opposite relationship. It indicates both that educational opportunities have become equalized and that severe declines in agricultural occupations have not been counterbalanced with sufficient growth in local off–farm jobs. Because those farming occupations that are left are clustered distantly from urban centers, farm origin has no effect on the tendency to migrate, aside from its association with distance from an urban center and with educational level achieved. It is ironic that after two decades of expansion in educational provision and attainment, as well as of rural industrial development, state policies have not destroyed the relationship between locality and migration.

References

Bacon, P., J. Durkan, and J. O'Leary. 1982. *The Irish economy: Policy and performance 1972–1981*. Dublin, Ireland: Economic and Social Research Institute.

Breen, R. 1984a. Status attainment or job attainment? *British Journal of Sociology* 35(3): 363–86.

———. 1984b. *Education and the labour market: Work and unemployment amongst recent cohorts of Irish school leavers*. Dublin, Ireland: Economic and Social Research Institute, Research Paper No. 119.

Census of Population in Ireland. 1961. Volume 3. Dublin, Ireland: Stationery Office.
_____. 1971. Volume 3. Dublin, Ireland: Stationery Office.
_____. 1981. Volume 4. Dublin, Ireland. Stationery Office.
_____. 1986a. Volume 1. Dublin, Ireland: Stationery Office
_____. 1986b. Classification of Occupations. Dublin, Ireland: Central Statistics Office.
Clancy, P. 1982. *Participation in higher education – A national survey*. Dublin, Ireland: Higher Education Authority. Dublin.
Commins, P., P. Cox, and J. Curry 1978. *Rural areas: Change and development*. Dublin, Ireland: National Economic and Social Council, Paper No. 41.
Conniffe, D., and K. A. Kennedy, eds. 1985. Employment and unemployment policy for Ireland. Dublin, Ireland: Economic and Social Research Institute.
Hannan, D. F. 1970. *Rural exodus*. London: Chapmans.
_____. 1978. *Displacement and development: Class, kinship and social change in Irish rural communities*. Dublin, Ireland: Economic and Social Research Institute, Research Paper No. 96.
_____. 1986. *Schooling and the labour market*. Shannon, Ireland: Curriculum Development Unit.
Hannan, D. F., R. Breen, B. Murray, N. Hardiman, D. Watson, and K. O'Higgins. 1983. *Schooling and sex roles: Sex differences in subject provision and student choice in Irish post–primary schools*. Dublin, Ireland: Economic and Social Research Institute, Research Paper No. 113.
Investment in Education. 1966. Report of the Survey Team Appointed by the Minister for Education in October 1962, Stationery Office, Dublin, Ireland.
Johansen, Harley E., and Glenn V. Fuguitt. 1984. *The changing rural village in America: Demographic and economic trends since 1950*. Cambridge, Mass.: Ballinger Press.
Kelly, M. 1971. *Young workers in a country town: A social survey report on young workers in Tuam*. Dublin, Ireland: An Foras Forbartha.
Kennedy, K. 1975. *The Irish economy*. Studies. Economic and Social Series No. 10. Brussels, Belgium: E. C. Commission.
Kennedy, R.E. 1973. *The Irish: Emigration, marriage and fertility*. Berkeley, Calif.: University of California Press.
Rottman, D. R., D. F. Hannan, N. Hardiman, and M. Wiley. 1982. *The distribution of income in the Republic of Ireland: A study in social class and family–cycle inequalities*. Dublin, Ireland: Economic and Social Research Institute, Research Paper No. 109.
Sexton, J. J. 1983. *Recent trends in youth unemployment*. Dublin, Ireland: Economic and Social Research Institute Policy Research Series, Paper No. 5.
Walsh, B. W. 1968. *Recent population problems reconsidered*. Dublin, Ireland: Economic and Social Research Institute, Research Paper No. 42.

_____. 1980. Recent demographic changes in the Republic of Ireland. *Population Trends*, No. 21. London: Office of Population Censuses and Surveys.

Walsh, J. A. 1984. *To go or not to go. The migration intentions of Leaving Certificate students*. Dublin, Ireland: Carysfort College.

Whelan, C., and B. Whelan. 1984. *Social mobility in the Republic of Ireland: A comparative perspective*. Dublin, Ireland: Economic and Social Research Institute, Research Paper No. 116.

PART 4

Ways to Survive and Thrive

11

CHANGING RURAL COMMUNITIES: RECONSTRUCTING THE LOCAL ECONOMY OF A NONMETROPOLITAN COMMUNITY

Marilyn W. Aronoff

To sociologists in the late 1950s, rural communities in the United States seemed to have entered a period of decline. The classic presentation of Springdale in *Small Town in Mass Society* (Vidich and Bensman 1958) argued that community autonomy was undermined as power was concentrated in institutions outside the local community. This, together with a long-standing attraction of population from rural to metropolitan areas, raised doubts about small communities' abilities to survive. In this view (Martindale and Hanson 1969; Stein 1960), rural communities seemed to be in their final stage of decline as the long-standing transformation of "community" ties into "societal" relationships was accomplished (Bender 1978; Hunter 1978).

From the vantage point of the 1990s, it is clear that these dire prognoses were wrong. Rural communities have refused to disappear in contemporary society and continue to draw both our attention and our curiosity. In fact, recent history has involved rural communities in a variety of contradictory experiences, some of which threaten their future (Lovejoy and Krannich 1981) while others offer the promise of incorporation into greater economic prosperity (Bradshaw and Blakely 1979). Rural communities' vulnerability to external events was exposed in the global recession of the 1970s and the U.S. Farm Crisis of the early 1980s (Fitchen 1988; Fendley and Christenson 1989; Ginder, Stone, and Otto 1986; Heffernan and Heffernan 1986; Murdock et al. 1987; Summers 1982; Wilkinson 1986a). Both crises left small towns in nonmetropolitan areas struggling with externally generated economic problems. By contrast, the upsurge in migration to nonmetropolitan counties in the decade of the 1970s revealed an enduring residential preference for rural/nonmetropolitan areas (Zuiches 1982). Innovations in transportation and communication, which made physical distance less of an obstacle to growth (Bradshaw and Blakely 1979), offered another potential source of nonmetropolitan community revival.

Thus, rural/nonmetropolitan communities endure as meaningful locations for social life, but their continued existence has not been built on a foundation of local autonomy (Lovejoy and Krannich 1981). Instead, they are defined in the context of interdependence with external units (Christenson, Fendley, and Robinson, Jr. 1989) that will inevitably become global in scope (Fendley and Christenson 1989). The central question raised in this chapter is how such communities can act locally to promote their own interests. Faced with the likelihood of externally induced change, it is important to determine what local strategies help rural residents remain a viable community while retaining a rural/nonmetropolitan identity.

The potential for nonmetropolitan communities to initiate workable processes of change has been the focus of several recent studies (Fendley and Christenson 1989; Garkovich 1989; Pulver 1979; Richards 1984; Shaffer and Summers 1989; Summers 1986). In a comprehensive and well–conceptualized review of the literature on rural community development, Summers (1986, 353) notes that ". . . the extent to which collective actions have a specific local focus varies among communities . . . ," and that ". . . unified and single public–interest collective action is not a defining characteristic of communities but rather a variable attribute, and the isolation of conditions that lead to this variation is an important research need." Fendley and Christenson (1989) develop a concept of "rural reflation" to denote strategies through which communities can increase residents' income and employment by using knowledge of their own unique assets to obtain available external resources. Under contemporary conditions of global interdependence, local communities must promote their own distinctive qualities in order to create a niche that can withstand competition. Local vitality can be created by residents who are willing to be innovative as they build on local financial and human resources. Under these conditions, communities can assume new responsibility for controlling development that at least partially serves their own interests.

These perspectives provide a concrete referent for the more general concern with sources of rural economic viability and revitalization in current writings on rural community development (cf. Shaffer and Summers 1989). In the process of development that enhances local vitality, rural communities must use local resources advantageously in view of changing external opportunities (cf. Christenson and Robinson, Jr. 1989; Fendley and Christenson 1989). Summers (1986, 357) proposes that: "Vital communities possess social constructions, with underlying assumptions which encourage and permit the orderly and efficient use of economic resources, ensure their maintenance, and allow adaptation to changes in the environment." Following their directions, it seems that contemporary sociological theories of community can help identify the structures within communities that increase capacities for productive local action where local communities depend on external sources of power. In this chapter, I will draw on a number of sociological approaches to community that help us to understand nonmetropolitan communities as interdependent entities, and the processes through which these communities develop awareness of their local capacities to direct change. On the foundation of this sociological framework, I will discuss material drawn from a case study of one nonmetropolitan county in Michigan to illustrate the processes through which communities seek to create development options that enhance economic viability while they sustain a nonmetropolitan local identity.

An Inventory of Community Theories

Although sociologists claim community as one of their basic ideas, their disagreements about how to define it are legendary (Bell and Newby 1971; Bernard 1973; Effrat 1974; Hillery 1955). The difficulty rests in part on a real consequence of social change. Sociology's emergence in the nineteenth century, at a time of profound historical transformation in Western society, disrupted the association between close social relationships and places of habitation that was represented as an essential feature of life in village communities. The transformation resulted in a division in sociologists' approach to community that has been difficult to bridge. Recognizing that human beings create social organizations in particular places, some sociologists focused on the spatial dimensions of community. Other sociologists defined the foundations of community in the human tendency to organize around a shared identity that joins members of a group in a sense of common purpose and common "fate" (cf. Bender 1978; Bernard 1973; Effrat 1974; Loomis and Beegle 1975).

This basic division has produced a proliferation of concepts and approaches, and a level of debate that promotes polemics rather than syntheses (cf. Effrat 1974). In addition, since territorial boundaries are more easily recognized than common ties, spatial conceptions of community have received far greater attention from sociologists (Bell and Newby 1971; Hillery 1955). In order to understand processes of interdependent local change and revival in contemporary rural communities, however, both components are critical: As local social systems, the spatial context of rural communities is the place where people experience change and explore new opportunities. Similarly, as solidarity groups, communities are the focus for human energies that can weather periods of crisis and can drive social changes. Only a conception of community that includes both territory and social meaning can mobilize the resources that rural communities have to sustain a way of life that is distinctive but no longer isolated from the larger society (Goudy and Ryan 1982; Wilkinson 1986b). It is the capacity to build on experiences of interdependence that enables a group to understand and use its local identity as a basis for development that is compatible with local interests.

Paradoxically, while communities have become more interdependent, they have not lost their meaning for residents. A sociological theory that explains the processes of identity formation that exist despite organizational interdependence will clarify the bases of local community action. In fact, sociological approaches to community have been more successful in increasing our understanding of social and spatial interdependence than in comprehending changing sources of community meaning and their contribution to local development. The interest in community identity has been dominated by long-standing debates about the merits of polar typologies that dichotomize characteristics of rural and urban, or community and society. Recent critiques suggest that, while there is broad dissatisfaction with these polarities, sociologists have not found alternative approaches to the question of contemporary variations in rural community identity (cf. Gilbert 1982).

Two contrasting approaches, social systems theory and political economy, illuminate the impacts of interdependence on rural communities. Conceptions of rural/nonmetropolitan communities as social systems (Loomis and Beegle 1975; Warren 1963) or fields (Kaufman 1959; Luloff 1990; Wilkinson 1972) emphasized communities' interdependence with external organizations. They moved sociologists beyond the search for neatly bounded territorial units with an array of institutions capable of satisfying the full range of local needs. Interdependence was seen as a cause of reduced local autonomy, but not the total "Eclipse of Community" that had been predicted by a number of "Mass Society" theorists. The model of community as system or field encouraged modification as sociologists observed shifts in the balance of power between the internal and external relationships of local communities.

Roland Warren's work exemplifies this capacity. Warren's initial formulation (1963) stressed the expansion of "vertical systems," whose centers of power were outside the local community, as the inevitable enemy of the local community's own "horizontal system." Later, he recognized communal endurance (1972) and focused on the persisting importance of local communities under macrosystemic dominance (1978).

Social–system approaches to conceptualizing interdependent local change are limited in part by the broad and ahistorical character that marked their connection to Parsonsian social theory. Political–economic approaches to rural communities examine local communities in the historical context of capitalism (cf. Gilbert 1982). In this perspective, communities are seen as spatial representations of conflicts generated in the larger system, and manifested locally in the conflict between different interests over land and development (Molotch 1976). These theories brought local community into an explanatory framework that had previously been reserved for work life, and focused attention on power relationships and interdependencies that had been obscured in the search for self–sufficiency. They are interested in local action as an expression of contradictions in the system that can lead to change, for example in the populist coalitions between working class urbanites and rural food producers arising from discontent over processes of distribution in the food system (Buttel 1980). Political–economic frameworks provide an alternative understanding of the sources and directions of rural community interdependence, and an antidote to less critical conceptions of the social systems paradigm. Although both approaches are concerned with local action, neither one devotes primary attention to explaining the sources of local community identity or their contribution to grassroots action.

The Social Construction of Rural Communities

A third approach, the social construction of communities, is derived from research in urban communities. It incorporates some of the strengths of social systems theory and political economy with a distinctive focus on the meanings local areas have for their residents. Thus far, it has had little influence on the understanding of contemporary rural communities (cf. Summers 1986). Social construction is built on the meanings created about space at multiple territorial levels, ranging from city blocks to metropolitan regions. As such, it unites a recognition of the multiple levels of territory that can be simultaneous environments for contemporary community residents with the human capacity to give meaning to these diverse communities and potentially to act collectively in response to those identities. On this foundation, it can provide a critical addition to rural community theory, and can help us understand the ways in which local residents can address the realities of interdependence while creating locally relevant community development based on a conception of local resources and local identity.

The phrase "social construction of communities," the title of a book by Gerald Suttles (1972), provides the name for this approach. It was built on the work of a group of University of Chicago Urban Sociologists including Morris Janowitz, Gerald Suttles, and Albert Hunter. Interestingly, for Rural Sociologists, "social construction" may represent a missed opportunity, a road not taken, perhaps because of its early tie to urban settings. It shares with Rural Sociology the effort to refute Mass Society assumptions that communities could exist only if they were autonomous and self–sufficient. Morris Janowitz (1952) analyzed urban neighborhoods as "communities of limited liability" that provided only a part of residents' needs, but remained important sources of local involvement.

Gerald Suttles (1972) expanded this perspective into a processual theory of the urban community. He argued that communities, far from existing in isolation from the larger society, were created in reaction to its demands and opportunities. He saw interdependence of community and society as an expectable condition that sets some of the parameters for community self–definition. Suttles recognized that urban communities range in size from a handful of personally recognized neighbors, to larger urban neighborhoods, to planned communities within cities, to larger segments of metropolitan regions. In any case, they emerge as areas of partial allegiance and need, defined through residents' response to definitions, regulations, and opportunities of external organizations. Suttles rejected earlier romantic images of communities as natural or primordial expressions of human solidarity. Instead, he identified their potential to contribute to popular movements for social change in their existence as the products of voluntary and self–conscious efforts of urban residents.

Suttles's approach to the social construction of local communities complements the understanding of local community interdependence noted for social systems theory and political economy. It makes a critical addition to community theory by explaining the processes through which territorial areas acquire meaning for their residents. These processes are essential components of nonmetropolitan community efforts to rebuild economies by reinterpreting local identity to fit external circumstances of interdependence. On the basis of research on urban neighborhoods, Suttles (1968, 1972, 1984) incorporates and revises Walter Firey's (1945) emphasis on the importance of sentiment and symbolism in generating community attachment. Values, material culture, and social patterns provide material around which residents create representations of their communities. These efforts, based on intrinsic human abilities to work with symbols, produce communities about which residents care. As such, they are incorporated into political and social initiatives for social change.

These symbolic activities are not necessarily unifying, and competing groups can draw on mutually exclusive symbols available in the local environment when they undertake competitive political efforts (Kasinitz 1988). These urban community struggles parallel the contradictions in the relationships between old timers and newcomers in nonmetropolitan communities as they try to channel rival symbols into the political process. These capacities are basic elements in the processes through which residents of contemporary nonmetropolitan communities mobilize to produce local change.

In an extension of Suttles's work, Albert Hunter (1978) presented a developmental typology of the hierarchy of local commitments and sentiments arising at different levels of the process of social differentiation. Hunter's typology demonstrates at which levels community processes will be defensive, built on negative, reactive, and obstructionist responses to the external world, as in "defended neighborhoods," and at which levels residents will be responsive to positive constructions that can capture resources from external agencies and use them to promote the goals of their "conscious communities." The ability of local organizations in rural–nonmetropolitan counties to mobilize their efforts in a self-conscious and positive way to extract available resources from external political entities is a primary source of capacity in optimizing locally oriented development.

The "social construction" approach provides conceptions that fit the experience of contemporary rural communities facing the problems of interdependence and struggling to create or maintain meaningful local identities in the service of development. The approach builds on the strengths of social systems theory and political economy, but adds processes of social meaning that are important elements in the effort to develop nonmetropolitan economies to benefit rural inhabitants. I will illustrate these processes with one nonmetropolitan county in Michigan. The essentials of my argument are as follows: This county has suffered recently from externally generated causes of economic decline. The decline has increased the importance of the county as the social unit that can most productively channel local efforts to promote development. County residents recognize interdependence as a reality and try to use external resources for local developmental goals. By reinventing a nonmetropolitan social identity compatible with external realities, they have developed a niche that maximizes their competitive edge. The social constructionist theory of community emphasizes the methods of empowering the community to build on its foundations and to change in ways that maximize opportunities for development in the local interest.

Gratiot County

My interest in Gratiot County's experience with economic crisis and economic redevelopment emerged, initially, in a comparative study of Michigan nonmetropolitan counties affected by the U.S. farm crisis of the early 1980s (MAES 1988). To counties in Michigan, such as Gratiot, where agriculture contributes significantly to the local economy, the 1970s brought high levels of international demand for local farm products. These demands were accompanied by liberal credit terms, both for international purchasers and for domestic farm operators, who were eager to meet the needs of their expanding markets. However, by the early 1980s, the rising rates of inflation due to these policies resulted in tighter credit, decreased advantage for U.S. farm exports, widespread financial instability, and farm foreclosures. In Michigan, severe flooding in the fall of 1986 exacerbated the broader farm financial crisis and further stressed the state's nonmetropolitan residents. My participation in the Michigan Agricultural Experiment Station (1988) study of the impact of these dual crises on a range of counties suggested that Gratiot's responses promoted countywide cooperation without overriding the identities of the smaller communities. My selection of Gratiot County as a potential exemplar of cooperative development strategies is not without precedent. Clinton's (1978) study, for example, is also based on deliberate selection of a county whose experiences seemed to be atypical in a positive way, and thus worthy of further investigation. In the following pages, I will examine Gratiot County's efforts to produce a coherent local strategy for development, but I will not claim that these attempts produce long-lasting economic growth.

Gratiot County is a nonmetropolitan county in central Michigan. Rich farmland insures that agriculture is an important source of the county's income and its rural character. Key crops include dry beans, soybeans, sugarbeets, corn, and wheat, along with vegetables, dairy products, poultry, and beef cattle (MDA 1987). The total population is approximately 40,000 residents, and its largest city numbers just over 10,000 people. As a nonmetropolitan county founded on a fluctuating mixture of agriculture and industry, Gratiot is socially apart, though not isolated from economic patterns of adjacent metropolitan counties. Three adjacent metropolitan areas, located within 50 miles of the county, offer additional employment to county residents. Although the highway to the state's major northern recreation area runs through the county, Gratiot has no special natural attraction of its own to support a local tourist industry.

Gratiot County's history presents images of crisis and survival as elements of county tradition that remain as foundations of contemporary county identity (Tucker 1913). Its economy has been permeable to externally generated crises, as well as to disasters of weather and climate that threaten any agricultural economy. The phrase "Starving Gratiot," derived from the near catastrophe faced by early European settlers, remains as an emblem of county life as a hard life, and county people as capable of facing and surmounting or integrating disaster. The county's current struggle for redevelopment is a response to two recent periods of economic decline. After a period of relative prosperity following World War II, two decades of crisis began in the early 1970s. Industrial collapse came first, beginning in 1973–74, when a number of large mobile home manufacturing plants closed or relocated. The chemical plant that had been the county's largest employer was ordered to close in 1976 after it was discovered to be the source of polybrominated biphenyl (PBB) that had accidentally contaminated state cattle feed, and subsequently Michigan's human food chain, as well as producing toxic contamination in Gratiot County, itself (cf. Aronoff and Gunter 1990). Average Gratiot County yearly unemployment rates of 15.64 percent in 1974 and 20.79 percent in 1975 were reported in the *Gratiot County Herald* (22 July 1976, 1). Even as the recession spread throughout the State of Michigan, Gratiot's unemployment rates exceeded those of most other counties (*Gratiot County Herald* 13 March 1975, 12a).

Agricultural prosperity during these years was followed in the early 1980s by collapse of worldwide demand for domestic farm products, which led to financial hardship for county farmers and related agribusiness enterprises. While the concentrated impact of these dual crises in agriculture and industry has lessened recently, sporadic plant closures have occurred in some of the local communities, and periods of severe drought and flood have occurred in agriculture. None of these crises could be attributed in a simple sense to local failures, but they were the reality that county residents faced as they struggled to redevelop the local economy.

County Economic Development: Localizing the Economy

In Gratiot County, preoccupation with change, growth, and decline have been long-standing, but present-day development differs from earlier approaches guided by Chambers of Commerce or Cooperative Extension Agencies. Contemporary "development" is itself an element of interdependence, stimulated, directed, and constrained by external regulations at state and federal levels.

Greater Gratiot Community Development, Inc. (GGDI) was established in 1978 to facilitate and coordinate developmental efforts throughout the county. It represents an emergent community of limited liability that gained strength in the context of external opportunity. Since that time, it has created a coherent development strategy that its current executive director labels "localizing" the economy. Building on local knowledge, this approach seeks to promote county resources for local advantage. Building on fertile soil as a natural resource, they seek to diversify crops and integrate food processing with agricultural production. Because they believe that well-run local companies are less likely to leave the county after one or two bad seasons, the corporation seeks to promote local growth, new ideas, and new relationships for established local companies. Finally, in attracting new industry to the county, which it defines as the true mark of economic growth, the county uses its single most potent resource: its own nonmetropolitan identity. Drawing on the character of its people as disciplined, hardworking, efficient, and friendly workers and neighbors, it seeks new businesses that are looking for that kind of workforce, and find it sufficiently attractive to make investment in the county an appealing alternative in comparison with metropolitan amenities. Special attention has been paid to encouraging the development of industries, such as the manufacture of recreational boats, that generate part-time employment for farmers because their seasonal labor demands complement the calendar of agricultural production.

Figure 1. Small business enterprises promising rural memorabilia at bargain prices created jobs, favored the local tax base, and supported the net migration to rural Michigan in the 1970s and 1980s. (Photograph by Nan E. Johnson)

Although the development corporation's personnel point to successes in retention and expansion of existing industries, as well as attracting new enterprises to diversify county agriculture and expand manufacturing and services, they portray the contemporary development environment as intensely competitive, requiring constant effort to maintain momentum in the county's economic recovery. Some of the positive returns on recent development projects are reported in a "Tax Track" (GGDI 1988). A recent article in *Michigan Business* (November 1988, 17), a magazine that reports on development experiences statewide, notes that: "For every dollar Gratiot County municipalities invested in 1987 in Greater Gratiot Development, Gratiot County received $6.29 tax dollars in return . . ." In addition, ". . . GGDI–assisted projects have created 606 full–time industrial jobs and 233 commercial jobs since the agency's inception in 1978: The Director is quoted as saying: 'The report clearly demonstrates that economic development efforts within the county are an ever–increasing positive force both for tax gain and employment.'"

Interdependent Development and Local Economic Viability

Greater Gratiot Development exemplifies the social constructionists' claim that community self-definition emerges in the interaction with external units, whether they appear as positive resources or as irritants to local residents. This process is dramatized in Gratiot County with the inception of externally generated industrial and agricultural crisis, to the use of state initiatives to enable the county to establish the countywide development agency. In response to early signs of economic decline in 1973, the County Board of Commissioners appointed a number of county residents to a Gratiot County Industrial Development Group, and appropriated funds to follow their recommendation to conduct a survey of county assets, "community by community," compile a brochure, and hire a county industrial promoter (*Gratiot County Herald* 20 December 1973, 1). Although the local newspaper cited this as "one of the pioneer efforts by Michigan counties to cooperate as a whole in planning and encouraging industrial growth . . . ," the organizational support for a countywide development effort could not be achieved with county resources alone (*Gratiot County Herald* 23 May 1974, 12a). It was not until state action created a Michigan Economic Development Incentive Concept (MEDIC) in the mid–1970s, and provided potential external funding, that the county could obtain sufficient resources to mount its own local development initiative. Beginning in 1978, three years of MEDIC funding, set up to decline annually, gave the county a chance to establish a viable development organization with a professional director, and a mandate to produce enough results to capture further support from the local communities. Initial state funding allowed the formation of a community development corporation, which has, itself, been a primary source for proactive promotion of a countywide economic and social identity.

A key element in converting interdependence to local benefit is based on the ability of local organizations to capture external resources. Fendley and Christenson (1989, 107) suggest that a foundation for successful economic redevelopment in nonmetropolitan economies depends on local leaders' access to external resources. Gratiot County's developmental efforts demonstrate this capacity. When they are available, government funds are sought and utilized to benefit local residents and promote local growth. Headlines in the *Gratiot County Herald* in 1974 and 1975, when the county was in the heart of its industrial collapse, proclaimed: "County gets more EEA [Emergency Employment Act] type $$ to create jobs for unemployed" [*Gratiot County Herald* 18 July 1974, 1]; "CETA [Federal Comprehensive Education and Training Act] funds add jobs in Gratiot" (*Gratiot County Herald* 30 January 1975, 1]. Another headline notes: "$8 MILLION DENIED. $2 billion awarded but well dry for Gratiot." The accompanying article deplores the fact that none of the eight Gratiot County applications for federal public–works monies for communities with high unemployment was awarded to Gratiot (*Gratiot County Herald* 13 January 1977, 1).

In the aftermath of the 1986 flood, residents suggested that the county had been successful in obtaining monies set aside to aid farmers with this disaster and with the larger farm crisis. More generally, county activists and public officials worked to obtain any appropriate external funding, and claimed that Gratiot's applications often appear most promptly and in the greatest number. A combined enthusiasm for resources and innovation is revealed in residents' enthusiastic participation in pilot projects ranging from "Downtown Development" to grade–school social science. Most recently, the county has secured a package of funds drawn from state and local sources to establish a business incubator. Beyond these efforts, county leaders seem to maintain close ties to state and federal representatives. Several state legislative initiatives in economic and commercial promotion have emanated from local legislators, and have subsequently benefited county residents, along with others in the state. On the model of the MEDIC start–up funds mentioned earlier, these projects seem to act as catalysts for further internal activity, rather than as initiators of dependent relationships. The continuing tradition of crystallizing county identity in the successful pursuit of external funding has resulted most recently in combining state and local funds to establish a business incubator that will nurture fledgling businesses to add to the stock of potential county employment (GGDI 1989).

A final example of what might be termed an external relationship is county leadership's willingness to use its local college, a piece of the outside world located within the county, as a resource for local growth. Relationships with the college seem to function to the county's benefit. Academic expertise and technical knowledge is sought in areas including crafting the local development strategy, and the college is promoted as a county asset in its development literature. In a small and homogeneous county, faculty and students can make valuable contributions to local deliberations. For the most part, they are neither deferred to automatically, nor is their advice defensively rejected. The ability to accept and work with external resources, rather than to experience the outside world exclusively as threatening, marks the boundary between the social constructionists' understanding of a transition from "defended" communities to "conscious communities," which are able to ". . . mobilize resources, internally and externally, to generate an enduring structure that becomes a legitimate representation of the community's interests in relationships with larger external institutions of mass society." (Hunter 1978, 150)

Constructing Rural Community Identity

For social constructionists, the interdependence of local communities with external units is a primary source of identity formation, rather than the inevitable "eclipse of community." This phenomenon is explained by the human capacity to impose meaning on the real world, and to incorporate social experience into a structure of human understanding. In Gratiot County an outcome of the industrial and agricultural transformations and related governmental policies and programs since the early 1970s has been the emergence of the county as an essential resource for economic development. In the aftermath of these events, local group energy has been invested in the creation of a countywide identity. Even in a small county with a low budget for promotional materials, the creation of bumper stickers reading "Go, Grow, Gratiot" symbolically represents the county and promotes county spirit alongside existing attachments to rural neighborhoods, townships, and local communities. The county, represented by the development corporation, is depicted as a "Team" (GGDI 1989) that utilizes the energies of local people throughout the county, without obliterating their loyalties to local communities or other competing interests. In fact, if the larger effort to revive the county's economy is successful, the broader affiliation makes loyalties to other components of county life more viable as well.

The social processes represented in the emergence and evolution of "Greater Gratiot" are an example of a local unit's capacity to draw on local wisdom to stimulate awareness of local resources. These are promoted to establish a specialized niche through which the county can establish better competitive advantage and promote economic growth that works to county advantage. They contribute to the emergence of the county as a "conscious community" of limited liability that can attempt to promote development in its own interest. The message conveyed by development corporation personnel and development corporation literature promotes an image of the county that maximizes its location, which is adjacent to a number of metropolitan regions, but manifests a standard of living and lifestyle that reflect a rural/nonmetropolitan way of life. The message that Gratiot County conveys to prospective investors is, we can offer the advantages of metropolitan life because we are near universities, cultural centers, specialized medical facilities, and so on, without incurring the problems of a truly urban environment. The coexistence of efficiency and positive developmental infrastructure is represented as surprisingly well developed for a county of its size. "Although Gratiot County is the only county in Michigan with a population of less than 140,000 to have three certified industrial parks, economic development officials here are already planning to expand . . ." (*Michigan Business* 1987, 51). The county tradition of "survival" is put forth in a contemporary representation of a little engine that can, in spite of its small size, make it up the mountain.

Drawing on local resources and the experiences of the crises of the 1970s and 1980s, development strategy uses elements of local identity to create viable economic growth and "ensures that the community can weather an economic downturn of any origin." (GGDI 1989). A commitment to practicality and pragmatism is presented as a locally claimed characteristic of "pragmatism," through which contemporary development strategy balances external realities with local resources. County businesspeople define themselves as practical, pragmatic, no–frills entrepreneurs who unite business skills with personal ties to the county and its residents. They see themselves as moderately self–interested, but not rapacious. As such, they can work for their own benefit, but also seek to work in the larger interest of the county. In a parallel formulation, the county economic development director answered that the only development schemes containing hidden agendas unbeneficial to the county and thus worthy of his suspicion were those in which the investor claimed no self–interest. Local values of survival and pragmatism become foundations for constructing an economic development logic; they provide an open but cautious basis of common sense to use in approaching future development opportunities that are compatible with county resources.

My interviews and observations in Gratiot County reveal an awareness of local identity that combines positive evaluations of the rural/nonmetropolitan way of life with more negative responses to images of life in cities. In conversation, positive evaluations of small-town and country settings, including close personal relationships that extended over time, adherence to traditional values, and an interest in affordable rather than ostentatious material possessions were expressed with an undertone of contrast to characteristics assumed to represent urban and suburban communities (Hummon 1986a, 1986b). A local celebration called "Rural–Urban Day" (Aronoff 1989) has helped to create the county's contemporary nonmetropolitan identity. The festivity is a countywide picnic in which small-city businesspeople celebrate agriculture's contribution to the economy. It establishes a symbolic representation of local values at the level of the county as a whole. It invites county residents to join together as friends and family in an event that celebrates a combination of nonmetropolitan warmth and efficiency that represents the source of contemporary county viability. These events and identities create the positive experience of nonmetropolitan life that mobilizes local energies and establishes the content for commitment to Gratiot County as a "conscious community." This identity promotes local consumer loyalty for shops and services in the downtown business districts of local communities, as well as the broader efforts of the development corporation as it works to create a niche for competitive local development.

Conclusion

The illustrative material drawn from one nonmetropolitan county's experience with economic crisis and redevelopment is intended to support my larger claim that theoretical perspectives drawn from the social constructionist approach to local communities provide an understanding of the sources of community viability. Viability is the outcome of a social process. Social construction provides the theoretical framework to understand the processes through which territory is made meaningful and used to local advantage as communities interact with external organizations and externally generated events.

Gratiot County exists as an interdependent local community involved in dynamic processes of change and self–definition. The county's meaning to local residents endures, but its meaning will be different at different points in time, and it will not mean the same thing to all residents. Gratiot County's experiences over the last two decades reflect the combination of internal and external relationships through which local units can attempt to direct change. Drawing on traditions of survival and resilience, the county connects its past identity with its present circumstances. Targeting modified agricultural production as a mainstay of its economic future, the county adapts a basic resource to harmonize with changing external opportunities in marketing and processing. Viewing external relationships as an inevitable constraint on their own initiatives, county units can attempt to limit their impact or maximize their benefits, at least in part in terms of their own definitions of local interest. What is fundamental is not the county's identity at this point in time, but the capacity for groups of people in territorial units to define local options for change by using local resources in the context of their awareness of external opportunities and constraints.

References

Aronoff, M. 1993. Collective celebration as a vehicle for local economic development: A Michigan case. Human Organization 52: 368-79.

Aronoff, M., and V. Gunter. 1990. It's hard to keep a good town down: Local recovery efforts in the aftermath of toxic contamination. *Industrial Crisis Quarterly* 6: 83-97.

Bell, C., and H. Newby. 1971. *Community studies: An introduction to the sociology of the local community.* London: George Allen & Unwin.

Bender, T. 1978. *Community and social change.* New Brunswick, N.J.: Rutgers University Press.

Bernard, J. 1973. *The sociology of community.* Glenview, Ill.: Scott, Foresman and Co.

Bradshaw, T. K., and E. J. Blakely. 1979. *Rural communities in advanced industrial society.* New York: Praeger.

Buttel, F. 1980. Agriculture, environment and social change: Some emergent issues. In *Rural sociology of the advanced societies,* ed. H. Newby and F. Buttel, 453–88. Montclair, N.J.: Allanheld, Osmun.

Christenson, J. A. 1989. Themes of community development. In *Community development in perspective,* ed. J. A. Christenson and J. W. Robinson, Jr., 26–47. Ames, Iowa: Iowa State University Press.

Christenson, J. A., K. Fendley, and J. W. Robinson, Jr. 1989. Community development. In *Community development,* ed. J. A. Christenson and J.W. Robinson, Jr., 3–25. Ames, Iowa: Iowa State University Press.

Christenson, J. A., and J. W. Robinson, Jr., eds. 1989. *Community development in perspective.* Ames, Iowa: Iowa State University Press.

Clinton, C. A. 1978. Shiloh: The little county that could – and did. *Rural Sociology* 43: 91–203.

Effrat, M. P., ed. 1974. *The community: Approaches and applications.* New York: The Free Press.

Fendley, K., and J. A. Christenson. 1989. Rural reflation: An idea for community development. *Journal of the Community Development Society* 20:103–15.

Firey, W. 1945. Sentiment and symbolism as ecological variables. *American Sociological Review* 10:140–48.

Fitchen, J. M. 1988. Agricultural change, community change, and rural poverty. *The Rural Sociologist* 8:104–19.

Garkovich, L. E. 1989. Local organizations and leadership in community development. In *Community development*, ed. J. A. Christenson and J.W. Robinson, Jr., 196–218. Ames, Iowa: Iowa State University Press.

Gilbert, J. 1982. Rural theory: The grounding of rural sociology. *Rural Sociology* 47: 609–33.

Ginder, R. G., K. E. Stone, and D. Otto. 1986. Impact of the farm financial crisis on agribusiness farms and rural communities. In *New dimensions in rural policy: Building upon our heritage*, 298–307. Washington, D.C.: U.S. Government Printing Office.

Goudy, W. J., and V. D. Ryan. 1982. Changing communities. In *Rural society in the U.S.: Issues for the 1980s*, ed. Don A. Dillman and Daryl J. Hobbs, 256–63. Boulder, Colo.: Westview Press.

Gratiot County Herald. Ithaca, Michigan. 20 December 1973, 1; 23 May 1974, 12a; 18 July 1974, 1; 30 January 1975, 1; 13 March 1975, 12a, 29; 22 July 1976, 1; 13 January 1977, 1.

Greater Gratiot Development, Inc. (GGDI). 1988. Tax Track, Ithaca, Mich.

_____. 1989. Flyer, Ithaca, Mich.

Heffernan, W. D., and J. B. Heffernan. 1986. The farm crisis and the rural community. In *New dimensions in rural policy: Building upon our heritage*, 273–80. Washington, D.C.: U.S. Government Printing Office.

Hillery, G. A., Jr. 1955. Definitions of community: Areas of agreement. *Rural Sociology* 20:111–23.

Hummon, D. M. 1986a. City mouse country mouse: The persistence of community. *Qualitative Sociology* 9(1): 3–25.

_____. 1986b. Urban views: Popular perspectives on city life. *Urban Life* 15: 3–36.

Hunter, A. 1978. Persistence of local sentiments in mass society. In *Handbook of contemporary urban life*, ed. David Street and Assoc., 133–62. San Francisco: Jossey–Bass Publishers.

Janowitz, M. 1952. *The community press in an urban setting.* New York: Free Press.

Kasinitz, P. 1988. The gentrification of "Boerum Hill": Neighborhood change and conflicts over definitions. *Qualitative Sociology* 11:163–82.

Kaufman, H. F. 1959. Toward an interactional conception of community. *Social Forces* 38: 8–17.

Loomis, C. P., and J. A. Beegle. 1975. *A strategy for rural change.* New York: John Wiley and Sons.

Lovejoy, S. B., and R. S. Krannich. 1981. Rural development: A critial perspective. *The Rural Sociologist* 1: 84–91.

Luloff, A. E. 1990. Communities and social change: How do small communities act? In *American rural communites*, ed. A. E. Luloff and L. E. Swanson, 214-27. Boulder, Colo.: Westview Press.
Martindale, D., and R. G. Hanson. 1969. *Small town and nation*. Westport, Conn.: Greenwood.
Michigan Agricultural Experiment Station (MAES). 1988. The impact of the farm financial crisis and the 1986 flooding on Michigan agriculture and rural communities. (Report to the Michigan Legislature). January 1988. East Lansing: Michigan Agricultural Experiment Station, Michigan State University.
Michigan Business. April 1987, 51; November 1988, 17.
Michigan Department of Agriculture (MDA). 1987. Food and agricultural development statistics (Gratiot County). Lansing, Mich.: Michigan Department of Agriculture.
Michigan Department of Commerce (MDC). 1989. Profile of Gratiot County. Lansing, Mich., 1 April 1989.
Molotch, H. 1976. The city as a growth machine: Toward a political economy of place. *American Journal of Sociology* 82: 309-22.
Murdock, S. H., F. L. Leistritz, R. R. Hamm, D. E. Albrecht, and A. G. Leholm. 1987. Impacts of the farm crisis on a rural community. *Journal of the* 1988. *Community Development Society* 18: 30-49.
Pulver, G. C. 1979. A theoretical framework for the analysis of community economic development options. In *Nonmetropolitan industrial growth.and community change*, ed. G. F. Summers and A. Selvik, 105-17. Lexington, Mass.: D.C. Heath and Company.
Richards, R. O. 1984. When even bad news is not so bad: Local control over outside forces in community development. *Journal of The Community Development Society* 15: 75-85.
Shaffer, R., and G. F. Summers. 1989. Community economic development. In *Community Development*, ed. J. A. Christenson and J.W. Robinson, Jr., 173-95. Ames, Iowa: Iowa State University Press.
Stein, M. 1960. *The eclipse of community: An interpretation of American studies*. Princeton, N. J.: Princeton University Press.
Summers, G. F. 1982. Industrialization. In *Rural society in the U.S. : Issues for the 1980s*, ed. D. A. Dillman and D. J. Hobbs, 164-74. Boulder, Colo: Westview Press.
———. 1986. Rural community development. *Annual Review of Sociology* 12: 347-71.
Summers, G. F., and K. Branch 1984. Economic development and community social change. *Annual Review of Sociology* 10: 41-66.
Suttles, G. D. 1968. *The social order of the slum*. Chicago: University of Chicago Press.
———. 1972. *The social construction of communities*. Chicago: University of Chicago Press.

———. 1984. The cumulative texture of local urban culture. *American Journal of Sociology* 90: 283–304.

Tucker, W. D. 1913. *Gratiot County, Michigan, historical, biographical, statistical.* Saginaw, Mich.: Seeman and Peters.

Vidich, A. J., and J. Bensman. 1958. *Small town in mass society: Class, power and religion in a rural community.* Princeton, N. J.: Princeton University Press.

Warren, R. 1963. *The community in America.* Chicago, Ill.: Rand McNally.

———. 1972. *The community in America*, 2d ed. Chicago, Ill.: Rand McNally.

———. 1978. *The community in America*, 3d ed. Chicago, Ill.: Rand McNally.

Wilkinson, K. P. 1972. A field theory perspective for community development research. *Rural Sociology* 37: 43–52.

———. 1986a. Communities left behind—again. In *New dimensions in rural policy: Building upon our heritage*, 341–46. Washington, D.C.: U. S. Government Printing Office.

———. 1986b. In search of community in the changing countryside. *Rural Sociology* 51: 1–17.

Wilkinson, K. P., D. J. Hobbs, and J. A. Christenson. 1983. An analysis of the national rural development strategy. *The Rural Sociologist* 3:384–91.

Zuiches, James J. 1982. Residential preferences. In *Rural society in the U.S.: Issues for the 1980s*, ed. D. A. Dillman and D. J. Hobbs, 247–55. Boulder, Colo.: Westview Press.

12

SOCIAL CHANGE AND DRESS AMONG THE KALABARI OF NIGERIA

Joanne Bubolz Eicher

Introduction

The Kalabari people of Nigeria have been exposed to non–Kalabari ways of life and cultural artifacts (both African and non–African) for several centuries as a result of internal Nigerian trade routes (Alagoa 1970) and Portuguese explorations, which opened Kalabari ports to European trade in the late 1400s. As prominent middlemen in the transatlantic slave and palm oil trade, the Kalabari have participated in a global economy and have experienced many changes in their daily lives. Their involvement in the world economy is shown by their profuse use of dress[1] and textiles from such other places as India, England, and the rest of West Africa. Through dress and textiles, the Kalabari provide a visible symbol of their invisible worldview.

To demonstrate the role of dress in understanding social change in Kalabari life, I briefly review Kalabari history before the 1880s and provide a background for the changes occurring from the 1880s to the 1980s. Next, I describe daily life in the 1880s and 1980s in order to analyze change and relate it to Kalabari traditional dress. A key concept in this analysis is *cultural authentication*, whereby borrowed items are selected, characterized, incorporated, and transformed to create a new combination (Erekosima 1979; Erekosima and Eicher 1981 and 1995).

Setting

The Kalabari comprise about one million people in an estimated total Nigerian population of 90 million. In the last century, they have shared with other Nigerians massive demographic, political, economic, and social changes. These changes have occurred as Nigeria has gone from precolonialism to colonialism, to independence, and then to postindependence.

The islands the Kalabari call home are at the southernmost part of Nigeria, about four degrees above the equator. The River Niger (combined midcountry from the Niger and the Benue Rivers) flows south into the Atlantic Ocean and forms a large delta area of tributaries and islands. Here the Kalabari live on islands among miles of mangrove swamps, where they experience two seasons, dry and rainy, with temperatures from 70–90° Fahrenheit.

The Kalabari are members of the Ijo–speaking group, one of 250 linguistic groups within Nigeria. As others who are now known as Nigerians, they lived under British control from the time of the Berlin Conference agreement in 1885 until independence in 1960. Kalabari express religious beliefs that encompass Christianity and an indigenous belief system (sometimes both simultaneously). A high proportion of Kalabari men are monogamous, although polygyny is practiced when affordable. Kalabari men, once primarily traders and fishermen, now participate in a widened set of occupations; many Kalabari women have joined them in employment outside the home. Many Kalabari work and live not only in nearby Port Harcourt, the capital city of Rivers State, but also migrate to other Nigerian cities such as Lagos, Kano, Kaduna, and Enugu. Whenever time permits and finances allow, they revisit their communities of origin.[2]

Kalabari History Prior to 1880s

Written records of the Kalabari date to the first contacts with them as traders in the 1400s. New Calabar (also called Elem Ama and Old Shipping) on the Rio Reall was one of the major trade centers for West Africans, Portuguese, Dutch, and English (Barbot 1746; Duarte Periera, 1937; Ryder 1965; Alagoa 1972, 135). Prior to this time, the Kalabari were probably never self–sufficient, but dependent on trading salt and fish for other foodstuffs and materials (Jones 1963, 9).

In addition to their reputation as traders, the Kalabari are also known for their loyalty to a lineage system that includes both consanguineal and adopted members. The basic descent group is called *wari* or "war canoe house." Adoptions pragmatically expanded the human resource base of the *wari*. Historically, the actual war canoe was a vessel for trade and war, large enough for 40 to 80 men, headed by a powerful man and his subalterns. Both slaves and freeborn manned the canoe. The head of the *wari* controlled trade between foreigners and traders from the hinterland by not allowing either to meet. Europeans exchanged goods first for slaves and later for palm oil, both coming from the Nigerian hinterland. As adopted slaves or freeborn men became experts in trade, they were sponsored by their chief to become independent traders and heads of war canoes of their own. In short, Kalabari slaves, originally from neighboring ethnic groups such as the Igbo, could be adopted into the family after proof as successful traders (Jones 1963; Horton 1969). Thus, the Kalabari developed an "expanded" family system (Erekosima 1989) and encouraged competition among the lineages who sought control of the river for trade and stimulated continuous inter– and intraethnic rivalry and conflict.

Marriages, whether monogamous or polygamous, involved a choice between large and small bridewealth. In an *iya* marriage (large bridewealth), children belonged to the father's lineage. In an *egwa* marriage (small bridewealth), children remained with the mother's lineage. In this Kalabari kinship system, individuals recount, often several generations back, complex sets of relationships for both mother's and father's forebears, depending on the bridewealth conditions (Talbot 1926; Horton 1969). Textiles played a role in bridewealth for both traditional and Christian marriages, as quantities of cloth were given by the prospective husband to his intended. Generally, only successful Kalabari traders who were chiefs were polygynous, since only they could afford the resources, including cloth, for more than one wife. A large inventory of cloth was a highly visible measure of wealth and relationships (Eicher 1988).

Also significant in an understanding of the Kalabari is their independent character, often noted by early travelers on the West African Coast. The Kalabari not only established and perpetuated a trade monopoly based on geographical position (Jones 1963), but also refused to take goods on trust (credit) from the Europeans, an act thereby reinforcing their independence (Hutchinson 1858, 101; Dike 1956, 125-26). This image of autonomy was emphasized by British Consul Hutchinson (1858): "In New Calabar the King and chiefs walk on the deck of any ship with an air of independence, similar to that assumed by a wealthy capitalist on the Stock Exchange at home" (as quoted in Geary 1927, 83).

Independence, the Nigerian historian Dike (1956, 161) pointed out, exhibited itself throughout the Delta, for inhabitants showed selectivity in responding to outside contact:

> The impact of Western European commercial enterprise on the Delta States, after three centuries of continuous contact, was more evident on the material than on the ideological plane. European institutions and dogma had remarkably small influence and traditional religious and political beliefs, though unwritten, still dominated the daily life of the nineteenth–century Africans.

For the Kalabari, one distinctive lifestyle was reflected in the material plane: their dress. They chose to incorporate borrowed items to create an ensemble uniquely identified as Kalabari. Just as they incorporated human beings to expand their kin groups, they incorporated material artifacts to expand their material resource base. From European tradestuffs, they chose such goods as cowrie shells, beads, iron bars, and much cloth from West Africa, Europe, and India (Adams 1823). They were seen as "very particular." For example, Dapper reported in 1668 that when the Kalabari selected gray copper armlets used for exchange purposes, they often rejected "two to three hundred out of one barrel," accepting them only if they were "oblong with a rounded curve and very well made" (Talbot 1926, 1:241).

Documents of the mid–1800s report Kalabari selectivity in dress and textiles. Rev. Waddell ([1863] 1970, 420), during his 1850 visit to New Calabar, commented on details of dress and demeanor: "Barboy, on whom we called, an intelligent man, was dressed in a long blue velvet shirt with red facings, in which he looked majestic." Count de Cardi (1899, 507), who traveled from 1862 to 1896 in West Africa, wrote that: "Another chief of no mean capacity is Bob Manuel, of Abonnema, exceedingly neat, almost a dandy in appearance. . . ." Consul Hutchinson (1858, 101) said: "All the people met in the town have an air of sturdiness in their walk, not to be seen elsewhere except at Lagos and Akra." De Cardi (1899, 508) contrasted the Kalabari with other groups in the area because the Kalabari covered their bodies and had a preference for Indian madras:

> Owing to some peculiarities in their dress, the New Calabar chiefs are very different to the chiefs in other parts of the Delta. They never appear outside of their houses unless robed in long shirts (made of real india [sic] madras of bold check patterns, in which no other colour but red, blue and white is ever allowed to be used) reaching down to their heels; under this they wear a singlet and a flowing loin cloth of the same material as their shirts.

Talbot (1932, 279) gave further information about the source of madras and its use in Kalabari life:

> Injiri—the local pronunciation of the word India—a cloth, the trade name of which is "real india" and which was first introduced to these regions by the Portuguese, was for many years the finest material obtainable and therefore became the dress of Kalabari chiefs and is still worn on ceremonial occasions.

Talbot reasonably credits the Portuguese with introducing madras, for historical records indicate that the Portuguese had reached and traded in Bombay and Madras by the same time they touched base in the Rio Reall. This attribution is complicated by the fact that the word "Portuguese" has been used by riverine people to designate anyone not native to the area, whether European or other Africans, such as Sierra Leonians (Alagoa 1988). If Talbot's argument is accepted, the tradition of this textile in Kalabari life could date to the early 1500s. Although there was (and is) a potentially wide range of colors and patterns available for madras, Talbot describes the Kalabari as being discriminating about these.[3]

This preference for madras appears to have been related to their indigenous belief system that has been described by Horton (1960, 1962, 1963, 1965, 1969, 1970). Three categories of spiritual beings are pivotal within the Kalabari worldview: water people (*owu'amapu*), the community deities (*am'oru*), and the ancestors (*duein*).[4] Dress and textile arts of the Kalabari are related to these philosophic beliefs, especially the interplay between power and creativity as represented by gender roles, a theme first noted by Horton in his article on the Kalabari Ekine Society (1963) and later elaborated by Erekosima (1979).

The water people (*owu*) are associated with controlling the many rivers and tributaries that surround the Kalabari environment. Any activity involving economic pursuit, such as successful trade, is generally attributed to the water people, who are said to govern an individual's good and bad fortune and innovation. For example, the *owu* are accountable for the imported textiles and dress items brought to the Kalabari world by trade, as well as for ingenious uses of these items in new ensembles (Daly, Eicher, and Erekosima 1986).

The community deities (*am'oru*), representing collective life, bear good will to the Kalabari, generate welfare, and refine the culture. The Kalabari tutelary deity, *Owame–kaso*, is female, representing creativity (ibid.). *Owame–kaso* is said to wear an emblem of refinement, "print" cloth (a cotton textile printed with figurative motifs), which she prohibits the Kalabari to wear.[5] Because they do not want to anger her, the Kalabari assiduously observe the prohibition and wear Indian madras (*injiri*) and a range of other "nonprint" textiles (Eicher 1988). Thus, textiles as symbols of Kalabari participation in world trade were incorporated into their belief system.

The ancestors (*duein*) represent kinship existence in the Kalabari world. Cloth, coral and gold jewelry, and ceremonial hats of leading elders become emblematic property of the kin group at the death of the elders, who then join the ancestors (*duein*). Sociopolitical power in Kalabari terms rests in the hands of adult males. Technically only males become ancestors at death. Sociopolitical status is represented by men's dress, which includes a variety of hats that focus attention on the head and forehead, where power is said to reside (Erekosima 1989).[6]

Kalabari Life in the 1880s and the 1980s
The 1880s

I will use the first and last decades of the century from the 1880s to the 1980s to analyze change in Kalabari life.[7] The 1880s are important because overcrowding, overpopulation, and internal rivalries forced major migrations from the island of New Calabar. The control of economic, political, and religious life came increasingly from the outside.

Scanty descriptions of the physical environment indicate a relatively simple, indigenous technology with dependence on natural resources for shelter and food. With the exception of Kalabari chiefs' houses at the turn of the century, native materials were used to construct ordinary housing of thatched roofs with walls of sticks and mud or palm mats and poles. Chiefs built large two–story houses (often with large verandas) of imported materials, such as zinc and colored glass, and frequently filled them with imported English furniture.

As the Kalabari had more contact with outsiders, exposure to imported tradestuffs, such as clothing and certain household items, increased (Jones 1963, 74). When exports shifted from slavery to palm oil, ships waited longer in harbors for their puncheons to fill, up to five months as compared to one month needed for loading slaves; this delay allowed Kalabari traders more time to interact with the outsiders (ibid.). English traders did not ordinarily go ashore, but invited the Kalabari to visit and trade with them aboard ship. These occasions provided the Kalabari with opportunities to hear and learn English, observe European dress, and request favored items of dress. Some items were given as gifts: the pull-boys of the canoes were given cloth; chiefs were given other items of dress. In addition, a specific pattern of madras became named for the Kalabari trader who first bought and traded it in the Kalabari community. Cloth so named bestowed additional prominence on the family; today, many patterns still retain names originally given to them.[8]

Involvement in a world economy by the Kalabari was indicated by the source of imported textiles and design of garments. For example, there were: wrappers worn by both men and women, made of cotton madras, silk, and velvet from India; printed woolen flannel from England; and handwoven cloth from the Gold Coast, Yorubaland, and the adjacent Igbo town of Akwete. Male garments appear patterned after Englishmen's clothing of the middle nineteenth century (Case 1987).

By 1884, during the reign of the Kalabari ruler Amachree IV, migrations to Buguma, Abonnema, and Bakana were complete, and New Calabar was left deserted. Competition for control of trade was developing from forces outside the Kalabari when the charter of the Royal Niger Company was established by England in 1886, lasting until 1899. This charter excluded any trader not a member of the Company, African or English, from trading on the River Niger. With the establishment of the Nigerian Protectorate, the presence of the English became increasingly pronounced. In 1900, when King Amachree IV died in Buguma, the English were clearly in political control. This control was visibly symbolized by the completion in 1904 of permanent buildings for the colonial government at Degema, across the river from Abonnema.

The English were not only controlling trade and government, but also trying to control religious beliefs by introducing Christianity. Missionaries sought converts within Kalabari communities, but had little success before 1890. However, they gained many converts from 1890 to 1912, which consequently spurred the development from 1912 to 1918 of a revolutionary Kalabari interpretation of Christianity. Syncretism and revival of traditional beliefs followed from 1918 on (Horton 1970).

Missionaries apparently had little impact on Kalabari dress in any of the periods of influence because the Kalabari men already "covered their nakedness," a usual missionary concern. (In the case of women, the impact of missionaries may have been to influence them to wear blouses). Most importantly, the items of Western dress worn by the Kalabari were not imposed upon them by political force or religious zeal. Instead, the Kalabari themselves exercised considerable choice based on the items available to them through trade.

Throughout this period of time, competition among the war canoe houses continued. Rivalry through warfare decreased as the British increased commercial, political, and religious control of the Kalabari world. However, lineage competition continued through display of power and wealth in dress, textiles, and household furnishings obtained in trade. According to oral testimony by Kalabari informants, families treasured the family heirlooms of textiles, coral, and gold that they kept to display at the death of a chief. (During the twentieth century, the practice of conspicuous display at a funeral was expanded to include any prominent elder, and this has continued into the 1990s [Eicher and Erekosima 1987; Daly 1987]).[9]

Written descriptions of Kalabari dress are augmented by photographs. A few published photographs are found in a history on Southern Nigeria (Anene 1966). Additional unpublished photographs, displayed on the sitting room walls or in family albums, can be found in Kalabari homes in

Port Harcourt and Kalabari communities. Sometimes, either handwritten inscriptions or typed captions with dates are found on the back or front of the photograph. Some photographs have been duplicated for extended family members to display—thus copies of the same photograph are frequently seen.[10] Both photographs and written descriptions appear more frequently for Kalabari males, who, as traders, chiefs, and house heads, were in contact with male outsiders, who photographed and recorded their observations. The few images of women available show them photographed with a male, (presumably a husband), wearing a "wrapper" (a rectangular piece of cloth wrapped around the lower torso, in a common West African style) with a blouse or another textile on the upper torso. Because photographs are more available for the males during the century of my analysis, I emphasize male attire in this chapter.

Anene's (1966) analysis of Southern Nigeria from 1885 to 1906 includes photographs showing how Kalabari men borrowed and combined foreign items of dress to create a uniquely Kalabari ensemble. Three selections (two undated and one dated 1905) allow comparison and contrast of Kalabari dress with that of the Efik king (Obong) of Calabar[11] and the king of Okrika. In the first photograph (fig.1), the seated Kalabari Chief Young Briggs from Abonnema is wearing an *attigra* gown (that comes from the Igala area north of the Kalabari in Nigeria) with an elaborately decorated crescent hat called an *ajibulu*. The full–length gown, tailored from handwoven cloth, is still worn by Kalabari chiefs on formal occasions. Standing beside him, his son wears an ankle–length gown called a *doni*, fashioned of fabrics such as damask, with no collar but with a front opening requiring four studs. Under the *doni*, he wears an *etibo* (a knee–length shirt with neckband and no collar) and a madras wrapper.

In contrast, Prince Archibong II, the Efik ruler from 1864 to 1867, sits bare–chested and enthroned, with a wrapper around his waist and a crown on his head (fig. 2). Being bare–chested in public is not appropriate for a Kalabari man, as de Cardi (1899, 508) observed when he noted that Kalabari men would not leave their houses unless fully dressed. The photograph of the king of Okrika (fig. 3), who was deported in 1896, shows him wearing a rumpled gown and a crushed and dented top hat. Neither the style of the gown nor the disheveled appearance show any similarity to Kalabari dress displayed in photographs of that time. Fastidiousness of dress and person, a mark of Kalabari appearance today (Daly, Eicher, and Erekosima 1986), was presumably also a similar requirement in the late 1800s, for de Cardi commented that Bob Manual was "almost a dandy" (1899, 507) and Waddell used the adjective "majestic" to describe Barboy (Talbot 1926, 1:256). Neither description applies to the king of Okrika's photograph.

Social Change and Dress Among the Kalabari

Figure 1. Chief Young Briggs of Abonnema, coast *warrant chief*, with his son, Chief Frank Briggs. The elder chief wears an *attigra* gown and a decorated *ajibulu* hat. His son wears an ankle-length *doni gown*. Photo made in 1905, courtesy of A. Fombo in J.C. Anene (1966), *Southern Nigeria in Transition, 1885–1906* (p.413).

The ensemble worn by Kalabari males separated them from their neighbors, for the items assembled from their history and the range of their trading contacts resulted in a distinctive appearance. The *attigra* gown came from within Nigeria; but the shirt originated in Europe. Hats and textiles emanated from England and India. The photographs discussed above were dated in the 1880s and later, but we can infer that the apparel and accessories represented ensembles developed and recognized as Kalabari well before those dates. In view of the adroit trading practices of the Kalabari in the early and mid–1800s, such ensembles must have been well–established symbols of successful Kalabari trading at the peak of their commercial achievements.

The Kalabari signified their awareness and knowledge of the outside world through items of dress. Descriptions of Kalabari life at that time reveal a strong commitment to their communal values, as the Kalabari rejected missionary attempts at conversion and resisted increasing control by the English in political and economic matters. Kalabari dress represented their independence of thought and action and their view of a tripartite cosmology of the water people, community deities, and ancestors.

Figure 2. Prince Archibong II, the obong of Calabar, circa 1865. The obong is photographed wearing a wrapper and crown but bare–chested. Courtesy of A. Fombo in J.C. Anene (1966), *Southern Nigeria in Transition, 1885–1906* (p.337).

The water people were seen as responsible for foreign trade, and good fortune in life associated with that trade which included cloth and items of dress that the Kalabari found appealing to wear in combinations unique to them. The community deities specifically designated one trade textile, *injiri* (madras), to be worn by the Kalabari, and another type, "print," as the property of the tutelary deity. Kalabari ancestors were respected by the act of amassing fortunes from trade that included dress and textile items to display in order to indicate lineage prestige.

The 1980s

At the visible level, life in the 1980s differs from life in the 1880s for the Kalabari. Buguma, Abonnema, and Bakana are large and prominent island communities found alongside several smaller but viable Kalabari island settlements. Port Harcourt, a multiethnic city, is a work base for many Kalabari businesspeople, professionals, civil servants, and traders, who maintain a home in their village and return frequently on weekends. Some traditional modes of life are found in the island communities, but many Western conveniences exist alongside them.[12] For example, houses include

Figure 3. The king of Okrika on his deportation in 1896. Courtesy of A. Fombo in J.C. Anene (1966), *Southern Nigeria in Transition, 1885–1906* (p. 412).

elaborate and modern two–story dwellings with air–conditioning, a few two–story dwellings from the early 1900s, and simple mud–walled houses with traditional thatching or aluminum roofs.

From Monday morning until Friday noon, island residents go about their everyday work and children go to school. Beginning at Friday noon, motor launches from Port Harcourt arrive more frequently than during weekdays. Family and *wari* persist as significant foci in Kalabari life, to which the Port Harcourt resident returns on weekends, especially for such major events as funerals, traditional masquerades, or chieftaincy installations. Crowded boats bring those who have come to participate in a funeral ceremony, the most common weekend social activity, which begins by a display of the corpse on a "state" bed, an initial wake on Friday night, a burial by Saturday noon, a family parade through the community, and a final dance a week later (Eicher and Erekosima 1987). Jammed into the boats along with the passengers are crates of Coca Cola, Sprite, hard liquor, yams, and rice for traditional hosting of family and friends during these occasions. The Port Harcourt workers not only reinforce kinship bonds on their weekend visits, but also provide financial support that keeps much of the community economy afloat.

Dress of travelers usually indicates the purpose of their visit home, for Kalabari traditional garb is socially mandatory for adults in all social strata when attending traditional events. There are wide variations in income and social standing, but no matter what the income level, Kalabari adults wear Kalabari dress when needed. Less fortunate individuals may have only one Kalabari outfit; more fortunate often have a large wardrobe to select from. Thus, women wear a blouse and double wrapper set called *bite sara*, the most frequent example being a white eyelet blouse with madras wrappers (Iyalla 1968; Daly 1983, 1984); men, the knee–length, shirt–like garment called an *etibo* with a madras wrapper beneath it; or perhaps an upper–torso tailored garment called a *woko* of gabardine, worn either with matching gabardine trousers or with a madras wrapper. If dressed in Western style upon arrival in their home community, both men and women change to traditional attire to pay respect to families in mourning, to stroll around the town, and to attend church services on Sunday. No matter how limited or extensive one's wardrobe, Kalabari men and women take pride in being turned out properly in Kalabari dress for weekend activities (Daly 1984; Daly, Eicher, and Erekosima 1986; Erekosima 1989).

Kalabari men's dress indicates a hierarchy that parallels age–grade and political status. The rules of dress for these ensembles are as follows: *asawo* or the "young men that matter" wear the shirt called an *etibo* with an *injiri* wrapper; the *opu asawo* (gentlemen of substance) wear the outfit called a *woko* with either a wrapper or matched trousers and appropriate accessories of hat, cane, and jewelry; and *alabo* (the chiefs) wear the gown called a *doni* with shirt and wrapper, plus a hat and cane. The king wears a madras gown with a matching madras wrapper called an *ebu*. *Attigra* gowns are by custom reserved for chiefs and the king, to be worn at ceremonies (Erekosima and Eicher 1980; Erekosima 1982; Erekosima 1989, 1995). When finances are meager, clothing may be borrowed, when possible, or approximated. For example, for young or impoverished males, a white European–style dress shirt may be used in place of a white *etibo* for a top garment. However, a madras (*injiri*) wrapper will always be worn with either shirt or *etibo*. The ensembles of *woko, doni, ebu,* and *attigra* with appropriate headgear can be borrowed from the corporate store of family heirlooms for ritual occasions, such as required for participation as a family mourner in a funeral. Adult males recognized as *opu asawo* and *alabo* will have the necessary finances to own the garments and accessories required for their position and the occasions when they are called upon to wear them.

When in mourning, the immediate family of the deceased (males and females, children and adults) meet special dress requirements for taking the body home from the mortuary to lie in state for the initial wake, for the burial, for the last wake, parade, and funeral dance (Eicher and Erekosima 1987). Other adolescent males and females, not yet married, not yet adults, thus not yet part of the adult social structure, sometimes wear western dress, such as jeans, trousers and shirts, western style "frocks," skirts, and blouses, depending on current fashion and the occasion. At large funeral wakes, youth occasionally wear western styles for the event to dance to loud, popular music from stereos; others choose to wear traditional dress. In contrast, adults almost without exception wear traditional garb to dance traditional steps to the beat of traditional drums or to stereos playing traditional music. Family members and close friends of the deceased, youth and adults, dress in traditional dress for the church funeral service, burial, family parade, and final dance.

How is change related to the way the Kalabari dress? Signs of change indicating involvement in an industrial world are displayed in the island communities by new community buildings and personal homes. Kalabari people had access to a wider range of jobs in the 1980s than in the 1880s and to more creature comforts in housing and transportation. Many Western-style material possessions in Kalabari life are available and prized, both in Port Harcourt and in the island communities; possession of such conveniences varies according to personal wealth. Thus, change in many areas has been eagerly embraced and internalized; aspects of Kalabari life resemble life in larger Nigerian, West African, and Western worlds. With new occupations and modern ways of living in the 1980s, the Kalabari wear Western dress when interacting with the Western world.

However, the Kalabari exhibit their link to traditional Kalabari beliefs about the water people, community deities, and ancestors when they wear Kalabari dress to attend funerals, masquerades, chieftaincy installations, and other island celebrations. These occasions allow the Kalabari to express their loyalty to community and kin and to reaffirm their Kalabari identity.[13]

Dress and textile items involve material goods that entered Kalabari life through the process of trade over a period of time extending back to the late 1400s. These items both glorify Kalabari commercial prowess of that time and exemplify cultural authentication, the process whereby borrowed objects become transformed and indigenously meaningful. Where beliefs and practices stem from the Kalabari past (with Western ideas either rejected or modified extensively), the arts of dress and textiles visibly symbolize Kalabari beliefs and identity.

The continuity of their worldview is represented by the continuity of male traditional dress in the 1980s. *Attigra* and *doni* gowns, *etibo* shirts, and *ajibulu* hats, for example, are almost duplicate examples of 1880s garments. Although Kalabari men and women of the 1980s have traveled far

Figure 4. An example of an *attigra* gown worn with an *ajibulu* hat during a masquerade performance in the 1980s. This chief carries an elephant tusk and fan and has a circlet of leopard's teeth. (Photograph by Carolyn J. Eicher.)

beyond the boundaries crossed by their forebears who were traders, when they return home they wear the ensembles of dress and display the textiles that echo the past and reinforce their pride in being Kalabari.[14] They have incorporated items from worldwide sources, placing them in creative juxtaposition, making a composite not English, Portuguese, Dutch, or Indian, but Kalabari.

Curtin (1984, 1) has observed that most changes within a society come from external stimulation, with trade and exchange providing perhaps the the most important stimuli, for "no human group could invent by itself more than a small part of its cultural and technical heritage." This observation has meaning for the Kalabari material world of the 1980s. However, as Dike (1956) observed, European influence was "remarkably small" in the area of African traditional and political beliefs. The Kalabari use their traditional dress ensembles of culturally authenticated items, assembled from years of trade, as visible symbols of an invisible worldview.[15]

Acknowledgments

Among the many interests that J. Allan Beegle has had in teaching, research, and his personal life is a concern with the topic of rootedness as expressed by ethnic identity. My doctoral research under his direction dealt with the topic of Finnish ethnic identity in the "cutover" area of the Upper Peninsula of Michigan, where much outmigration had occurred.

Although the weather was severe and making a living was precarious, many families declined to migrate and some, we found, returned to live in what they called "God's country." We thought the heritage of being Finnish would prove to be a significant reason to stay or return, but the data did not support that hypothesis. Nevertheless, I gained experience as a fieldworker and went on to other endeavors. Among these endeavors has been a research involvement since 1963 in Nigeria, where dress and adornment serve as a visible ethnic identifier along with such other identifiers as language. My teaching and research at Michigan State University and at the University of Minnesota have focused on dress as a significant variable in everyday life. It is a pleasure to come full circle to focus on ethnicity again in this chapter.

I wish to thank several institutions for their support during various drafts of this manuscript. The University of Minnesota and Bush sabbatic award funds supported my stay in England at Oxford University under the aegis of the Centre for Cross Cultural Research on Women at Queen Elizabeth House. Another draft was undertaken while I was at the University of Alberta. Helpful critiques of the manuscript came from Suzanne Baizerman, Margaret Bubolz, Helen Callaway, Tonye Erekosima, Nan Johnson, Annette Lynch, and Mary Ellen Roach–Higgins. I am grateful to each of them for their insights. In addition, I wish to thank Susan Michelman for her useful comments on gender. My debt to Kalabari friends and informants who have provided me the opportunity to do fieldwork among them is great. I treasure their friendship and help, beginning with my first visit to Buguma in 1966. Seven more field trips since 1980 to Buguma and Kalabari communities of Abonnema, Degema, Idoh, Tombia, Bakana, Krakrama, and Kula and my association with the Erekosima family have given me a rich source of data.

Funding for my research over the years has come from many sources. Sincere appreciation is extended to several units at the University of Minnesota: the Graduate School, Office of International Education, Minnesota Agricultural Experiment Station, College of Home Economics, Bush Sabbatic Award program. In addition, support was given for 1981 fieldwork from Midwest University Consortium for International Activities (MUCIA). Equally generous funding for field research came from the Kalabari community in Buguma: the Buguma Internal Affairs Society, Chief O. K. Isokariari, The Honorable Edwin Dakoru, and Mrs. Nume Taiwo West.

Members of the John Bull compound in Buguma have been invaluable in many areas of support. Three key individuals are Chief I. D. Erekosima, who has overseen many facets of the research process as well as providing documentation of many types; his son and my colleague, Dr. Tonye V. Erekosima, who first invited me to visit Buguma to introduce me to the Kalabari and their rich and complex heritage; Madame Elizabeth Princewill, a fount of knowledge and a gracious hostess. In addition, Chief Donald Diboyesuku has offered me the hospitality of his home in Buguma in 1983, 1984, 1987, and 1989, and his contribution to my research is gratefully acknowledged. I also wish to thank Professor E. J. Alagoa and Professor Robin Horton for their cooperation with my fieldwork endeavors and willingness to supply information and answers whenever possible.

Notes

1. I define dress as presented in a paper by Eicher and Roach–Higgins (1989) as follows: "an assemblage of body modifications and supplements displayed by a person in the presentation of self. This self is located within a physical body that has a visible appearance and a continuity often referred to as an identity."
2. This migration does not easily dissolve or weaken ethnic identity and loyalty for Kalabari or other Nigerians. Commitment to and identification with ethnic roots and the home community persist for migrants, as equally for those well–educated, successful, and with prominent jobs, as for those subsisting marginally. Cities are seen as places of transitory existence; "home" is the village of one's forebears; kin groups expect the successful individual to come home regularly, to build, improve, and maintain a house, and to support kinfolk. This observation is based on my familiarity with Nigeria as a whole, as well as with the Kalabari people. Migration to urban areas for work is common, but the loyalty to one's home appears to remain paramount in one's life and extends to one's offspring as well, even though the offspring may not have been born in the home village.
3. DeCardi noted their color preference for red, blue, and white madras in the late 1800s. These same color preferences existed in the 1980s, slightly widened, as I was told by exporters in India whom I interviewed in 1988. They reported that Kalabari preferences are limited to nine specific colors (indigo, red, burgundy, white, beige, orange, green, yellow, and black), combined in a limited number of particular plaid patterns. The marked preference of the Kalabari for madras is noteworthy. Even though other West African peoples, such as adjacent Rivers groups and the Igbo, wear madras, they also wear many varieties of printed textiles.
4. Horton uses the terms *village heroes* for *am'oru*, *ancestors* for *duein*, and *water people* for *owu'amapu*. Erekosima translates the word *am'oru* as *community deities* instead of village heroes, as he maintains this interpretation is more accurate, and its meaning more accurately includes the female tutelary deity, *Owame–akaso*. The first published reference using the modified terminology can be found in Daly, Eicher, and Erekosima (1986).

5. Barley (1988, 82 n.59) incorrectly assumes that this prohibition against using printed textiles has broken down because the photograph of King Amachree IV "shows the king seated on a chair covered with a textile that depicts large flowers." The textile Barley describes is what the Kalabari call "damask," which has floral textile designs woven in the fabric and does not belong to the Kalabari category of cotton "prints."
6. Headgear of the carved figures in the ancestor shrines in the major family compounds is most often a hat, sometimes a masquerade headdress that was owned by the lineage (Barley 1987; Erekosima 1988).
7. Documentation for the 1880s comes from written accounts by both non–Africans and Africans (including Kalabari), Kalabari oral history and testimony, and photographs.
8. A thorough documentation of cloth names has yet to be undertaken. Daly (1984) discusses "named" cloth and the works by Renne (1985); Erekosima and Eicher (1981); Eicher and Erekosima with Thieme (1982); Eicher, Erekosima and Liedholm (1982) also refer to the naming of the Kalabari cut–thread cloth. I have been shown many cloths used by the Kalabari that are identified by name, a common practice throughout West Africa. Other West African groups name cloth by describing or commenting about the pattern, giving such names as "polo" (the English equivalent of the American candy called "Lifesavers") or ministers' houses (a social comment referring to a pattern seen as the shape of a house). Among the Yoruba, the cloth name may be in the form of a proverb (Boyer 1983). I am not familiar with other groups who name cloth after a person or lineage, as is done among the Kalabari. A discussion of naming of motifs of wax–printed textiles for the West African market can be found in Ruth Nielsen (1979).
9. Field data collected in 1988 indicates that the practice of display of family heirlooms of cloth and ornament most probably began first with chiefs. According to accounts given to me in 1988, large displays of cloth and other personal possessions were heaped on the corpse of a chief, with a majority of the possessions buried with the corpse. Later, the practice of display was apparently extended to other deceased elders and the burying of possessions terminated (Eicher 1988).
10. Dates in parentheses for each photograph are exactly as I found on them. At this point, I am accepting the date presented as accurate.
11. The Obong of Calabar is from the Efik ethnic group who live in what is called "Old Calabar," to the east of New Calabar and the Kalabari ethnic group. Apparently Dutch and English traders provided a confusion in place names. The Efik and Kalabari are not related.
12. A description of one community, Buguma, provides an example of changes in material resources from the 1880s to the 1980s. The island town (estimated population of 200,000) is known as Buguma City, to emphasize its increasing urban amenities. Before the 1980s, there were no motor vehicles. Now a few cars travel the main road (having reached the island by tortuous road and ferry), along with minivans and motorbikes that provide a land transport alternative to some nearby villages. Two western-style hotels were built in 1984; at

the same time, construction of the new King Amachree IV Memorial Hall began on the town square. Opposite the Memorial Hall is the drum house of the prestigeful men's society known as Ekine, and in the middle of the square is a towering sculpture of the founder of Buguma, King Amachree IV. Along with a bank, post office, and police post are three large Christian churches (Baptist, Anglican, and African), a smaller Faith Tabernacle Church, ten prayer houses, and a shrine to Owame-kaso (the tutelary goddess). Educational facilities include a nursery school, several primary and four secondary schools. After secondary school, whenever possible, children are educated for contemporary professions and occupations, and often sent to a university in Nigeria or abroad. A government hospital, one private clinic, and several native doctors provide medical attention. Dwellings vary from modest mud and thatch roofed structures to several-story cement block or concrete structures that are as up-to-date as finances allow; some posh by any standard, with modern, convenient bathrooms, kitchens, appliances, and furniture. Municipal facilities for piped water and electricity exist but rarely function. Water is usually carried from town wells; only residents with private generators for their compounds enjoy a constant and steady supply of electricity. Those without generators use kerosene for lamps and cooking, hot charcoal for irons, and foot-pedaled sewing-machines. For women, making a living includes petty trade, hairdressing, catering for small food stalls and bars, and cutting designs in madras, a textile art traditional only to the Kalabari. Both men and women teach; both own shops that specialize in imported textiles, small household and personal supplies, and foodstuffs. Primarily men perform commercial services, such as watch and shoe repair, photography, and tailoring traditional Kalabari dress. A few men and women specialize in making traditional, ceremonial headgear.

13. Two subcategories of Kalabari identity are also displayed in traditional dress: lineage and gender distinctions, both of which existed in the 1880s, and have been mentioned briefly. Textiles used in wrappers appear as symbols of lineage. A trader's name is identified with his lineage, and some names of textiles are lineage names, such as Wokoma or Owunari. Thus, the continued use of such named textiles constantly reinforces the pride of the designated lineage. In addition, a lineage gains prestige at special events when ceremonial dress is worn: the textiles and accessories display its socioeconomic power. Similarly, textiles displayed on funeral beds and walls symbolize lineage identity and power.

Gender distinctions have also been mentioned in the discussion of position of the male. Women's dress also has a ranking system that indicates biological and procreative roles as so defined by the Kalabari. Erekosima (1982, 1984, 1989) analyzes men's dress and sociopolitical position. Daly (1983, 1984) analyzes stages of female development and dress. Discussion comparing Kalabari gender differences as shown through dress can be found in Michelman (1987), who analyzes body, dress, and dance of both males and females.

14. This observation is similar to one from Loomis and Beegle (1975, 22) regarding the significance of the local community: "Although Americans move about

much more than their parents, the most meaningful interactions generally transpire within the confines of the local community."
15. When this chapter was first presented at the symposium honoring Professor Beegle in Athens, Georgia, in 1988 and later in a review by Nan Johnson, the question arose whether or not the "sartorial imperialism" was inevitable in regard to the traditional dress of the Kalabari. The answer to this question has two parts. First, the term "sartorial imperialism" implies domination or compulsion and does not apply to Kalabari dress. Instead, the Kalabari, as I indicate by the historical data in this chapter, exercised voluntary choice in their selection of cloth and apparel, in both design and style, from those items available through trade. Second, the continued use of what the Kalabari themselves call "Kalabari dress" has continued vigorously into the 1990s. I predict it will continue because both Kalabari men and women talk about Kalabari dress and wear it with much pride when strolling in their island communities on weekends, for funerals, chieftaincy installations, or other celebrations. My field observations during the decade of the 1980s indicate that adolescents and adults wear Western dress during their periods of schooling and when engaged in work situations in Port Harcourt. When they play traditional roles in funerals or other rituals, they wear Kalabari dress.

References

Adams, Capt. John. 1823. *Remarks on the country extending from Cape Palmas to the River Congo.* London: n.p.

Alagoa, E. J. 1970. Long distance trade and states in the Niger Delta. *Journal of African History* 11(3): 319–29.

———. 1972. *A history of the Niger Delta.* Ibadan, Nigeria: Ibadan University Press.

———. 1988. Personal communication.

Anene, J. C. 1966. *Southern Nigeria in transition, 1885–1906: Theory and practice in a colonial protectorate.* Cambridge: Cambridge University Press.

Barbot, John. 1746. A description of the coasts of North and South Guinea. In *A collection of voyages and travels,* vol. T, 3d ed., ed. A. Churchill. London: H. Lintot and J. Osborn.

Barley, Nigel. 1987. Pop art in Africa? The Kalabari Ijo ancestral screens. *Art History* 10 (3): 369–80.

———. 1988. *Foreheads of the dead: An anthropological view of Kalabari ancestral screens.* Washington, D.C.: Smithsonian Institution.

Boyer, Ruth M. 1983. Yoruba cloths with regal names. *African Arts* 16(2): 42–44, 98.

Case, Juli. 1987. Western influence on Kalabari men's dress. Undergraduate Research Opportunities Program, Department of Design, Housing, and Apparel, College of Home Economics, University of Minnesota, Minneapolis.

Curtin, Philip D. 1984. *Cross cultural trade in world history.* Cambridge: Cambridge University Press.

Daly, M. C. 1987. Iria Bo appearance at Kalabari funerals. *African Arts.* 21 (November): 58–61, 86.

———. 1984. *Kalabari female appearance and the tradition of Iria.* Ph.D. dissertation, University of Minnesota, Minneapolis.

———. 1983. The Kalabari tradition of Iria: Examples of cloth use and the female lifecycle. *Newsletter of the Textile Council of the Minneapolis Institute of Arts.* Minneapolis, Minn. 24 July.

Daly, M. C., Joanne B. Eicher, and Tonye V. Erekosima. 1986. Male and female artistry in Kalabari dress. *African Arts* 19 (May): 48–51.

de Cardi, Le Comte C. N. 1899. Appendix I: A short description of the natives of the Niger Coast protectorate with some account of their customs, religion, trade, etc. In *West African studies*, ed. Mary Kingsley, 442–511. London: Macmillan and Co., Ltd.

Dike, K. O. 1956. *Trade and politics in the Niger Delta.* London: Oxford University Press.

Duarte Pereira, Pacheco. 1937. *Esmeraldo de situo orbis.* Trans. G. H. T. Kimble. Series 2, no. 79. London: Hakluyt Society.

Echeruo, Michael J. C. 1977. *Victorian Lagos: Aspects of nineteenth century Lagos life.* London: Macmillan Education, Ltd.

Eicher, Joanne B. 1988. Field notes.

Eicher, Joanne B., and Tonye V. Erekosima. 1987. Kalabari funerals: Celebration and display. *African Arts* 21 (November): 38–45, 87.

———. 1989. Kalabari funeral rooms as handicraft and ephemeral art. In *Man does not go naked: Textilien und handwerk aus Afrikanishen und anderen landern*, ed. B. Engelbrecht and B. Gardi, 197–208. Festschrift for Dr. Renee Boser–Sarivaxevanis, Basel, Switzerland.

———. 1995. Why do they call it Kalabari? Cultural authenticity and the demarcation of ethnic identity. In *Dress and Ethnicity*, ed. Joanne B. Eicher. Oxford/Washington: Berg Publishers, Ltd.

Eicher, Joanne B., Tonye V. Erkosima, and Carl Liedholm. 1982. Cut and drawn: Textile work from Nigeria. *Craft International* (summer): 16–19.

Eicher, Joanne B., and Tonye V. Erekosima, with technical analysis by Otto Charles Thieme. 1982. Pelete bite: Kalabari cut–thread cloth. (exhibit catalog). St. Paul: University of Minnesota, The Goldstein Gallery.

Eicher, Joanne B., and Mary Ellen Roach–Higgins. 1992. Describing dress: A system of classifying and defining. In *Dress and gender: Making and meaning*, ed. Ruth Barnes and Joanne B. Eicher. Oxford, England: Berg Publishers Ltd.

Erekosima, Tonye V. 1984. The changing patterns of status among Kalabari men, Buguma Centenary Symposium. Eds. Tonye V. Erikosima, W. H. Kio Lawson, Obeleye Mac Jaja. Lagos, Nigeria: Sibon Books, Ltd.

———. 1979. The tartans of Buguma women: Cultural authentication. Paper presented at the African Studies Association, Los Angeles, Calif.

———. 1982. The use of apparel and accessories for expressing status in Nigerian societies: The Kalabari case studies as an educational technology. Presented at the annual meetings of the African Studies Association.

———. 1988. Reply to Nigel Barley on "Pop art in Africa? The Kalabari ancestral screens." Personal letter.

———. 1989. Analysis of a teaching resource on political integration applicable to the Nigerian social studies curriculum: The case of the Kalabari men's traditional men's dress. Ph.D. dissertation, Catholic University of America.

Erekosima, Tonye V., and Joanne B. Eicher. 1980. Kalabari men's dress: A sophisticated African response to culture contact. Paper presented at the African Studies Association, Philadelphia, Penn.

———. 1981. Kalabari cut–thread and pulled–thread cloth: An example of cultural authentication. *African Arts* 14(2): 8–51, 81.

Geary, Sir William N. 1927. *Nigeria under British rule*. London: Methuen & Co., Ltd.

Horton, Robin. 1969. From fishing village to city–state: A social history of new calabar. In *Man in Africa*, ed. Mary Douglas and Phyllis M. Kaberry, 37–58. London: Tavistock Publications.

———. 1960. The gods as guests: *An aspect of Kalabari religious life*. Lagos: Federal Government Printer.

———. 1962. The Kalabari world–view. Africa 32:97–220.

———. 1963. The Kalabari Ekine society: A borderland of religion and art. *Africa* 33: 94–114.

———. 1965. *Kalabari sculpture*. Apapa, Nigeria Department of Antiquities, Federal Republic of Nigeria

———. 1970. A hundred years of change in Kalabari religion. In *Black Africa*, ed. J. Middleton, 192–211. New York: MacMillan Co.

Hutchinson, T. J. 1858. *Impressions of West Africa*. London: Longman, Brown, Green, Longmans, & Roberts.

———. 1861. *Ten years wandering among the Ethopians*. London: Longman, Hurst and Blacket.

Iyalla, B. S. 1968. Womanhood in the Kalabari. *Nigeria Magazine*, 98 (November), 216–23.

Jones, G. I. 1963. *Trading states of the oil rivers: A study of political development in eastern Nigeria*. London: Oxford University Press for the International African Institute.

Loomis, Charles P., and J. Allan Beegle. 1975. *A strategy for rural change*. Cambridge, Mass: Schenkman Publishing Company.

Mabogunje, Akin L. 1987. *Nigeria*. Africa south of the Sahara: 1988. London: Europa Editions, 754.

Michelman, Susan. 1987. Kalabari male and female aesthetics: A comparative visual analysis. Master's thesis, University of Minnesota, Minneapolis.

Nielsen, Ruth. 1979. History and development of wax–printed textiles intended for West Africa and Zaire. In *The Fabrics of Culture*, ed. Justine Cordwell and Ronald Schwarz, 467–98. New York: Mouton Publishers.

Renne, Elisha. 1985. Pelete bite: Motif and meaning. Master's thesis, University of Minnesota, Minneapolis.

Ryder, A. F. C. 1965. Dutch trade on the Nigerian coast during the 17th century. *Journal of the Historical Society of Nigeria* 3: 195–210.

Talbot, P. Amaury. 1926. *Peoples of Southern Nigeria* Vols. 1–3. London: Oxford University Press.

_____. 1932. *Tribes of the Niger* Delta. London: The Sheldon Press.

Waddell, H. M. [1863] 1970. *Twenty–nine years in the West Indies and Central Africa*. 2d ed., with new introduction by G. I. Jones. London: Frank Cass & Co. Ltd.

13

THE CALL OF THE SUGAR CANE: AGRICULTURAL CHANGE, COOPERATIVE–CAPITALISM, AND MIGRANTS IN NORTHWESTERN URUGUAY

Gaston J. Labadie

Introduction

The City of Bella Union (the Spanish name translates as "beautiful junction"), Department of Artigas, is in the northwestern tip of Uruguay, on its borders with Argentina and Brazil. The city is surrounded by two of the largest rivers in the area, the Uruguay on the west and the Cuareim on the northeast.

At the beginning of the century, Bella Union was dedicated to cattle breeding. With an early wave of immigrants in the 1920s and 1930s, there was a shift toward citrus fruit production and grape vineyards. During the 1940s and 1950s, summer crops such as tomatoes, green peppers, and others dominated agricultural production, along with cotton, wheat, and a wood–based industry. All of these crops were largely replaced or supplemented by sugar cane production after the 1950s. Currently, the Cooperative Agropecuaria del Norte Uruguayo (CALNU) of Bella Union is one of only two cane refineries in the nation. It is a cooperative that buys from its members, the producers, who individually and privately produce the sugar cane on their farms.

With 11,576 inhabitants according to the 1985 Census, the City of Bella Union is the largest in this region. Its population grew at an annual rate of 4.9 percent between 1975 and 1985, almost nine times faster than did the nation as a whole (0.55 percent). The even more dramatic annual growth rate of 13.6 percent for the rural population (from 1,705 inhabitants in 1975 to 4,028 in 1985) made Artigas the only department in Uruguay with a rural population increase.

Net inmigration (an excess of inmigrants over outmigrants) was the chief reason why the population exploded in Bella Union and its rural hinterland. Both inmigration streams, but especially the rural one, favored males over females. Indeed, there were nearly twice as many males as females living in this rural hinterland in 1985. Although agricultural employment was their main "pull factor," these rural inmigrants were largely skilled workers, since the 1985 Census showed the rural literacy rate for the Department of Artigas to be an impressive 93.1 percent. Professional and technical workers comprised over 25 percent of the rural labor force in Artigas, according to the 1985 census.

This chapter is a first attempt to show how agricultural development improved the lot of rural peoples in the Department of Artigas so much as to attract others to move in. To this end, I will show that three significant elements in this story of success include: the role of the Uruguayan government in developing economic policies to protect a domestic farming system from foreign competitors; the economic contribution from an agricultural cooperative designed to benefit laborers, growers, and refiners; and the spatial advantage of a "beautiful junction" at three national borders, where macroeconomic policies play a significant role.

The Political Economy of Sugar Refinement in Uruguay

Before 1950, the importation of sugar to Uruguay was regulated haphazardly. Then Parliament passed a law to declare a national interest in becoming self–sufficient in sugar consumption and to protect the domestic markets producing and refining sugar (Correa 1986; Moraes 1988, 133; Plouvier 1987). From this law, tariffs and quotas were levied on imported raw sugar so that the amount of foreign raw sugar received by domestic refineries in a given year would be proportional to what had been harvested nationally the year before. Generous credit lines were also created, and a regulatory commission was installed. Sale prices of domestically grown raw sugar were set at 20 percent over production costs, so that a profit would be assured to local growers. These prices were regulated by the commission until 1978, after which time they were negotiated between the domestic producers and the refineries.

Either by private or governmental initiatives, the profit was large enough to encourage the cultivation of sugar cane in Uruguay. The amount of raw sugar produced from cane in Uruguay rose from 1,700 tons in 1952–53 to 56,300 tons in 1985 (table 1). The supply of raw sugar from domestic crops rose for cane but fell for beets. There were two important consequences: the supply of raw sugar from either crop fell if it was foreign–grown (table 1), despite the cheaper prices available for raw sugar in the global market (table 2); and CALNU seized the national monopoly on refined cane sugar from its only competitor, the nationally owned refinery.

Table 1.
COMPOSITION OF SUPPLY OF SUGAR IN URUGUAY (IN THOUSANDS OF TONS).

Year	Sugar Cane	%	Raw Sugar Imported	%	Total
1952–53	1.7	2.5	54.8	81.9	66.9
1955–56	1.6	1.9	67.8	79.3	85.5
1960–61	5.4	5.1	78.1	73.5	106.2
1965–66	9.4	9.6	29.3	29.8	98.2
1970–71	14.4	11.8	60.3	49.2	122.5
1975–76	27.2	21.1	—	—	128.9
1980–81	41.3	46.4	9.2	10.3	89.1
1985	56.3	66.7	3.4	4.0	86.5

Sources: Correa 1986, Plouvier 1987.

Table 2.
PRICE EVOLUTION OF SUGAR (SELECTED YEARS).

Year	US$/KG Uruguay	International Price US$/KG	Uruguay/ International
1964	.34	.13	2.64
1965	.14	.05	2.98
1970	.34	.09	3.78
1975	.74	.45	1.64
1978	.56	.18	3.04
1981	1.19	.59	2.03
1984	.65	.12	5.42

Sources: Correa 1986; Plouvier 1987.
Note: Prices are OIA TNS raw FOB at Caribbean Ports, they are not CIF prices.

How can a privately and cooperatively owned sugar refinery triumph over such a formidable rival? A partial demystification of this political–economic miracle is rooted in the history of CALNU. In the early 1960s, the sugar–refining industry in Bella Union was controlled by a single U.S.–owned firm named American Factors. Partly because its capacity to refine raw sugar was below the locally produced supply, American Factors' monopoly over raw sugar cane exacerbated its conflicts not only with growers, but also with labor unions (the refinery was not paying the regulated prices, but lower ones; see Moraes 1988). These tensions fomented an indigenous social movement crosscutting social classes but coalescing around the five or so families who owned the major sugar cane plantations in the area of Bella Union. They co-authored a manifesto entitled *El Norte Uruguayo en Marcha (The Uruguayan North Moves Forward)*, which was signed by nearly all inhabitants of the area. The document outlined the importance of a cooperative refinery for the economic development of the region and called for, *inter alia*, a program of rural electrification to reduce the costs of irrigating fields; an expansion of irrigated fields to include not only sugar cane, but also citrus groves and grape vineyards; and a greater effort to do research aimed at boosting yields from all of these crops.

Spain lent the initial funds to start the CALNU refinery. Then an open public meeting was held in Bella Union in 1965, whereat it was decided that further capitalization and maintenance of the cooperative was to be divided among the producer–members, who agreed to contribute 10% of their annual income from their sugar cane crop. Excess capital contributions would be reimbursed in proportion to patronage. The cooperative received tax exemptions and special credit/interest rates from lenders. A number of local business and professional leaders cosigned the loan agreements. Having avoided sponsorship by only one or two rich local families, the social movement that produced CALNU freely vested its truly collective power in the organization of the cooperative.

The social movement giving birth to CALNU grew from dissatisfactions foisted by one foreign–owned refinery upon all local agricultural classes. By closing its future meetings to any Uruguayan politicos, however, CALNU resisted attempts by political authorities to co-opt its leadership. This resistance served the selfish interests of CALNU's leaders, whom the political leaders wanted to unseat.

CALNU benefits its producer–members (who increased in number from 110 in 1966 to 430 in 1987) by providing credit, technology, and certainty. This cooperative facilitates loans that aid the producer to plant the sugar cane crop. It organizes and funds research on developing cane varieties with higher yields and different harvest times so as to increase the quantity of the harvest and the time to bring it in (*zafra*, which is now six months long). As stated above, a profit of 20 percent above production costs is guaranteed to the growers by national law; and since CALNU advances payment on the crops, growers planting various subspecies with different harvest times will receive more money extended over a longer period of the year.

The producers' greater certainty about the size and the periodicity of their cash inflows allowed them to invest in land purchases, and private ownership of farmland by the cultivators increased over other types of tenure (see Labadie 1988b). Although farms in the rural hinterlands of Bella Union are smaller than the national average, farm ownership here is now more common than in the Department of Artigas as a whole (72.4 percent vs. 52 percent of farm operators are owners; see DIEA 1980). Since farmers are more willing to improve land if they own it, the number of farms and tilled hectares receiving fertilizer, irrigation, or private technical assistance has increased (table 3), along with the number of tractors (from 125 to 267 tractors with 50–85 horsepower during 1970–80). Another benefit from the expansion of irrigated land has been a rise in the importance of rice, citrus fruits, and grapes, which have reduced the depen-

Table 3.
USE OF FERTILIZER, IRRIGATION, AND TECHNICAL ASSISTANCE IN BELLA UNION.

	1961	*1966*	*1970*	*1980*
Number of farms that fertilize vs. total number of farms	UNK	38.6	54.0	73.4
Fertilized area vs. total area	5.0	9.2	13.6	44.4
Irrigated area vs. total area	6.2	9.1	13.6	20.3
Received private technical assistance	UNK	UNK	19.6	59.7

Source: Agrarian Censuses.
Note: UNK = unknown

dency of the local agricultural economy on sugar cane alone. Two other cooperatives have been spawned: CALAGUA, a cooperative that irrigates about 2,500 hectares, half in sugar cane and half in horticultural fruits; and CALVINOR, a cooperative that grows grapes for wine and direct consumption [(for details on their interlocking memberships and directorates, see Labadie (1988a)].

The capitalization of the cane, fruit, and rice commodity systems increased productivity, as is shown by the steady decline in the number of workers per hectare since the mid–1960s (table 4) and by the fall in the relative share of the labor force in self-employment (Balan 1980). Paradoxically, it has also increased the demand for agricultural labor, as is seen in the rise in the volume of rural workers and in the number of workers/farm in Bella Union, especially since 1970 (table 4). In the rural hinterlands of Bella Union, employment in agriculture jumped from 64 percent of the labor force in 1975 to 81 percent in 1985. Even the demand for agricultural scientists (posed mostly by CALNU) multiplied the number of these professional workers in rural Bella Union by a factor of 3.6 during the decade.

The intensified demand for farm hands and agricultural scientists has been met by inmigration. Most inmigrants have come as seasonal wage laborers or temporary workers (*peludos*) but eventually have become permanent residents. The 1985 Census revealed the long–term importance of

Table 4.
AGRICULTURAL WORKERS, HECTARES CULTIVATED, AND WORKERS PER HECTARE AND FARM IN RURAL BELLA UNION (BY YEAR).

	1956	1961	1966	1970	1980
Workers	1,737	2,209	1,733	1,451	1,762
Hectares of agriculture	10,897	8,708	8,527	12,124	14,822
Workers/ hectare	15.9	25.4	20.3	12.0	11.9
Workers/ farm	5.0	5.0	4.0	3.0	6.0

Source: Agricultural Censuses; own calculations.

Table 5.
Proportion of Natives and Those over Five Years Old Who Lived in the Same Place in 1980: Selected Areas.

Area	% Natives	% Living in same place in 1980
Uruguay		
Non–Capital	91.4	95.6
Dep. Artigas	83.3	89.6
Bella Union:		
Whole area	51.3	72.6
Rural area	28.5	48.7

Source: 1985 Census, special tabulations.

Table 6.
Population Five Years and Older from Bella Union, Rural Area, According to Place of Residence Five Years Before.

Residence in 1980	Number of Residents	Percentage
Bella Union, rural area	1,728	48.6
Remaining interior rural	46	1.3
Total urban	1,386	39.1
Montevideo	155	4.4
Interior urban	1,231	34.7
City of Artigas	263	7.4
Remaining interior urban	968	27.3
Exterior	347	9.8
Without information	43	1.2
N	3,550	100.0%

Source: 1985 Census

inmigration to the rural hinterlands of Bella Union: only 28.5 percent of the residents responding to that Census were natives of the area but nearly half (48.7 percent) had been residents for at least the past five years (table 5). In fact, most of the inhabitants of rural Bella Union in 1985 (63.2 percent) were born in urban areas. As such, the "call of sugar cane" seems to have been heard more loudly by urban than by rural members of the labor force. The dominance of this urban–to–rural migration stream is a dramatic exception for Latin America (see Balan 1980).

Obviously, the call beckoning immigrants to rural Bella Union is the loud tinkle of monies to be made, primarily in the cane sugar commodity system. This call has been amplified by the constraints put on producers by their negotiations with the two agricultural labor unions; indeed, the shower of profits upon the former group has trickled down upon the latter. One consequence has been a burst in the number of seasonal jobbers and in the size of their paychecks. In 1985, there were 2,600 seasonal agricultural workers in the rural zone around Bella Union, about 200 workers transporting sugar, and about 480 seasonal workers in the CALNU sugar refinery during the *zafra*. CALNU had hiring policies favoring the employment of relatives of its members as well as of inhabitants of the area and nearby small towns. The fact that the wages paid by CALNU were quite high by rural standards meant that profits generated by the national protectionist law and the local cooperative were kept within the region. These advantages were shored up by CALNU, when, in the late 1960s, it asserted its monopsony over sugar cane in Bella Union by purchasing its rival refinery, American Factors.

Even as the wages were rising in an absolute sense, their purchasing power was being sharply eroded by inflationary factors (table 7, top panel). However, the "real" purchasing power is higher than the "official" value of money in the surrounds of Bella Union. In truth, most goods consumed within Bella Union and its surrounds can be bought more cheaply from Argentina or Brazil, and both men and women commonly work as smugglers when the *zafra* season is over. Thus, if we correct the rural wages using the Consumer Price Index for Brazil, we see that they rose significantly after 1970. The rising purchasing power in the rural and urban zones of Bella Union were magnified by the drop in real wages in the interior of Uruguay. This change strengthened the "call of sugar cane" beckoning urban migrants to rural Bella Union.

The inmigration into Bella Union has not been limited to persons of labor force age, for there has been a significant inmigration of people aged 70 or more, even from Montevideo. This may be family "chain migration," return migration, or retirees seeking to stretch the value of their

Table 7.
DAILY WAGES IN BELLA UNION BY TYPE OF JOB AND YEAR.

Year	Plain Laborer	Tractor Driver	Support Personnel	Cane Cutters
A) In constant Uruguayan real Pesos of 1970				
1970–71	83.7	94.9	136.0	366.5
1975–76	60.8	61.5	82.3	354.9
1980–81	53.4	55.7	67.0	244.0
1985–86	61.5	64.0	76.0	223.5
B) In Uruguayan Pesos of 1970 corrected for real exchange rate between Uruguay and Brazil [a]				
1970–71	67.1	76.1	109.1	293.9
1975–76	59.9	60.6	81.1	349.5
1980–81	138.7	144.6	174.0	633.8
1985–86	141.7	147.5	175.1	515.0

Source: All wages from APCANU; all other from BCU.
[a] Real Exchange Rate relates prices of the Brazilian CPI to the Uruguayan CPI, taking into account the exchange rate between the two countries. Exchange rates were 1970=100, U:B(P), 124.684, 101.534, 38.499, 43.395, respectively.

savings by consuming the cheaper products available from across the border. Indeed, Census data give evidence of all of these types of elderly inmigrants.

Conclusions

These changes toward the capitalization of the sugar commodity system in Bella Union have paralleled those in other Latin American countries since the early 1960s, but in at least four important respects, they are distinctive. First, the capitalization of the sugar commodity system in this area of northwestern Uruguay has not resulted from an increase in production for foreign markets, given the prices that result from protectionist economic policies, since the sugar can be sold only in the internal market. Nor has it happened through the usual backwardly vertical integration of the commodity system (from the processors to the growers). Third, it has been organized by a privately owned cooperative that has served collective economic interests crosscutting the various agricultural classes.

Fourth, more urbanites than rural populations have been drawn into, and retained within, the rural sectors of Bella Union by economic incentives. An important question is whether this local success in relatively "even development" can be replicated elsewhere.

This can happen only if certain conditions present in Bella Union can be met. One special key has been the skill of the agricultural leaders in Bella Union in obtaining start–up funds for CALNU from external (international) creditors. Another crucial element has been the diversification into crops other than sugar cane (e.g., tomatoes, rice, citrus fruits, and grapes) enabled by CALNU's support of irrigation works for producer–members. This has freed Bella Union's prosperity from a dependency on the state's continuous protection of the sugar cane commodity system from foreign competition. This independence has been reinforced by the ability of CALNU's leadership to avoid co-optation by representatives of national political parties. However, the most important ingredients have been an exchange rate favoring the Uruguayan peso over Argentine and Brazilian currencies and the location of Bella Union at this trinational junction, where the Uruguayan peso can jingle so loudly.

Note

I thank DIEA and DGEC for providing unpublished data. D. Zucases generated special tabulations and ably assisted with the 1985 Census. Other state agencies, such as VERNO and PDBU, have provided support and information, as well as many other qualified informants, whose collaboration I cannot possibly acknowledge by name in this chapter. I am deeply grateful for the assistance provided by E. Trigueros with the Agrarian Census data and by C. Mendivil in the analysis of national Census data. Nan Johnson and Jan Flora have provided useful comments on an earlier version of this chapter, and Nan Johnson has contributed greatly with editorial suggestions.

References

Balan, J. 1980. Migraciones temporarias y mercado de trabajo rural en America Latina. Estudios, 3, Buenos Aires: CEDES.

Correa, A. 1986. La industria azucarera enel Uruguay. Montevideo: Unpublished thesis, FCEA, Universidad de la Republica

Direccion de Investigaciones Economicas Agropecuarias (DIEA). 1955, 1961, 1965, 1970, and 1980. Censo General Agropecuario. Unpublished results at the section level.

———. 1988. Modelos de produccion canera: Estimaciones econometricas. Montevideo: MGAP.

El Pais. 1987. CALNU: Algo mas que Caña: de Azucar. Suplemento Panorama Agropecuario.

Labadie, G. J. 1988a. The call of the sugar cane: Agricultural change, producer cooperatives and immigrants in northwestern Uruguay. Paper presented to the VII World Congress of Rural Sociology, Bologna, Italy. June, 1988.

_____. 1988b. Bella Union: Integracion vertical, cooperativas y sus efectos distributivos. Paper presented to the V Meetings of the Latin American Sociological Association, Montevideo, Uruguay. December, 1988.

Moraes, M. I. 1988. Raices historicas de la agricultura intensiva en Bella Union. Montevideo.

Plouvier, L. 1987. Azucar. In Estudio Sectorial Agropecuario. Montevideo, Uruguay: Food and Agricultural Organization, April, 1987, TCP/URU/6651.